T5-CPV-535

DISCOVERING THE OTHER
Humanities East and West

INTERPLAY 4

Proceedings of Colloquia
in Comparative Literature and the Arts

Editors:
Moshe Lazar
Ron Gottesman

Published under the auspices of
THE COMPARATIVE LITERATURE PROGRAM
and THE CENTER FOR THE HUMANITIES
University of Southern California

DISCOVERING THE OTHER
Humanities East and West

edited by

Robert S. Ellwood

UNDENA PUBLICATIONS
Malibu 1984

INTERPLAY 4

CB
251
.D 57
1984

Library of Congress Card Number: 82-50983
ISBN: 0-89003-152-5 (cloth)
0-89003-151-7 (paper)
© 1984 by Undena Publications

All rights reserved. No part of this publication may be reproduced or transmitted in any form or by any means, electronic or mechanical, including
photo-copy, recording, or any information storage and retrieval system,
without permission in writing from the author or the publisher.

Undena Publications, P. O. Box 97, Malibu, CA 90265

TABLE OF CONTENTS

INTRODUCTION

This volume represents a selection of papers presented at a seminar entitled "Humanities in East Asian and Western Cultures: Crosscultural Studdies" held at the University of Southern California in the fall of 1979, and made possible by a generous grant from the Henry Luce Foundation, New York. The basic purpose of the seminar was to investigate the influence of the East on Western writers and artists, of the West on Eastern creativity, and other closely related topics. The seminar itself was a microcosm of its topic, for it was deliberately constituted to include highly qualified scholars and artists of both occidental and Eastern background, both academic and non-academic, and both East Asian specialists and non-specialists with a lively interest in the meaning of East Asian tradition for their disciplines. Participants were from the University of Southern California and other selected colleges and universities in the area: in addition, several distinguished speakers from as far away as Japan were invited to present lectures. The co-principal investigators for the seminar were Professor Ronald Gottesman, Director of the USC Center for the Humanities, and myself.

Cultural exchange between East and West is an ancient and perennial feature of the human landscape. It is older than the Age of Exploration, older than Marco Polo, older than Ashoka and Alexander the Great. But in recent centuries it has been running at flood tide. Far more than a matter of neat, voguish intellectual and aesthetic movements, the interaction of East and West, even in the humanities alone, has been a vast, messy, confusing, irreversible typhoon steadily gathering force in the modern cultural world. Its protagonists have been brutal warriors as well as poets, travelling scientists and doctors as well as painters, students going abroad and philosophers who stayed home. Its concerns include, as these papers reveal, the impact of Zen on an American poet who lives on a mountain and the bitter experience of Chinese students and immigrants who, though heirs to a proud culture, underwent daily humiliation in a time and place where they were just another lesser breed, suitable to labor as laundrymen and houseboys. They embrace the cumulatively measurable effect of the Chinese classics on the authority of biblical chronology in Europe, and of western scientific knowledge on Confucian authority.

The meeting of East and West has been an explosive issue giving rise to passionate feelings for millions in our age, not excluding members of the seminar. In these papers will be found many powerful, emotionally-charged statements, some of which are much at odds with equally strong assertions by other writers and some of which were vehemently challenged at the time they were originally presented in the seminar. But all of this is part of the real-world meeting of East and West: its effect had been "to spread skepticism, bewilderment, and free thinking." It could also be asserted that, in response, it has produced reactionism, authoritarianism, and premature dogmatism, as well as progress (however that is defined) in both East and West. The reader is invited to enter this rainbow world through the minds and words of some of its most sensitive and articulate experiencers, its writers and artists and their interpreters.

I am indebted to many for helping to make this volume possible: the members of this seminar, the editors of the Interplay Series in which it appears, and to Mr. Yasuo Sakata, indefatiguable coordinator of the seminar and assistant in the preparation of this manuscript for publication. In particular, I would like to thank Professor George Hayden, of the Department of East Asian Languages and Cultures of the University of Southern California, for extensive editorial help, and John Ramsay Bickers for editorial assistance.

Robert S. Ellwood
Bishop James W. Bashford Professor
of Oriental Studies
School of Religion
University of Southern California

January 12, 1982

I

BACKGROUND STUDIES
IN EAST ASIAN CULTURES

TRADITION AND INVENTION
IN MODERN KOREAN POETRY

Peter H. Lee

It is widely accepted that there was a revolution in poetry in the beginning of this century in Korea as advocates of the so-called new style poetry attempted to break with the tradition and convention of their poetic past. Liberation from the inherited corpus of poetry was in itself a formidable task and was, moreover, impeded by the conditions in which Korea found herself in those years.

The advent of a poetry that can be considered essentially modern in spirit was preceded by a transitional period, the period of songs and new poetry during the last decade of the nineteenth and the first decade of the present century. The opening of ports in 1876 prompted the rise of songs (*ch'angga*) to warn the people of the danger of foreigners and to emphasize the need of enlightenment and reform. In 1888 the first Sunday school taught Christian hymns, and from 1906 on music became a part of the elementary school curriculum. And contemporary newspapers carried a large number of such songs, most of them denouncing corruption in the government and stressing the urgency of independence, enlightenment, and patriotic fervor. Song writers still used such traditional verse forms as the *sijo* and *kasa,* or the song form, whose predominant pattern was 7, 5 syllables, influenced by the popular Japanese songs (*shōka*). They were groping for a new verse form but did not successfully break away from the limitations of the traditional prosody, the alternation of 4's and 3's, and the use of traditional forms of speech and allusions.[1]

The "new poetry" movement is usually traced back to the publication of "From the Sea to Children" (1908) by Ch'oe Nam-sŏn (1890-1957). At the

---

[1] Chŏng Han-mo, *Han'guk hyŏndae simunhaksa* [*History of Modern Korean Poetry*] (Seoul: Ilchisa, 1974), pp. 78-151; Kim Yun-sik, *Han'guk hyŏndae siron pip'an* [*Criticism of Modern Korean Poetics*] (Seoul: Ilchisa, 1975), pp. 162-187.

age of thirteen, Ch'oe published editorials in the leading dailies of the day
and between 1904 and 1910 went to Japan for short sojourns, where he is
said to have read Turgenev's prose poems and perhaps Byron.[2] In November
of 1908 he published the first cultural magazine, Sonyŏn (Children, 1908-
1911), to launch a new literary movement and to educate the masses in the
new civilization of the West. The first and sixth stanzas of "From the Sea
to Children" go in the literal version:

> Splash, splash, slap, roll.
> The sea lashes, smashes, crushes.
> Great mountains like T'ai, boulders like houses,
> These flimsy things, what are they to me?
> "Do you know my power?" The sea roars,
> Lashes, smashes, crushes,
> Splash, splash, slap, rumble, boom.

☆

> Splash, splash, slap, roll.
> I scorn the world and people,
> But there is one I love most.
> My love, brave and innocent children,
> Come and nestle in my bosom lovingly.
> Come, children, let me kiss you.
> Splash, splash, slap, rumble, boom.

The poem's typographical arrangement on the page, with white space on
the upper and lower margins and 106 punctuation marks, must have startled
readers. It compels a dramatic comprehension of the eye, imposing the poet's
intention on the reader: that it is for the voice and for the eye, that the poet
needs the collaboration of the printer, and that his arrangement (and reading)
is final.

All traditional Korean poetry was meant to be sung. Its forms and styles
therefore reflect melodic origins. The association of the verbal and musical
rhythm can be seen in the refrains of the medieval poems. Nonsense jingles
or onomatopoetic representation of the sounds of musical instruments, such
as the drum, attest to the use of refrains long after the disappearance of its
musical origin and function. The singer is the lyric persona, the performer
and interpreter. A distance between poet and persona also determines his
relationship with the audience. This relationship is essentially dramatic, as the
singer through his masks assumes different ritual roles, in much the same

---

[2]He is said to have been inspired by Byron's *Childe Harold's Pilgrimage*, canto 4,
CLXXI-CLXXXIV, for which see Samuel C. Chew, ed. *Childe Harold's Pilgrimage*
(New York: The Odyssey Press, 1936), pp. 202-203.

manner that the poet speaks through his personae. The Korean singers, like the oral poet, recalled the past, acting as memory for society, a carrier of culture, a celebrant of its norms and values. The role of singer as interpreter becomes clear in the arrangement of premodern manuscripts which admitted no punctuation, quotation marks, or sometimes stanzaic divisions. It was the function of the singer to interpret the poem through the proper emphasis on the words and phrases. Thus pictorial presentation played little role. The imposition of the poet's will and interpretation reflects a change in the relation between author and audience: "From the Sea to Children" radically reduces the distance between them. It breaks with the tradition of the generalized and impersonal, presenting itself with the immediacy of the distinctive and individual, although I doubt that Ch'oe fully understood the implications of his choice.

The poet of the past seldom used stanzaic forms of unequal length. True, there are cycles of short poems, most of which, however, regularly repeat the recurring patterns of stresses and syllable count, as, for example, in a *sijo* cycle, "Songs of Five Friends" by Yun Sŏn-do (1587-1671), addressed to the water, stone, pine, bamboo, and moon, or his *Angler's Calendar* (1651), comprising forty poems on the joys of the fisherman throughout the four seasons. In this poem, minor irregularities occur in the first stanza, where the second and sixth lines are identical, but not in other stanzas. The number of syllables in a corresponding line throughout the poem is the same, and the first and last lines of each are identical. More important, it is not the line, the unit of composition in the past, but a stanza, that constitutes the form. The first and seventh lines, for example, consisting wholly of onomatopoeia, intended for their musical effect and magical echo, cannot be a full sentence. The use of a run-on line, which discourages pause, is to build up large units of rhythmical movements, the stanza. (It is interesting to recall that in *Cathay*, published in April 1915 in London, Pound used a line to comprise a full sentence, persuaded by Fenollosa's plea for the sentence as the natural unit of poetic perception.)[3]

In the past, poems written in the vernacular usually did not have titles, while those in Chinese did. Titles are often supplied by the compiler. Shorter poems such as *sijo* are usually classified by their musical tunes, subjects, authors, or chronology, again without titles. The use of formulaic diction and *topoi*, a predictable combination of imagery, the occurrence of season words, and inner progression told the audience the subject, occasion, mood, and tone of the poem.

---

[3] Donald Davie, *Ezra Pound: Poet as Sculptor* (New York: Oxford University Press, 1964), pp. 41-43.

"From the Sea to Children" is startling for other reasons. Both the sea and children are seldom employed in classic East Asian poetry. There are streams and rivers, including such large ones as the Yellow River and the Yangtze, but the sea somehow did not excite the imagination of the poet (A notable exception may be the rhymeprose, "The Sea," by Mu Hua [c.300].) Even the Japanese, long a seafaring people, did not leave memorable verse on the subject. Likewise, children made scant appearance. Often the speaker in the *sijo* addresses a "boy": "Boy, lead a cow to the northern village" (Cho Chon-sŏng, 1553-1627), or "Boy, fetch your old net!" (Yun Sŏn-do). But, "boy" in such instances refers to an unmarried man younger than the speaker, a servant, friend, or even one who shares the speaker's mood and tastes, an ideal audience who sees things with the eyes of the youth, or a youth in whom the speaker recalls through memory his own past, thus combating the onslaught of time.

The first and last lines of each 7-line stanza consist of what can only be termed an onomatopoetic assualt on the reader, four examples in the first line, five in the seventh. No classical poem would have begun with four imitations in sound of lexical meaning. They are the sounds of the sea's motion, and their repetition in the beginning and end of a stanza points to the basic structural principle: the poet is appealing to our aural imagination, and their power, as in charms, lies in their sounds. Three out of nine such examples are dated. Wornout allusions include Mt. T'ai (st. 1), an eastern sacred mountain in the west of Shantung, synonymous with the great mountain, and the First Emperor of the Ch'in (st. 3), the unifier of China and a tyrant who burned books! These, together with a few others, written in Chinese logographs and appearing amid the otherwise pure vernacular, like the Latinate in English, are orotund, grave, and emphatic. Of course, certain locutions are archaic, including inversions, which tend to detract from the force of the line.

The last but equally significant innovation is personification. In Tu Fu's famous "Spring Prospect" (757), "flowers draw tears";[4] but that is pathetic fallacy to bridge the gap between man and nature. In allegorical verse in Korea, such emblematic flowers as the chrysanthemum (or plum) hold an imaginary dialogue with gaudy but ephemeral spring flowers. But here the speaker is the sea, which addresses children, the future hope of a new generation. As the title of the journal and the poem suggest, "From the Sea to Children" celebrates the power of the young, beacons in the darkness, who will carry out a necessary social and literary revolution. The sea is a bridge between nations, an outpost for the new civilization from the West. The sea's

---

[4]Burton Watson, *Chinese Lyricism* (New York: Columbia University Press, 1971), p. 162.

majesty, creativity, and power are what the youth of Korea need in their task of forging a modern expression approximating simple, colloquial language and a modern civilization.

I have belabored what may seem obvious to bring out new features in this poem--the difference in voice, the way the new voice is achieved by subject, diction, figures, and prosody, and the relation between author and audience. Despite changes in the assumptions of poetry, Ch'oe's view of the function of poetry was traditional and public. Like earlier song writers, his primary concerns were the introduction of Western civilization, the enlightenment of people, and the arousing of national consciousness; hence his eagerness to draw out the meanings of the sea and children and moralize upon them. From the quarrel with others he made rhetoric. Contemporary political and social realities were overwhelming, and he was intent on pointing out the fact that the time was out of joint. He witnessed the death of old structures, the collapse of tradition and the loss of country, but could not erect an alternative. It was up to the subsequent generations further to explore and develop the task Ch'oe had begun.

Several months before the unsuccessful and costly movement for Korean independence came a powerful Western influence on Korean poetry in the form of French symbolism. In late 1918, the *Western Literary Weekly* published translations from Verlaine, Gourmont, and Fyodor Sologub, followed by the description of the French and Western literary scenes. Kim Ŏk (1895-?), the principal translator, introduced the tenets of symbolism, the art of indirection, and magical suggestiveness. He proposed that the poet's job is not to name but to suggest an object (Mallarmé)[5] and quoted Verlaine: "never the color, always the shade,/ always the nuance is supreme!" ("Art Poétique"; st. 4, lines 1-2).[6] To him Rimbaud's "Les Voyelles" is the supreme example of musical verse in the symbolist technique and a line from Baudelaire–"perfumes, sounds, and colors correspond" ("Correspondences," st. 2, line 4)[7]–the ultimate of modern poetry; but he fails to see the correspondences between the material world and spiritual realities and those between the different human senses. He then concludes that *vers libre* is the supreme creation of the symbolist, defining it as "the music of language to express the poet's inner life," and states of mind. He

[5] *Oeuvres Complètes* (Paris: Gallimard, 1945), p. 869 (from "Résponses à des enquêtes sur l'évolution littèraire ").

[6] "Car nous voulons la Nuance encore,/ Pas la Couleur, rien que la nuance!" Translation from C. F. MacIntyre, *French Symbolist Poetry* (Berkeley: University of California Press, 1961), p. 35.

[7] MacIntyre, p. 13.

ignores Baudelaire's aspiration toward mysticism, or art as another cosmos which transforms and humanizes nature.[8]

Kim also expressed his own view of translation as art along with something of his poetics. Art, Kim says, is a product of the spirit; a work of art is an expression of the harmony between body and soul. Just as a people has a unique language, so does the individual. As his breathing and pulse have short and long, so does each poet his unique diction, style, and rhythm. Such individual characteristics demand a harmonious and musical form, which he sought in free verse or in the characteristic rhythms of the Korean language. He adumbrates the concept of the independence and autonomy of the poet as conscious artist and craftsman, and he says elsewhere that poetry captures a moment of experience in a harmonious whole. Later he adds that the poet must find the adequate medium to express the Korean sensibility, probably a counterpart to the emphasis on the intellect in creation advocated, for example, by Poe, Baudelaire, and Mallarmé. Kim Ŏk and other translators active in the late 1910's and early 20's reacted against sentimentality, rhetoric, description, didacticism, and political and public themes and attempted to mingle music and image to create strange and sad beauty in their works.

Kim's absorption with Symbolism culminated in March 1921 with the publication of the *Dance of Anguish* (*Onoe ŭi mudo*), the first volume of translations from Western poetry. It introduced Verlaine, Gourmont, Samain, Baudelaire, Yeats, and others. Like Ueda Bin's *Sound of the Tide* (*Kaichōon*, 1905) and Nagai Kafū's *Corals* (*Sangoshū*, 1913), the book was at once acclaimed for its beautiful translations in the language and became the favorite reading of aspiring poets till the forties. Translating from the Japanese, English, French, and Esperanto Kim produced a mellifluous, soft, and dreamy language, often using the colloquial honorific verbal endings.[9] Exoticism, strange and sad beauty, suggestive of the melancholic mood of a dying season, boredom, anguish, and abandonment of self to a state of death—all this appealed to the poets who sought models to express their frustration, emptiness, and despair after the collapse of the 1919 independence movement.

Two years later, Kim published the *Songs of a Jellyfish* (*Haep'ari ŭi*

[8] René Wellek, *A History of Modern Criticism: The Late Nineteenth Century* (New Haven: Yale University Press, 1965), pp. 435, 437, 441. See also David Perkins, *A History of Modern Poetry* (Cambridge, Mass.: Harvard University Press, 1976), pp. 48-52.

[9] For example, Verlaine's "Chanson d'automne." Kim was an active member of Korea Esperanto-Asocio, founded in September 1920, wrote the first manual, *Esperanta Kurso Ramida* (1931; 2d ed., 1946), and himself translated some Western poems into Esperanto, for which see Kim Yun-sik, *Kŭndae Han'guk munhak yŏn'gu* (Studies in Modern Korean Literature] (Seoul: Ilchisa, 1973), pp. 112-163.

norae; June 1923), the first volume of new verse by a single poet, comprising eighty-three pieces. As the predominant mood of the *Dance of Anguish* is autumn so that in the *Songs of a Jellyfish* is one of autumnal sorrow, with a homesick wanderer starting out for an aimless journey in search of a lost spring, "blue blue May" ("My Sorrow"), a home, or a lost country. The lost youth blowing sadly on the pipe an old tune is a fit metaphor for the state of mind of the poets of the twenties. His strong sense of form (the 7, 5 pattern—7[3,4], 7[3,4], 7[3,4], and 5), frequent use of metaphors and personifications, and emphasis on musicality—all this was the heritage of Symbolism and an advance he brought to the development of modern Korean poetry.[10]

Most symbolist techniques, such as the communication of mood, the art of indirection, the creation of the symbol, the fusion of music and image, however, were already qualities of traditional East Asian poetry. What it helped advance were the creation of new forms, the poem as an intimate experience of the self—the conscious artist—rather than a rearrangement of inherited imagery, and the emphasis on the intellect in poetic creation, this last not always practised. The choice of autumn, especially autumn twilight, as the favorite time of poetry is nothing new. Autumn was the favorite poetic season in classic East Asian poetry, and the deliberate cultivation of the dark and mysterious, the sad and veiled, the fleeting and intangible were the highest aesthetic ideals. Hence the recurrence of special images or associated images (scattered stars, cold moon, white dew, departing swallows, fallen leaves), including the cry of a cricket, goose, quail, snipe, all intended to symbolize the speaker's state of mind. But these insects and birds seldom make their appearance in Korean imitations of symbolist poetry. A typical symbolist poem was intent on creating a world "dense with specificity but difficult to specify,"[11] an atmosphere or a mood "riddled with nuance," a poem of adjectives and adverbs rather than of verbs, devoid of locality. A poet tries to find his dispossession and entrapment in some landscape outside, but the vague and dim autumn atmosphere reflects at best the poet's failure to see clearly the nature of his anguish or the self's consciousness of anguish. He saw decay and death in the midst of life, but could find adequate means neither to register the dilemma nor to come to grips with the world.

The first authentic interpreter of the plight of the colonized people is Han Yong-un, who introduced Tagore's work in 1920.[12] Han adopted a

---

[10]Chong, pp. 339-393.

[11]Hugh Kenner, *A Homemade World: The American Modernist Writers* (New York: Knopf, 1975), p. 205.

[12]Kuo Mo-jo (1892-1978) read some of his poems in September 1914 in Japan, for

common, colloquial language and free verse to reveal how man can transcend the obstacles imposed from without as they penetrate his own selfhood en slavement, tyranny, wickedness, and censorship. As a poet of his time, he not only reflected the moment of his culture in crisis but went beyond suffering into an awareness that is at once old and new. Patriot, revolutionary, reformer, and prophet, at the age of fifteen (1894), Han took part in the Tonghak [Eastern Learning] rebellion, whose rallying cry was to expel foreigners so as to preserve native ways and beliefs and to liberate the masses from oppression. He then became a monk and realized that Buddhist reform could not be brought about without the regeneration of man. He strove to revive the faith, in which he saw the sprititual foundation of the salvation of Korean society. At the time of the 1919 independence movement, he helped draft the "Declaration of Independence," mainly written by Ch'oe Nam-sŏn, the author of "From the Sea to Children," and signed the document as one of the thirty-three patriots. In prison he wrote another essay in which he said that the desire for freedom and independence is an interest in every man, that aggression will eventually fail, and that Korean independence is vital to the preservation of peace in East Asia. He predicted that if Japan's military aggression continued, it would eventually collide with the United States and China.

In 1926, he published *The Silence of Love* (*Nim ŭi ch'immuk*) comprising eighty-eight meditative poems. *Nim* is a complex word in Korean. In love poetry it refers to the beloved, in allegorical poetry, the king, and in religious verse, God. In Han's poetry, *nim* is the object of our love, be it the nation, life, the Buddha, or enlightenment. His poems are built upon the dialectic of engagement and withdrawal, motion and stillness, action and nonaction, life and death, *nirvana* and *samsara*, enlightenment and illusion. The Foreword begins:

> The loved one is not only the beloved; it is also everything yearned for. If all living beings are the beloved for Śākyamuni, philosophy is the beloved for Kant. If the spring rain is the beloved for the rose, then Italy is the beloved for Mazzini. The loved one is not only that which I love but also that which loves me.[13]

---

which see Julia C. Lin, *Modern Chinese Poetry* (Seattle: University of Washington Press, 1972), p. 202. Hsü Chih-mo (1885-1931), the founder of the Crescent Moon Society, compared him to "a sun over Mount T'ai." Tagore wrote two poems for Korea, "The Song of the Defeated" and another which went, "In the golden age of Asia/Korea was one of its lamp bearers./And that lamp is waiting to be lighted once again/for the illumination of the East," published in the *Tong'a Daily*, April 2, 1929. Kim Yun-sik, pp. 199-295.

[13] All Han's poems are translated by Sam Solberg.

"The Silence of Love" goes:

> You *have gone*. Ah, my love, you *have gone*.
> Shattering the green brilliance of the mountain, hard as it
>   might be, cutting off all ties, *gone* along the narrow path
>   that opens out to the maple grove.
> The old vows, firm and splendid as flowers of golden metal,
>   have turned to dust and *flown off* in the breath of a
>   sigh.
> The memory of a sharp first *kiss* reversed the compass
>   needle of my fate, *stepped backward and faded*.
> I was deafened by your perfumed sounds and blinded by
>   your flower-like face.
> Love too is man's lot; even though we have prepared with
>   fear of *parting* at meeting, *parting* comes upon us
>   unawares and the startled heart bursts with a fresh
>   sorrow.
> However, since I know that to make *parting* the font of
>   needless tears is to shatter love, I transferred the irre-
>   sistible power of sadness and poured it over my brow to
>   quench the old ill with fresh hope.
> Just as we fear *parting* when we meet, we believe we will
>   meet again when we *part*.
> Ah, even though you are *gone* I have never said good-bye.
> The sad melody of my song of love curls around your
>   silence.   [emphasis added except for the word 'kiss']

☆

The poem's speech situation and the identity of the speaker and the addressee signal the reader that more is intended than love arguments. Seman-tically, the poem's controlled indeterminacy allows the reader to explore other interpretive horizons, for example, the range of meaning and emotion of a single word, *nim*, in a given context and in the tradition and the col-lective experience of culture. Syntactic changes, repetition of key words (*ploce*),[14] and the phonaesthetic suggestiveness of words—manipulation of the sounds of Korean to reinforce meaning—help the reader experience the multiple significance of the narrative situation.

The poem seems to say: the immaterial is the material, and vice versa. Emptiness is not nothingness, but is not different from the material which constitutes the world. To attain this view is to attain wisdom. The absent lover is addressed as the lover present. His *nim* is the boundless *nim*, and it

---

[14] A. C. Partridge, *The Language of Modern Poetry: Yeats, Eliot, Auden* (London: Deutsch, 1976), p. 148.

is with him, who is truly non-existent but mysteriously existent, the state which is permanent and existent, that the speaker seeks reunion. To link the lines Han employs the rhetorical device of *ploce–nim* (7 times); go (4 times), part (5 times), as well as kindred verbs–fly off (once) and step backward (once). The reverberation of key words reinforces the rhythmical pattern and enables the poet to dispense with punctuation.

> The paulownia leaf that gently ripples down the windless air–whose footprint is it?
> The glimpse of blue sky through rents in the ominous black clouds driven away by the west wind after the tedium of the long rains–whose face is it?
> The mysterious perfume caressing the quiet sky over the old stupa, on its way from the green moss on the unflowering tree in the distant dingle–whose breath is it?
> The small freshet, its source no one knows where, that winding splashes against the stones–whose song is it?
> The afterglow adorns the setting sun with hands like white jade caressing the endless heavens, heals like lotus flowers set on the boundless seas–whose poem is it?
> The ash left after burning become oil again; my breast that burns and never stops–whose night does this weak lamp watch?

"I Cannot Know" asserts the relativity of all. "Footprint," "face," "breath," "song" and "poem" are the basic elements of the poet's life. The beloved who experienced this relativity has experienced *śūnya* as *śūnya*. He has glimpsed the unsurpassed wisdom, perfect enlightenment, of the Buddha, the true form (*tathatā*) of *śūnya*. His poems seem to make more sense when we see the true subject as the way of mystic experience, a witness to the truth. "The weak lamp" and "my breast that burns and never stops" may also be the lamp that awaits the rebirth of the fatherland or that burns brightly in his consciousness upon attaining the reality of relativity (*śūnya*). "The ash left after burning become oil again" is intended to imply the sorrow of loss of country, his longing and hope for its return, his timeless waiting, or his firm purpose for his country.[15] The blue sky he glimpses through "rents in the ominous black clouds" is the face of his beloved, but the long rains never stop. Here again the poem's source of melody and incantation is the repetition of key word "whose" (six times) and the interrogative sentence (six times) without a question mark.

[15] See Kim Hak-tong, *Han'guk kŭndae siin yŏn'gu* [*Studies in Modern Korean Poets*] (Seoul: Ilchogak, 1974), pp. 47-85; Song Uk, *Nim ŭi ch'immuk-chŏnp'yŏn haesŏl* [*The Silence of Love: Complete Annotations*] (Seoul: Kwahaksa, 1974).

Poets writing till the mid-twenties all wished in various ways to reflect the profound alternations in the conditions of Korean life. Some imported Romanticism, Decadence, and fin-de-siècle mood. Their experiments with new forms and new subjects in imprecise language, however, reflected at best their own frustrations. They struggled to establish a distinct identity, echoing the Romantic glorification of the poet, but their self-expression couched in the past convention resulted ironically in the abandonment of self. Unable to define their function in a society which was in flux, indifferent, and often antagonistic to the poet, they were content to devote themselves to suffering and self-examination. Seldom does a speaker address an audience or assume a role other than that of the estranged, lonely, and melancholy artist inhabiting a twilight world of dream.

Contrarily, Han Yong-un achieved his distinctive voice by the use of the past and the creation of the new. Drawing on Buddhist epistemology, the religion firmly rooted in the people, he enriched his works with the common store of reference. Unlike the Buddhist meditations of the past on the merits and virtues of Buddhas and Bodhisattvas, Han's poetry, couched in the language of love, is a spiritual exploration of the relationship between self and other, the one and the many. Like seventeenth-century English devotional poetry, Han's is a spiritual exercise, contemplating the origin and end of his beloved, the Buddha, and his country. The self cannot exist away from society. Man cannot be rootless, nor can he deny the claims of the flesh. His rhythmical language, individual and precise in sensuous detail, belongs to the shared convictions, communal hopes and anxieties of Koreans.

Kim Sowŏl is another poet who explores to the fullest the multiple meanings of the word *nim* and others of the same dimension. Under the tutelage of Kim Ŏk, he became a poet of nature and folk tradition, and the effectiveness of his works depends on the simplicity, directness, and intensity of the phrasing. His vitality and sensitiveness rose to the fullness of poetry in "The Summons of the Soul," which makes an impassioned appeal to the soul of his lady to return.

> O name broken piecemeal,
> Strewn in the empty void.
> Nameless name, deaf and dumb.
> That suffers me to die as I call it.
>
> The last word carved in my heart
> Was never spoken in the end.
> O you that I love,
> O you that I love.

Crimson sun hangs on the west peak,
The deer bell and call sadly.
There on the sheer steep peak
I call your empty name.

I will still call your name
Until sorrow chokes and unmans me.
My voice goes aslant rejected,
Lost between heaven and earth.

Were I to become a stone,
I would still call your name as I died.
O you that I love,
O you that I love.[16]

The "Name broken piecemeal," "Nameless name," "empty name," "your name," and "You that I love" repeated four times (sts. 2, 5) easily lend themselves to more than one reading. Although he assumed the anonymity of a folk song writer or the individuality of the lyric persona in more personal pieces, Kim Sowŏl never lost sight of the functions of the poet in an enslaved society: the preservation and extension of the possibilities of the language

This poetry of resistance voicing defiant sorrow over the ruined land illustrates the cry of self in wilderness, a keen awareness of time and place, a modern awareness of history. Yi Sang-hwa (1900-43), Shim Hun (1904-37), Yi Yuksa (1905-44), and Yun Tong-ju (1917-45) showed how to express in poetry their encounter with history and to expand the poet's consciousness and establish the authority of the poet. The speaker in Yi Sang-hwa's "Does Spring Come to Stolen Fields?" (1926) wishes to return to the earth as a child would to his mother. But mother as land, or land as mother, is unattainable.[17]

Shim Hun, in "When That Day Comes," reveals his aspiration to independence in impassioned language. The speaker says he "will soar like a crow at night/ and pound the Chongno bell with his head," and "skin his body and make a drum and march with it in the vanguard." Couched in the *adynata*, the topic of impossibilities, it is an affirmation of the spaker's unshakable belief in the day of liberation. The Chongno bell was struck on festival days in the past. The speaker looks forward to the day when the bell will resound

---

[16]*Poems from Korea* (Honolulu: University Press of Hawaii, 1975), p. 167, with minor changes. The title alludes to the poem of the same title written some time in the second half of the third century B.C., in the *Ch'u Tz'u: The Songs of the South*.

[17]*Poems from Korea*, pp. 163-164.

and "the thundering shout" of his people will celebrate the restoration. In his claim that "nature will share his joy and rise and dance with him," Shim Hun used a very ancient trope—a rapturous moment, a joy so violent, he will burst the confines of his body.[18]

Yi Yuksa was imprisoned seventeen times and perished in Peking prison.

> Beaten by the bitter season's whip,
> I am driven at the end to this north.
>
> I stand upon the sword-blade frost,
> Where numb sky and plateau merge.
>
> I do not know where to bend my knees,
> Nor where to lay my vexed steps.
>
> I cannot but close my eyes and think—
> Winter;
>   Winter is a steel rainbow.[19]

In "The Summit" (1939), the self stands alone on a precipitous, dizzying boundary. Chased and homeless, the poet does not blink at the terror and absurdity of history. Not by a shrill scream, but by a plunge into the depths of self, he recreates the condition of existence in extremity and makes us contemplate the final implications of our destiny.

All lines, with four stresses, are metrically self-contained. The poem's power comes from the use of personification (season's whip), metaphor (vexed steps; sword-blade frost), metonymy (bend my knees), and oxymoron (steel rainbow), as well as a combination of strong, harsh aspirated affricates and fricatives (*k'* aspirated velar stop, *ch'* aspirated palatal affricate, *tch* tensed affricate, *ss* tensed dental fricative, and *h* glottal fricative), which creates the rhythms and controls the meaning. The fusion of sound and sense evokes the encroachment of the ruthless season, as the speaker struggles to "outface/ The winds and persecutions of the sky." He is modern, because he reveals a vision of a moment of time, a new way of looking upon man's existence. He posits a frightening discontinuity, a nothingness, the modern "I" on the summit, a place where man makes a last stand. There are no certainties, only an authentic response. Like some Hemingway heroes, he has no pretence to sentiments or self-pity: he is faithful to his own experience, which has universal validity.

---

[18] *Poems from Korea*, p. 166. Maurice Bowra, *Poetry and Politics 1900-1960* (Cambridge: University Press, 1966), pp. 92-93.

[19] Unless otherwise noted, all translations are by the author.

The recurrent concerns of Yun Tong-ju, who perished in Fukuoka prison on February 16, 1945, are the sorrow of the oppressed, the presence of death, and the problem of the sensitive and frustrated individual besieged by existential despair and spiritual desolation. At times he feels a nostalgic dismay and pity at the image of his divided and displaced self, which the age besieges and obliterates:

> My face reflected
> In the rusted blue bronze mirror,
> So full of disgrace—
> Which dynasty's relic am I?
> ("Confession," 1942)

An unimpassioned witness of immense void, he realizes that it is futile to seek an illusive peace or relief.

> Who is calling me?
>
> I still breathe
> In the shade of a budding tree.
>
> I've never raised my hand,
> I've no heaven to mark.
>
> I have no place under any heaven.
> Why are you calling me?
>
> The morning I die after my task's done,
> Heartless leaves will fall—
> Don't call me.
> ("Awful Hour," 1941)

To be a poet is "a sad mandate"; but he has accepted his terrible fate and has found new ways of identifying his inner anguish and spiritual predicament with national crisis. His poems reflect that moment of his culture in crisis, and his short life is an embodiment of difficult times for his people.

To Han Yong-un and later poets of resistance, the loss of country was an omnipresent condition of consciousness. Seeking enlightenment for the fate of his self and his fellowmen, Han found the most adequate lyrical correlative in a Buddhist contemplative poetry. By using a single word of myriad dimensions, he successfully communicated the full measure of his anxieties, questionings, and final illumination. These poets were witnesses of national humiliation and degradation, especially the banishment of Koreans from the public realm—"action" made up of the interactions of men, the basis of political life, leaving only "labor" and "work."[20] Tormented by exile and unfulfillment, these poets knew how to stand alone for a brief but meaningful life. But their pessimism was finally balanced by affirmation, celebration of a triumph of self that was purchased with sacrifice and suffering.

Poets through the thirties continued the exploration of new diction and prosody made necessary by "a new self and conception of self."[21] Chŏng Chi-yong, the first truly successful modern poet, is a master of his medium and a continuing presence. If some younger poets try to undermine him, it is because they want to slay their father, whose mastery of language and form is breathtaking. His 123 poems written from 1925 to 1941 deal mainly with the sea, mountain, city, country, and religion. Wishing to recall the virtues of classical strength and lucidity, he rendered particulars exactly and explored the unlimited implication of words. He scorned a belated Romanticism and his astringent remarks made his view of poetry clear: "The mystery of poetry is the mystery of language," "Only the poet can infuse the blood and breath into language," "If a poem weeps first, the reader would not have time to contemplate the tears," or the "Poet must indefatigably explore his spirit."

His "Window," first of two poems on the subject, deals with the death of his child.

> Something cold and sad haunts the window.
> I dim the pane with my feverless steam;
> It flaps its frozen wings, as if tamed.
> I wipe the glass, wipe again,
> Only black night ebbs, then dashes against it,
> Moist stars etched like glittering jewels.
> Polishing the window at night
> Is a lonely, spellbinding affair.
> With your lovely veins in the lung broken,
> You flew away like a mountain bird!

No other poet had written a poem so arrestingly "modern" in sensibility. Chŏng finds his material in his own life. But he deepens the meaning of the experience by letting the powerful description speak for itself. Strong detail and rhythms that exactly suit the feeling work to achieve the effect. From the first line, which begins matter-of-factly, to the last exclamation, he makes us see and feel the objects evoked in a fresh, surprising, and inventive way.

---

[20] Hannah Arendt, *The Human Condition* (Chicago: University of Chicago Press, 1958), esp. p. 221.

[21] Richard Ellmann, *The New Oxford Book of English Verse* (New York: Oxford University Press, 1976), p. xxiii.

The last two lines, together with the traditional association of the soul with bird, set his experience at a distance, thus magnificently controlling his sadness.

Chŏng's first collection (1935) was followed by *The White Deer Lake* (1941), where the poet leads the reader to the harmonious world of nature. The title poem, comprising nine sections in prose, is suited to the experience in a colloquial style and vivid presentation. The theme may be conventional— for it belongs to a system of similar works—but the emotional weight of right words in their contexts produced a work wholly "modern." The judicious blending of Sino-Korean and native words, so strongly individual, and concreteness of phrasing suggest the speaker's "discovery of his thought in the process of saying it"[22]—a cultured, heightened talk. Upon seeing the motherless calf, the speaker thinks of having to "entrust his children to a strange mother" (sect. 6). He also contemplates his ultimate homecoming: "I don't mind turning white as a birch after death" (sect. 3). The audacious listings of alpine plants, explored for their sounds and tones, may be unpoetical in themselves and in the hand of a lesser poet, but here they are given a new life (sect. 8):

> Flowering ferns, bracken, bellflowers, wild asters, umbrella plants, bamboo, manna lichens, alpine plants with star-like bells—I digest them, get drunk on them, and fall into a doze. Yearning for the crystalline water of White Deer Lake, their procession on the range is more solemn than clouds. Beaten by showers, dried by rainbows, dyed by flowers, I put on fat.

Section 9 goes:

> The sky rolls in the blue of White Deer Lake. Not even a crayfish stirs. A cow skirted around my feet disabled with fatigue. A wisp of chased cloud dims the lake. The lake on whose mirror I float daylong is lonesome. Waking and sleeping, I forget even my prayers.

The lake is a symbol of stillness and purity. The speaker describes "a condition of the spirit where the self is completely dissolved in the lucid apprehension of nature."[23] The self and nature reflect each other, waking and sleeping become one. The collection represents the symbolic progress of the

---

[22] Perkins, p. 593.

[23] U-Chang Kim, "Sorrow and Stillness: A View of Modern Korean Poetry," *Literature East and West*, XIII (June 1969), 154. For a criticism of Chŏng's poetry see O T'ak-pŏn, *Hyŏndae munhak san'go* [*Essays in Contemporary Literature*] (Seoul: Korea University Press, 1976), pp. 85-139.

spirit to the condition of lucidity, a fusion of man and nature, as in classic Chinese mountain poetry. The arduous ascent to the summit of Mount Halla, where the White Deer Lake sits, also stands for the stages of spiritual pilgrimmage in archetypal themes of journey, quest, and initiation.

Pak Tu-jin (born 1916) emerged in the early forties as heir of Chŏng Chi-yong and a member of the "Green Deer Group" (others being Pak Mogwŏl and Cho Chi-hun). Through a skillful use of such elemental imagery as mountain, river, ocean, star, sun, and sky, he summons hope for new life, a prelapsarian world, or a cosmos of perfect harmony.

> Mountain, mountain mountain, you have kept a long, tedious silence for myriad years. Mountain, could I wait for the flame to leap out of your soaring peaks and prostrate ridges? Could I hope to see the day when foxes and wolves leap in joy with deer and rabbits to find bush clover and arrowroot?
>
> ("Hyanghyŏn")

He relies for effect on the appeal of incantation—alliteration, consonance, assonance, onomatopoeia, together with balanced structure, the rhythm and sonority carried by reverberation—recurrence of the sibilant, liquid, nasal, and trilled consonants, association of words, and rhetorical questions. The same rhetorical devices recur in "Sun" (1949):

> Rising sun, sun uprising, clean laved face of the comely rising sun; across the mountains, over the mountains you consumed the dark, you comely uprising sun with your ruddy, unfledged face.[24]

Does the poem express the speaker's hope for the fulfillment of his ideal? The mode of presentation of his yearning through syntax—inversion of normal word order—and repetition helps express his mood. It transcends the world of logic (he dispenses with connectives) and creates one full of energy and zest through the use of powerful rhythm.

Earlier poems of Pak Mogwŏl (1916-1978), written in folk song rhythm, created the local color of the South in effortless elegance and control.

> On a distant hill,
> Blue Cloud monastery,
> with an old tile roof

[24]Trans. Sam Solberg.

When spring snow melts
On Mount Purple Mist

Along the hill's twelve bends
Elms breaking into leaf

In the bright eyes
Of a green deer

A cloud
Rolls.

Unlike traditional spring poems, "Green Deer" does not evoke feelings of melancholy, loneliness, and the passage of time. Spring is full of life—snow melts, the birds are healthy, elms sprout, and a green deer watches. The phrasing is economical as in the classic *sijo*—clear, swift, uncluttered, but suggestive, and fragmented syntax reinforces rapid transition. It evokes a quiet warm spring day veiled in a mist, but only the poet can observe a rolling cloud in the deer's eyes. The poem progresses from the far away (distant hill) and unperturbed state (symbolized by "blue" in Blue Cloud monastery) to a close-up; and as the vision gets closer, the poem uses fewer words, the last stanza in the original consisting of two syllables in each line. The paratactic movement of the recording eye allows the reader to be more actively involved as he tries to imagine, organize, and discover the significance of the scene from his own experience. The landscape, subject, and sensibility are Korean, and the poem presents a few images in a fresh and new way.

The love of nature, which stands for country—the fatherland—is a genuine native heritage. If in the West nature has often been viewed as indifferent, crude, deceptive, and bestial, East Asian man is never separated from his natural envrionment by intellectual discrimination or by emotional response: he is invariably perceived as one with nature and his life patterned after natural harmony. Even if the land is stolen, the moon, cloud, and wind are not. Indeed, no tyrant has claimed them as his own; they can be won only by the imagination. Advocates of Symbolism such as Kim Ŏk and his pupil Kim Sowŏl, we recall, reverted to their native tradition—folklore, folkways, folksongs—for greater resonance in their works. Likewise, Chŏng Chi-yong, a student of Blake and Whitman and a convert to Catholicism, returned in his mature poetry to his own tradition to attain harmony between man and nature. He therefore placed himself in the great tradition of East Asian nature poetry written in the first person singular that allows the claims of the self. Again, poets of resistance who won poetic victories with loss of blood depicted the spiritual landscape drawn on nature imagery, a veiled expression of nostalgia for the stolen country. Pak Mogwŏl, throughout his career, assimilated local color and used a plain language incorporating dialect.[25]

Among poets who came of age after liberation, some attempted to assimilate more of their history, its virtues and vices, as well as of actuality. Their imagination was fired by events and issues of the time, especially the malicious repetition of history—division of the country, repression, and censorship. Shin Ton-yŏp (1930-1969) viewed the history from the liberation through the post-Korean war period as a serious falling-off from the innocence and harmony of earlier times, in terms of an exploited victim of imperialistic powers that had crushed the harmonious life of an agrarian society.

> Keep life simple as wild asters,
> as when you weeded bean rows, barefooted.
> Let us go back to our primitive land,
> to the village dance of legend-rich past,
> danced under the moon with swirling skirts,
> to the fresh earliness of the rippling stream,
> to the land of our heart.
>
> ("To Hyang," 1959)[26]

He fondly evoked such a helpless rural plant as "day lily," in which he heard the voice of his ancestors or the age of innocence unsullied by modern civilization, much like the Adamic myth in American literature. But Shin oscillates between his utopian nostalgia and concerns for actuality. The use of past events, characters, especially folk heroes who mirror the mind of an historical period is a recurrent device in modern poetry. In his narrative poem *The Kŭm River* (1967), Shin chose to identify himself with the heroes of the Tonghak rebellion for their courage and conviction, devotion and toil, and final martyrdom. His special use of the past raises the question of the idea of society and the justification for power. The cause of the plight of Korea in the past and present is seen as the misuse of power by authority— injustice, suppression, and corruption—in disregard of the welfare of people. The fact that poetry has to take up a problem so unpoetical is evidence of social instability.

In "Snow Falls in the South" (1967), Hwang Tong-gyu (born 1938) also contemplates the defeat of Chŏn Pong-jun (1854-1895), a leader of the Tonghak rebellion.

[25] Yeats' Ireland, Eliot's Boston and the Dry Salvages Off Cape Ann, Frost's Vermont, Steven's Florida, Williams' Paterson, Tate's South, Olson's Gloucester, and even Black Mountain and New York—all this is in an attempt to endow poetry with a sense of place and to combat chaos with a world discovered by the imagination.

[26] Trans. U-chang Kim.

Pon-jun is weeping, illiterate, illiterate,
Utterly illiterate.
If only he knew how to read the classics,
If only he knew how to cry softly!

If Chŏn had remained a farmer without attempting social-political reform to
benefit the people, he would not have been beheaded. But if he had had a
classical education like a member of the ruling class, would he have dared
what was fated to be a failure? His failure was an epitome of the tragedy of
a lesser power, which brought about the collapse of the old order, the loss
of the country, and finally division. Hwang Tong-gyu therefore views history
at a distance, with irony, for the situation has not changed after some eighty
years. His country is still ruled by whims and decrees, power and terror.
Bearing testimony to the corruption of justice, he will live on to express his
compassion for humanity. His later poems encompass the barbed wire that
besieges his consciousness and snowflakes falling from the sky—a symbol
of consciousness, an emblem of purification and the esemplastic (unifying)
power of the imagination.

Ah, those are sick words.
My soles shiver.
I'm determined to become a simple man!
When dry winds,
Daylong,
Chase snow here and there,
In the evening,
Every snowflake is muddy—
When the sun-shaped sun suddenly down,
My dream shattered,
Prostrate on the ground,
I wipe away my eyes, nose, and mouth.
Terrifying even to myself,
Am I turning into
Muddy snow
Driven about and trampled again?

"I'm determined to become a simple man," the speaker says in "Snow under
Martial Law"; but can a poet afford to, even if he knows he will turn into
"muddy snow/ Driven about and trampled again?" There is nothing agree-
able or ideal in the poem. The conversational tone, disjunctive progression,
rapid transition, and reliance on symbols and sequence of emotions for
meaning—all seem to be at the service of arousing a similar emotion in the
reader. The poem also explores the ambiguity of homonyms, *nun* meaning

"snow" (three times) and *nun* meaning "eye" (once, but *nun* in line 7 could also mean "eye"). The speaker shows no feeling of piety for repetitive history: it is only terrifying—those sick words make one's soles shiver.

If there is enough blood in this language, it is because the poet drew not only on his self but also on the common predicament of his people. His is a voice that expresses what his fellow men know but do not think of saying or could not say. Traditional rhetoric in the poetry of protest, with assumptions and responses about the dialectic of engagement and withdrawal, society and nature, action and contemplation cannot adequately sustain the modernist tradition, a bold but plain language focusing on a contrast between personal and social realities and his dream. He knows there is no easy affirmation, but he must define, as best as he can, his own role in relation to the flux and audience.

This is not a protest for the sake of novelty, difference, or surprise, but a passionate concern for the survival of his culture. Unlike some politically naive poets in the west who mistook fascism for aristocracy (Yeats, Eliot, Pound, Celine, Brecht, to name a few),[27] Korean poets have a firm grasp of the reality of historical changes and try to find a parallel or contrast to illuminate the actuality. Hence the mediation of history, landscape, and reality are inseparable. In fact, both the poet-in-nature and the poet-in-society participate in culture to affirm the same allegiances to the human condition. Again, unlike some western poets who wished to escape from or efface the self (for example, Eliot, Pound, Williams, the confessional poets,[28] the Projectivists) ours cling tenaciously to the center of consciousness. The fact that none succumbed to the allure of the Savage God (suicide)[29] seems to show how ours shunned excess, a misguided expression of free will. Some practitioners elsewhere write poetry that is submerged, elusive, floating, or simply silent ("disengagement from life"),[30] as if to abdicate the role of the poet in time. But a poem is written by somebody, it comes from some place, it is related to others, and it must mean something. Marked by a rigorous exclusion of sentimentality, self-pity, and impatience, however startling a risk our poets may have taken with language, their assumptions about the educated common reader's knowledge have not caused an outcry.

[27]Donald Davie, *The Poet in the Imaginary Museum*, ed. Berry Alpert (Manchester: Carcanet New Press, 1977), p. 169.

[28]For a sympathetic reading of confessional poets see Steven K. Hoffman, "Impersonal Personalism: The Making of a Confessional Poetic," *ELH* 45 (1978), 687-709.

[29]Irving Howe, *The Critical Point on Literature and Culture* (New York: Horizon Press, 1973), pp. 170-180.

[30]Robert Pinsky's phrase, see *The Situation of Poetry* (Princeton: Princeton University Press, 1976), p. 166.

A little more than seventy years ago modern Korean poetry was born with "From the Sea to Children." The primary concerns of poets have been: could the self be free in an enslaved society? How could one create a national literature and a national mind without a nation? How could a poetry be consonant with the time and with the Korean reality? And how could a poetry, which found its material in suffering in a specific time and place, be at once local and universal, contemporary and perennial? The struggle against the tradition meant a struggle with the language, a search for new ways of expressing political and spiritual predicaments. The cultural and moral crises fostered experiments and stimulated the modernization of language—the adoption of common speech, the distinction of tenses and numbers, the identification of the subject, the use of free verse, and the widening of subject matter. Early in the development of modern poetry, however, poets learned that technical innovation alone did not create a new poetry or a new self. They also learned that the poet must take up his place in society and culture, if he is to be heard. The poets who matter have delved into the resources of language to establish contacts with audiences and to secure desired effects. Knowing that the meaning of words is the history of words, they have performed their function by adding new dimensions to the language—hence my emphasis throughout on the form, rhythm, meaning, and rhetoric.

The violation of normal language—anomalies of syntax and linguistic structure, together with elliptical associations and elusive metaphors, also attests to the existence of repression, for modern Korean poetry is a poetry produced under a continuous censorship. But we recognize the poets' gestures and a voice that speaks to us. Poets who matter move into the life of their readers, identifying their inner anguish with our common human plight. A poet of his time reflects the moment of his culture; he is a spokesman for the values by which his fellow men must live. Poetry of engagement and relevance is a product of a fierce honesty that scorns the threat of annihilation and creates affirmations; as Eliot says, only through time is time conquered. The major poets of modern Korea perfected the art of being themselves, a Korean voice issuing from Korean themes and the Korean soil. Informed by a powerful moral vision, they sang life without deception and illusion. They returned to tradition to redeem the past and to verify a new world they created ("Make it New," *Analects*, II, 11), a poetry of universal validity and appeal. As Lao Tzu said (XXV), the farthest journey is return.

University of Hawaii at Manoa

SOME FEATURES OF JAPANESE THOUGHT *

Hajime Nakamura

Owing to the rapid development of industrialization in contemporary life, traditional values are being lost gradually in many countries all over the world. Japan is no exception. It is our concern to know how traditional values that are preserved and embodied in daily life of the Japanese can be useful in an international community in the future.

I. THE PHENOMENAL WORLD AS ABSOLUTE

Let us begin with the observation that the Japanese are willing to accept the phenomenal world as Absolute because of their disposition to put more emphasis upon intuitive sensible concrete events than upon universals and abstract ideas. This emphasis upon the fluid, arresting character of observed events regards the phenomenal world itself as Absolute and rejects the recognition of anything existing over and above it. What is widely known among modern Japanese philosophers in the last century as the "theory that the phenomenal is actually the real" has deep roots in Japanese tradition.

It was characteristic of the religious views of the ancient Japanese that they believed that spirits reside in all things. They personified spirits other than those of human beings, considered them ancestral gods, and tended to view every spirit as divine. This gave birth to Shinto shrines, for in order

* Sources of the materials cited in this article are the following works: Hajime Nakamura, *Ways of Thinking of Eastern Peoples: India, China Tibet, Japan*, revised English translation, edited by Philip P. Wiener (Honolulu: East-West Center Press, 1964); Hajime Nakamura, *History of the Development of Japanese Thought*, 2 volumes (Tokyo: The Japan Foundation 1967); The Seventeen-Article Constitution, translated into English by Hajime Nakamura, in *Prince Shōtoku and Shitennōji Temple* (Osaka: The Hosan-Kai of Shitennoji Temple, 1970), pp. 30-33.

to perform religious ceremonies the gods and spirits were fixed in certain specified places. The most primitive form of this practice consisted in the invocation and worship of spirits in some specific natural object, mountain, river, forest, tree, or stone. Even to this day there remain shrines of this type. This way of thinking runs through the subsequent history of Shinto down to the present day. "Nowhere is there a shadow in which a god does not reside: in peaks, ridges, pines, cryptomerias, mountains, rivers, seas, villages, plains, and fields—everywhere there is a god. We can receive the constant and intimate help of these spirits in our tasks; many courtiers are passing."

Buddhist philosophy likewise was received and assimilated on the basis of this thinking. To begin with, the Tendai sect in Japan is not the same as China. Tendai scholars in medieval Japan, using the same nomenclature as that used in continental Chinese Buddhism, arrived at a distinctly original system of thought, called *Honkaku Hōmon*, which asserts that the appearances of doing things in the phenomenal world are aspects of the Buddha. On the Asian continent, the word for Enlightenment, *"Honkaku,"* meant the ultimate comprehension of what is beyond the phenomenal world, whereas in Japan the same word was brought down to refer to "understanding things within the phenomenal world." In this way, the characteristic feature of Tendai Buddhism in Japan is an emphasis upon things rather than principles.

It is natural that the Nichiren sect, an outgrowth of Japanese Tendai, also puts emphasis upon an empirical turn of thought. Nichiren asserts that "in the earlier half of the whole Lotus Sutra, the directions are called the pure land and this place is called the soiled land, while in the latter part of this Sutra, on the contrary, this place, this world, is called the main land, and the pure land in the ten directions is called the soiled land where Buddha has had an incarnation." The Nichiren sect states that, although Tendai takes the standpoint of "Action according to principles," Nichiren emphasizes "Action according to things."

The way of thinking that seeks for the Absolute in the phenomenal world plays an effective role in the assimilation of the Zen sect as well. The Zen Buddhism of Master Dōgen seems to have been influenced by the traditional Japanese way of thinking.

The Sanskrit word *"dharmatā"* means "truth." In connection with this, Dogen says that the truth which people search for is, in reality, nothing but the world of our daily experience. Thus he says. "The real aspect is all things. All things are this aspect, this character, this body, this mind, this world, this wind and this rain, etc., this sequence of daily going, living, sitting, and lying down, this series of melancholy, joy, action, and inaction, this stick and wand, this Buddha's smile, this transmission and reception of the doctrine, this study and practice, this evergreen pine and ever-unbreakable bamboo."

For Dōgen, therefore, the fluid aspect of impermanence is in itself the absolute state, the changeable character of the phenomenal world is of absolute significance. "Impermanence is the Buddhahood . . . The impermanence of the person's body and mind is verily the Buddhahood. The impermanence of the [land] and scenery is verily the Buddhahood."

Starting from such a viewpoint, Dōgen gives some phrases of Buddhist scripture interpretations that are essentially different from the original meanings. Dōgen said, "Buddhahood is time. He who wants to know Buddhahood may know it by knowing time as it is revealed to us." Elsewhere he asserts, "There is not the one mind apart from all things, and there are not all things apart from the one mind."

Dōgen is critical of the Zen Buddhism of China. The words of a Chinese Zen Buddhist, Yao-shan Wei-yen (745-828), contains the phrase "at a certain time." Dōgen interprets this phrase unjustifiably as "Being Time" and comments as follows: "So-called 'Being Time' means that time already is being and all being is time." A certain Japanese philosopher was delighted in finding a predecessor of Heideggar in Dōgen.

Again and again Dogen emphasizes that the true reality is not something static but dynamic. "It is a heretical doctrine," Dogen says, "to think the mind mobile and the essence of things static."

II. The Acceptance of Man's Natural Disposition

The Japanese in general are inclined to search for the absolute within the phenomenal world or in what is immediately observable. Man's natural dispositions rank highest in the Japanese way of thinking.

Just as the Japanese are apt to accept external and objective nature as it is, so they are inclined to accept man's natural desires and sentiments as they are, and not to strive to repress or fight against them.

Love, for example, was the favorite theme of ancient Japanese poetry. Love, among the ancient Japanese, was sensual and unrestrained, an expression of the true meaning of life. In general, their sentiments were direct and open, without suppression. Japanese poetry is, accordingly, rich in love poems, and seems vastly different from the general tendency of the poetry of the Indians and the Chinese.

In ancient China there were also some love songs included in the *Book of Poetry* [*Shih Ching*], but later Confucianists did not want to admit that they were love songs and explained them away in this fashion: These are not true love poems; they are poems composed by ancient sages to administer good politics, using allusions to love affairs.

Motoori Norinaga (1730-1801), the great scholar of Japanese classics, laughed at this moralistic attitude of the Chinese Confucianists. He recognized the distinction between the Japanese and the Chinese in this respect: "The fact that the *Book of Poetry* [*Shih Ching*] lacks love poems reveals something of the customs of the people of that country [China]. They only make an outward show of manly appearance, concealing the womanishness of their real selves. In contrast, the abundance of love poems in our empire reveals the way to express one's genuine dispositions."

How does this tendency affect the Japanese way of adopting foreign cultures?

Ogyū Sorai (1666-1718) recognized the intrinsic value of old literary works, whose value should not be observed by their risqué contents. He maintained that since poetry expressed natural feelings, the farfetched moralizing on the poems by Chinese critics was not relevant. He said: "The *Book of Poetry* [*Shih Ching*] is composed of the language of songs, just as later poetry is. Later scholars regard the *Book of Poetry* as an exposition of the principle of punishing vice and rewarding virtue. That is why one is at wit's end when it comes to interpreting the lascivious poetry of Cheng and Wei. The moral teachings of justice are so rare in this *Book* that they are negligible. If the neo-Confucianists' opinion is accepted, then why should the sage have resorted to such a roundabout way [of presenting political-moral principles in the form of love songs], instead of writing directly a separate book of moral instruction? So the opinion of these Confucianists shows that they are ignorant of the essence of poetry."

Dazai Shundai (1680-1747) called man's natural feelings the only genuine ones, which he listed as "likes and dislikes, suffering and rejoicing, anxiety and pleasures, etc." He maintains that there is not a single human being devoid of these feelings: "For the noble or the low, there is no difference in this respect. Love of one's parents, wives, and children is also the same for all. Since these feelings originate from an innate truthfulness, never stained with falsity, they are called genuine feelings." His standpoint is pure naturalism. "Those actions are done without being taught, without learning, without force but with freedom from all thoughts, are the work of natural disposition. This is called truthfulness."

According to the way of saints, one is a man of noble character only if one does not act improperly but "observes decorum concerning the body [regardless of] whether or not one sees a woman and imagines her lasciviously and takes delight in her beauty. That is exactly what it means to discipline one's mind through proper decorum."

Apparently this is a metamorphosis of Confucianism in Japan. Dazai, the Japanese Confucianist, defiantly declared: "I would rather be a master of acrobatic feats than a moralist."

As a nationalist, Hirata Atsutane (1776-1843) said, "One should indeed stop acting like a sage and completely abandon the so-called mind, or the way of enlightenment. Let us, instead, not distort or forget this spirit of Japan, the soul of this country, but train and regulate it so that we may polish it up into a straight, just, pure, and good spiritual Japan."

On the whole, Japanese Buddhism inclined towards peaceful and quiet enjoyment. The practice of prayer, for instance, was an occasion for the aristocrats of the Heian period to enjoy contemplative pleasures.

The Pure Land teachings, preached by Hōnen (1133-1212), disregard the distinction between the observance and the infringement of disciplines. Its emphasis is solely upon the practice of the invocation of Amitābha.

In traditional Mahāyāna Buddhism, the eating of fish or meat was not allowed. When Hōnen was asked whether fish is all right to eat or not, he replied: "If one who eats fish should be reborn into the Pure Land, a cormorant would certainly be the one. If one who does not eat fish should be reborn into the Pure Land, a monkey would indeed be the one. Whether or not one eats fish is of no consequence; it is the one who invokes Amitābha Buddha that is bound to be reborn into the Pure Land."

It is a well-known fact that, after Japan opened itself to the world in 1868, practically all the sects of Japanese Buddhism broke away from those disciplines.

The most outstanding example of the repudiation of the disciplines is drinking. The Indian Buddhist considered drinking a very serious religious sin; that was why "no drinking" was counted among the five precepts and was strictly observed, not only by priests and ascetics, but also by lay believers. In India the discipline of no drinking was strictly observed from the time of early Buddhism to that of Mahāyāna Buddhism. (The late degenerate period of esoteric Buddhism was an exception.) This discipline was strictly observed in China also, but was abandoned in Japan.

Hōnen, in reply to the question, "Is it a sin to drink? " answered: "In truth you ought not to drink, but drinking is, after all, a custom of this world." Neither Shinran nor Nichiren considered drinking as necessarily evil. Nichiren preached, "Drink only with your wife, and recite *Nam-myō-hō-renge-kyō* [Adoration to the Lotus Sutra] !" The Shungen sect maintained that if one inserts a slip with the following magic formula, even evil wine is transformed into good wine:

> The gods know, and
> Gods also drink
> The pure-water wine
> Of the sacred Mimosuso River.

Together with drinking, sexual relations between men and women also had their place in Japanese Buddhism.

Even now, Shōten [Ganesa] and Aizen Myōō [The God of Love] are widely worshipped as objects of popular religion for the consummation of one's love. Shōten, or the God of Ecstasy, who was originally Ganesa in India, was adopted and metamorphosed by the esoteric Buddhists. The images of Ganesa now existent in India, in contrast, are by no means obscene; the religious custom of worshipping the images of the elephant-faced god/goddess in an embrace is confined perhaps to Japan, Mongolia, and Tibet only.

Whereas the majority of the Indians and the Chinese try to distinguish the world of religion from that of the flesh, there is a latent tendency among the Japanese to identify the one with the other. In this way the same characteristics which mark the form in which Confucianism was accepted are also said to mark the acceptance of Buddhism.

The Japanese are probably the only Asiatic people who have forsaken almost all of the Buddhist disciplines. How should we account for this fact?

Since the olden days there has been a strong tendency among the Japanese to hold fast to a specific and closed social nexus or community. The repudiation of disciplines may seem on the surface to be incompatible with such a tendency, but the two are not necessarily in conflict. Religious disciplines are not always in agreement with customary morality.

Not to eat meat, not to drink, and not to marry are important problems when viewed from the standpoint of religion, but from the standpoint of defending the interests of the closed social nexus or community they do not count for much. Quite prevalent among the Japanese, however, are the dual attitudes of ignoring the religious disciplines on the one hand and of self-sacrificing devotion to the interests of the closed nexus or community of the other. Such attitudes gave rise to the idea that the assertion of natural desires and the abandonment of the disciplines do not necessarily mean the abandonment of the moral order.

III. EMPHASIS ON BENEVOLENCE

The tendency of the Japanese to accept the facts of life manifests itself in the form of the acceptance and high esteem for man's natural disposition. Buddhist ideas are preached with frank references to matters of love, for sexual love is not considered to be incompatible with religious matters. Not only has the significance of the human body been recognized, but also the idea of taking good care of one's body has become prominent in Japanese Buddhism.

The Japanese also put special emphasis upon the love of others. Kumazawa

Banzan, a famous Confucianist of the 17th century, calls Japan "the land of benevolence." The love of others in its purified form is named "benevolence [Sanskrit: *maitrī, karuṇā*]." This idea was introduced into Japan with the advent of Buddhism, and special emphasis was laid upon it from the first. Among the many sects of Japanese Buddhism, the Pure Land Sect, which typically emphasizes benevolence, enjoys great popularity. Pure Land Buddhism preaches the benevolence of Amitābha Buddha, who saves the bad man as well as the ordinary man. Most of the high priests of the sect have especially optimistic outlooks and benign attitudes.

Needless to say, the idea of benevolence had an important significance in Chinese Buddhism. Zen Buddhism, however, developed because the Chinese people's Buddhism did not seem to emphasize the idea of benevolence very much. This is probably because the Chinese Zen sect, under the influence of Taoism and other traditional ideologies of China, was inclined to strict clerical seclusion and resignation and neglected the positive approach of practising deeds of benevolence.

At the time the Zen sect was brought to Japan, however, it came to emphasize deeds of benevolence, just as the other sects in Japan did. Eisai, who introduced Rinzai-Zen, put the idea of benevolence first. "You should arouse the spirit of great benevolence . . . and save mankind everywhere with the pure and supreme disciplines of the Great Bodhisattva, but you ought not to seek deliverance for your own sake."

Dōgen (1200-1253), although he does not often use the word "benevolence" specifically, chooses for instruction the phrase "speak kindly to others" and "words of affection" from among the various Buddhist doctrines of the past. "Speaking words of affection means to generate a heart of benevolence and bestow upon others the language of affection, whenever one sees them. To speak with the heart, looking at mankind with benevolence as though they were your own children, is to utter words of affection. The virtuous should be praised, the virtueless pitied. To cause the enemy to surrender, or to make the wise yield, words of affection are most fundamental."

"To hear words of affection in one's presence pleases and brightens one's countenance and warms one's heart. To hear words of affection said in one's absence goes home to one's heart and soul. You should learn to know that words of affection are powerful enough to set the river on fire."

In addition, he emphasizes upon the virtues of altruism and cooperation beneath which flows the pure current of affection. The spirit of benevolence was preached by the Buddhists and also made its way into Shinto, where it was bound up with one of the three divine symbols of the Japanese Imperial family. It was also popularized among the general public and came to be regarded as one of the principal virtues of the samurai. The love of others by no means comes out of self-complacency. On the contrary, it goes with a humble reflection that one is, like others, an ordinary man. This had already been stressed by Prince Shōtoku at the beginning of the introduction of Buddhism into Japan.

A debate arose as to whether the benevolent tendency is inherent in the Japanese or was developed afterwards. It is certain that we owe it, to a great extent, to the Buddhist influence. For example, in the peaceful period of the Heian era (794-1184), when Buddhist influence was strong, there was not a single instance of capital punishment. This is a remarkable fact. There has hardly been any period in any other country up to the modern era marked by the absence of the death penalty. Even nowadays there are far fewer cases of murder in those districts where Buddhist influence is strongest.

On the other hand, our love of human beings seems to have been closely tied up with the love of nature, which we owe greatly to the beautiful scenery of the natural surroundings. Our general impression is that the spirit of bene-volence was probably introduced into Japan with the advent of Buddhism and that it exerted a renovating influence upon the traditional attitude of the Japanese. So it may be safely asserted that a certain element of humanism existed among the Japanese originally, and that with foreign influences—mainly Buddhist—the element of compassion appeared as we have it in later history, down to the present day.

Japan had another peaceful period in the past. Tokugawa Ieyasu, the military ruler, won the Battle of Sekigahara in 1600, in which all *daimyō* in the country took part, and he established national supremacy. In 1615 Ieyasu captured Osaka Castle, destroying the Toyotomi family. After that nation-wide peace prevailed until 1866, when the Tokugawa armies were successfully repelled at Chōshū. For nearly 250 years there was no nation-wide war and no war was waged with any foreign country. People enjoyed a peaceful life, although they were oppressed and exploited by feudal lords. I think such a situation is quite rare in the history of the world.

IV. CONCORD

The Japanese attitude of esteeming the natural dispositions of man is closely connected with the Japanese esteem of "concord" or "harmony." The ideal of "concord" or "harmony" was traditionally emphasized by the forefathers of Japan. We ought to evaluate it in the international scope from a new view-point.

In Japan the desired social ideal has been unanimous moral solidarity of a community on an island scale. This was intuitively felt in the spiritual atmosphere of the primitive Japanese society. Later, when the centralized state was established, after conflicts among various tribes had ended, what was stressed in the first place as the principle of the community was "concord (or *wa* in Japanese)."

The leader of Japan on this eventful age was Prince Shōtoku (574-622), Regent of Empress Suikō. He promulgated the Seventeen Article Constitution; Article 1 runs as follows: "Harmony (or concord) is to be valued, and an avoidance of wanton opposition to be honored." The spirit of concord was stressed throughout all the articles of the Constitution.

According to Prince Shōtoku, if we discuss affairs with this feeling of harmony—desisting from anger—difficult problems will be settled spontaneously and in the right way. In this way alone is it possible for decisions to be reached at conferences. The democratic way of managing a conference was realized in the remote past. In the mythology which reflects the primitive society of Japan, the *kami* convened in divine assembly in the bed of a river. This tradition was followed and developed by later monarchs. Setting forth multifarious mental attitudes of rulers and officials, Prince Shōtoku denounced dictatorship and stressed the necessity of discussing things with others: "Decisions on important matters should generally not be made by one person alone. They should be discussed with many others." This trend developed into an edict after the Taika Reform (645), which thus denounced the dictatorship of a sovereign: "Things should not be instituted by a single ruler."

Where did the denunciation of dictatorship come from?

The ancient way of ruling represented in Japanese mythology is not dictatorship by a monarch or by the Lord of All, but by a conference of gods in a river bed. Where public opinion was not esteemed, a conference could not have been held successfully: hence the spirit of primitive life in Japan must have been inherited and developed by later rulers.

On the other hand, it is possible that influential Buddhists influenced the thought of the Prince by means of rules set forth in full detail in the scriptures, including decision by majority rule in the order. This ideal was preserved in the days when the emperors were in power: The Japanese Emperor system developed as something different from dictatorship.

Professor Northrop observed that when a dispute arises among Asians, one does not settle it by recourse to determined legal principles, but by the "middle way" of meditation between the determinate theses of the disputants, by fostering the all-embracing, intuitively felt formlessness common to all men and things.

This is exactly the situation we find among the people of Japan. There is a well-known Japanese proverb which is understood by everybody in practice: "In a quarrel both parties are to blame." This is not due to lack of esteem for law on the part of Japanese people, but to financial and other reasons. If people should go to court, they will lose much time; it may take them several years to settle even one case. They have to employ lawyers and spend much money. Even if they should win at court, they will eventually obtain very little. Hence resort to legal measures very often impairs the happiness and welfare of the people concerned and others around them. Barristers-at-law are not always respected as in the West, but are sometimes abhorred by the common people of Japan, who fear that they may take advantage of the people's lack of legal knowledge in order to make money. I myself personally know some Japanese intellectuals who claim to be businessmen at home but to be lawyers when they go abroad: they want to conceal their status as lawyers when they work among the Japanese.

As the objective causes which brought about such a tendency in the Japanese people, we may cite the social life peculiar to their land and climate. The primitive Indo-Europeans, being nomadic and living chiefly by hunting, were in contact with alien peoples. Here, human relations were marked by fierce rivalry. Peoples were in great migration; one race conquered another, only to be conquered by still another. In such a society, struggles for existence were based not on mutual trust but on rational plan and stratgem.

Japanese society, on the other hand, developed from small localized farming communities. The Japanese did away with nomadic life very early, and settled down to cultivate rice paddies. People living on rice must inevitably settle permanently in one place. In such a society families continue, generation after generation. Genealogies and kinships of families become so well known by their members that the society as a whole takes on the appearance of a family. In such a society individuals are closely bound to each other and form an exclusive human nexus. Here an individual who asserts himself strongly and egoistically will hurt the feelings of others and thereby do harm to himself. The Japanese learned to adjust themselves to this type of familial society and created forms of expression suitable to life in it.

This tendency is deeply rooted in the people and has led to their stressing of human relations, especially the spirit of harmony and concord. The Japanese have learned to attach much importance to the human nexus, tending to minimize the individual.

V. TOLERANCE

The attitude of esteeming concord or harmony brings forth the spirit of tolerance.

The Japanese have been distinguished for their spirit of tolerance since ancient times. Although there must have been instances of interracial conflicts in prehistoric Japan, there exists no archeological evidence that there were any highly violent armed conflicts. According to the classical records also, the Japanese generally treated conquered peoples tolerantly. There are many tales of war, but there is no evidence that conquered peoples were made into slaves *in toto.*

Such a social condition gives rise to the tendency to stress harmony among the members of a society rather than dominance based on power. This is not to deny entirely the presence of the power relationship in Japanese society since ancient times. The social restrictions and pressures upon the individual might have indeed been stronger in Japan than in many other countries. Nevertheless, in the consciousness of each individual Japanese, the spirit of conciliation and tolerance has been pre-eminent.

The spirit of tolerance of the Japanese made it impossible to cultivate deep hatred even toward sinners. In the Japan of the Buddhistic period there existed few cruel punishments. Since crucifixion appeared for the first time in Japanese history during the Sengoku period, or Age of Civil Wars, it was presumably started after the advent of Christianity and suggested by it.

For the Japanese, full of the spirit of tolerance, the idea of *eternal damnation* is absolutely inconceivable. Among the doctrines of Christianity the idea of eternal damnation was especially hard for the Japanese to comprehend.

The fact that the Japanese manifest more of the spirit of tolerance and conciliation than the tendency to develop an intense hatred of sins also transformed Pure Land Buddhism. According to his eighteenth vow Amitābha Buddha will save the whole mankind out of his great benevolence, excepting only "those who committed the five great sins and those who damned the Right Law (Buddhism)." Saint Hōnen of the 12th century said, "You should believe that even those who have committed the ten evils and the five heinous sins are eligible for rebirth in the Pure Land, and yet you should shrink from the slightest of all the sins."

What are the rational bases for such a spirit of tolerance and conciliation? The tendency to recognize absolute significance in everything phenomenal leads to an acceptance of the jusitification of any view held in the mundane world, and ends up with the adaptability of any view with the spirit of tolerance and conciliation.

Such a way of thinking appeared from the earliest days of the introduction of Buddhism into this country. Many Buddhist leaders of Japan recognized the justification of multiple religious faiths. Because of this spirit of tolerance and conciliation, the development of a single continuum of various sects was possible within Japanese Buddhism.

Such a conciliatory attitude seems ultimately to form part of Japan's cultural heritage. When Christian civilization penetrated Japanese society after the Meiji Restoration, those who welcomed it were not necessarily about to become Christians. For most people in Japan, nothing about Christianity was incompatible with their traditional religion. That was the reason, it appears, why Christian culture became widespread despite the extremely small minority that converted to the Christian religion.

Thanks to the spirit of tolerance, a massacre of heathens never took place in Japan. In this respect, the situation differs vastly in Japan from that in the West. As far as religion was concerned the idea of "harmony" is the foremost quality in this country's cultural history. Some apparently exceptional cases have occurred: one being an overall and thoroughgoing persecution of Catholics, the second being the persecution of local Jōdō-Shin believers, and the third being a severe suppression of Nichiren and the Non-Receiving-and-Non-Giving sect (one of the Nichiren sects which has refused to receive alms from or give alms to those other than the believers of the Lotus Sutra). These, however, were far from being religious persecutions in the Western sense of the word. These sects were suppressed and persecuted simply because the ruling class feared the subversion that might be worked by these sects upon a certain human nexus, that is, the feudal social order maintained by the ruling class. A mere difference of religious faith was generally a matter of no consequence for the Japanese unless it was considered to be damaging to the established order of the social nexus; whereas in the West, a religious difference in itself would give rise to a conflict between opposing parties.

The spirit of tolerance has come to be esteemed very highly in the contemporary world. With the development of technology and mass communication, all human beings of different countries are going to live in a closely-knit human nexus. In the past, peoples of different countries lived separately. Whatever might have taken place in a distant country, it did not affect people of the countries which lay far away from the event. Now the situation has changed. Any violence which takes place in anywhere in the world immediately affects people of other places. The world has become smaller and smaller. The term "world" has often been replaced by the term "globe," which gives us the impression that we are going to live in a limited area of space. We must pay due consideration to people of other parts of the world. In this context the ethics of "concord" or "social harmony," which was practically understood and practiced by our forefathers, although not systematized in terms of concepts, will give us clues for solving the problem of how to bring forth mutual understanding and collaboration among different peoples of the world and how to attain world peace.

In this respect we should re-examine and re-evaluate traditional Japanese values for the cause of the prosperity and peace of the world.

University of Tokyo

II

EAST-WEST CROSSCULTURAL RELATIONS

THE CONFUCIAN *FIVE CLASSICS* AS A CONTRADICTION OF THE MOSAIC PENTATEUCH: A Study of the Encounter Between East and West on the Subject of Chronology

David Wei-yang Dai

The Jesuit missionaries, following the policy of St. Francis Xavier and Matteo Ricci, conscientiously accumulated information about China. These regular official reports on missionary activities were sent from the mission field to the several headquarters of the Society in Europe. In order to encourage new missionaries and to increase contributions to finance their work, excerpts from these official reports and personal correspondence were widely published in Europe. An unexpected result was that many men of letters throughout Europe made use of these passages to support their anti-Christian and anti-Biblical arguments. One of their major targets was the absolute authority of the Bible, particularly the Mosaic account of the date of the Creation and of the Deluge. Through this transmission—the translations by missionaries and the writings of English and continental Enlightenment figures—the reliability of the chronology as given in the Pentateuch came to be challenged by the more ancient history recorded in Confucian *Five Classics*, These opposing assertions, the reckoning of the time of the Creation and the Flood on the one hand by the early church fathers and on the other by the Jesuit Chinese chronologists, are the focus of this paper.

A chronology that went far back was indicated in each of the major Jesuit books on China.[1] After collecting and organizing the various missionary reports in Rome, Juan Gonzales de Mendoza, a Spanish Augustinian missionary at the command of Pope Gregory XIII, published *Historia . . . del gran Reyno de la China* in 1585. According to Lach's research, "Mendoza and

---

[1] For a list of important treatises bearing on the subject, see Cordier, *Bibliotheca Sinica*, "Chronology," I, pp. 557-564; and "Origine et antiquité des Chinois," I, pp. 571-579.

Rada write of China and its dynasties historically . . . depend upon Chinese literary sources as well as informants. Both writers dismiss as legendary the stories of creation found in the chronicles at their disposal. Both begin their historical account of the monarchy with Yü the Great, the founder of the Hsia dynasty (traditionally dated 2205-1766 B.C.) . . . The Chinese, Rada thinks, 'begin to have kings shortly after the Flood,' . . . And Mendoza remarks, 'that there is opinion that the first that did inhabit this countrie, were the neuewes of Noe.' Thus with the introduction of the chronology of the kings, Mendoza helped to lay the background for the great argument which soon developed in Europe over the antiquity of Chinese civilization and the relative reliability of Chinese and Biblical chronology."[2] Later, Martino Martini, in his *Historiae Sinicae Decas Prima* of 1658, set his chrono-logical tables of the Chinese Empire starting in 1697 B.C., with Huang Ti [Yellow Emperor], but noted that two earlier Chinese Emperors, Shen-Nung and Fu-Hsi, were said to have reigned 255 years earlier, pushing the beginning of the Empire back to 2952 B.C. He therefore advocated the use of a longer Patriarchal Chronology based on the Greek Septuagint to allow sufficient time for the growth of the population and culture in China.[3]

It was only with the publication of *Confucius Sinarum Philosophus: sive, Scientia Sinensis* in 1687 that European scholars—Locke, Leibniz, and Newton, for example—began to respond to these Jesuit works on China.[4] *Scientia Sinensis* represented the cumulative, collaborative result of the Jesuit interpretations of Chinese culture. In particular, it included trans-lations of three of the Confucian *Four Books* as well as a section called the "Tabula Chronologica Monarchiae Sinicae ante Christum juxta Cyclos anno-rum 60." The date 2697 B.C. is still widely regarded in the West as the begin-ning point of Chinese history. This date, however, could not correlate with the widely accepted dates given by Bishop James Ussher for the Creation and the Flood. Before Ussher, Joseph Scaliger (A.D. 1540-1609) wrote his monu-mental work *De Emendatione Temporum* in 1596; it described the Julian period of 7980 years from 4714 B.C. to A.D. 3266, formed by the multipli-cation of the sun cycle every 28 years and the moon cycle every 19 years.[5]

---

[2] Donald Frederick Lach, *Asia in the Making of Europe* (Chicago: University of Chicago Press, 1965), Volume I, Book 2, p. 783.

[3] Virgile Pinot, *La Chine et la formation de l'esprit philosophique en France, 1640-1740* (Paris: P. Geuthner, 1932), pp. 200-220.

[4] *Confucius Sinarum Philosophus: sive, Scientia Sinensis, Latine Exposita, Studio et opera Prosperi Intorcetta, Christiani Herdtrich, Francisci Rougemont, Philippi Couplet, Patrum Societatia Jesu, Parisiis Apud D. Horthemels, 1687*. There are 18 copies in Amer-ican libraries (see *Union Catalog*).

[5] Martin Anstey, *Chronology of the Old Testament* (Grand Rapids, Michigan: Kregel Publications, 1973), p. 26.

The shorter Patriarchal Chronology, given in the Massoretic Text of the Old Testament, was adopted by Ussher in 1654. He dates the beginning of the world as occurring on Sunday October 23 in 4004 B.C. He also dates "the Second Age of the World" as "the 601 year of life of *Noah*, upon the first day of the first month (October 23 being our Friday), the first day, as first of the new world, so now of this new year; when the surface of the earth was now all dry, *Noah* took off the covering of the Ark (Gen. 8:13) . . . in 2349 B.C." [6] Bishop Lloyd revised Ussher's dates in 1701 and printed them in the margin of the Authorized Version of *Holy Bible with Chronological Dates and Index*.

In England, John Speed, in his *Prospect of the Most Famous Parts of the World* (1624), followed the medieval fable perpetuated in Sir John Mandeville's *Travels* of the two-eyed Chinaman, the one-eyed Christian, and the blind pagans. [7] Speed discarded, as did most of his contemporaries, the claims of the Chinese chronology. [8]

John Locke, who advocated the importance of chronology in *Some Thoughts Concerning Education*, [9] reviewed the several systems of computing the age of the world. *In An Essay Concerning Human Understanding*, Locke wrote,

> Hence we see, that some men imagine the Duration of the world from its first existence, to this present year 1689 . . . to have been 5,639 years, or equal to 5,639 annual Revolutions of the Sun, and others a great deal more: as the Aegyptians of Old, who in the time of Alexander counted 23,000 years, from the Reign of the Sun; and the Chinese now, who account the world 3,269,000 years old, according to their Computation, though I should not believe to be true, yet I can really imagine it with them, and as truly understand, and say one is longer than the other as I understand that *Methusalem*'s life was longer than *Enoch*'s. And if the common reckoning of 5,639 should be true, (as it may be, as well as any other assigned,) it hinders not at all my imagining what others mean, when they make the World a 1,000 years older, since every one may with the same Facility imagine (I do not say believe) the World to be 5,000

---

[6] James Ussher, *The Annals of the World: Deduced from the Origin of Time, containing the Historie of the Old and New Testament* (London: Printed by E. Tyler for the J. Crook, . . . and for G. Bedell, 1658), pp. 1 and 3. It is first published in Latin in 1654.

[7] John Speed, *A Prospect of the Most Famous Parts of the World* (London, 1627), p. 193. The first edition was published in 1624.

[8] Speed, p. 189.

[9] John Locke, *Thoughts Concerning Education*, Third Edition (London, 1695), pp. 318-320.

years old, as 5,639; and may as well conceive the duration of 50,000 years, as 5,639. . . .[10]

In demonstrating the large intervals of the Chinese time scale, Locke revealed his familiarity with the Jesuits' computation of Chinese chronology.[11] He evidently thought Chinese and Egyptian examples would be especially effective for the study of various chronological systems. As if it were a notion of God, Locke expected computations of the date of the Creation to be different and contradictory.

In Germany, Leibniz and Wolff were known for their interests in China. In his correspondence with the Jesuit Father Bouvet, Leibniz referred to Fohi as "Founder of the Empire."[12] Leibniz went on:

> China is a great Empire, no less in area than cultivated Europe, and indeed surpasses it in population and orderly government. Moreover, there is in China in certain regards an admirable public morality conjoined to a philosophical doctrine, or rather doctrine of natural theology, venerable by its antiquity, established and authorized for about 3000 years, long before the philosophy of the Greeks whose works nevertheless are the earliest which the rest of the world possess, except for our Sacred Writings. For both of these reasons, it would be highly foolish and presumptuous on your part, having newly arrived compared with them, and scarcely out of barbarism, to want to condemn such an ancient doctrine because it does not appear to agree at first glance with our ordinary scholastic notions.[13]

In his book *Leibniz and Confucianism*, David E. Mungello noticed the influence of the Jesuit's *Confucius Sinarum Philosophus* on Leibniz and reported that "Leibniz thinks that Chinese antiquity predates that of Europe and contains a 'natural theology' or knowledge of God derived simply from observation of nature, and that this characteristic, together with admirable moral exterior, has forced a China that in many ways surpasses Europe."[14]

---

[10] John Locke, *An Essay Concerning Human Understanding* (London: Eliz Holt, 1690), p. 92.

[11] According to John Harrison and Peter Laslett's *The Library of John Locke*, (Oxford: Oxford University Press, 1965), Locke owned at least 40 books on China.

[12] Gottfried Wilhelm Leibniz, *Discourse on the Natural Theology of the Chinese*, trans. Henry Rosemont, Jr. and Daniel J. Cook (Honolulu: The University Press of Hawaii, 1977), p. 157.

[13] Leibniz, p. 59.

[14] David E. Mungello, *Leibniz and Confucianism* (Honolulu: University of Hawaii Press, 1977), pp. 71-72.

In France, this controversy about dates also caught Pascal's attention. In his *Pensées*, Blaise Pascal (1623-1662), the student of Cornelius Jansen, the founder of his order,[15] posed the explosive question: "Which is the more credible of the two, Moses or China?" Pascal and his skeptical *alter ego* went on to debate:

> It is not a question of seeing this roughly.
> I tell you there is something to confuse and something to enlighten us.
> With this one word I destroy all your reasoning.
> "But China obscures things," say you; and I reply;
> "China obscures issues, but the *light* [emphasis mine] is there to be found; look for it."
> . . .
> For this reason we must look at it in detail; we must put the documents on the table.[16]

Pascal did not live to resolve this dilemma, but in Fragment 593, he signalled an abrupt and aribtrary conclusion with respect to "Moses or China," in the section "Against the History of China." In Fragment 618, he stated:

> I see then a crowd of religions in many parts of the world and in all times; but their morality cannot please me, nor can their proofs convince me. Thus I should equally have rejected the religion of Mohamet and of China, of the ancient Romans and of the Egyptians . . . .[17]

Although Pascal rejected all the other religions save Christianity, he kept his hope "that God will not leave other nations in this darkness for ever; that there will come a Saviour for all."[18]

Concerning the problem of rival antiquities, Du Pin in his *Bibliothèque*

---

[15] T. S. Eliot, "Introduction" in *Pascal's "Pensées"*, trans. W. F. Trotter (New York: E. P. Dutton, 1958), p. viii.

[16] Blaise Pascal, *Pensées*, Fragment 592. The French text in the Brunschwing edition of Pascal's *Oeuvres* (Paris, 1904), XIV, p. 33 reads (Lequel est le plus croyable des deux, Moise ou la Chine?) "Il n'est pas question de voir cela en gros; je vous dis qu'il y a de quoi aveugler et de quoi éclairer. Par ce mot seul, je ruine tous vos raisonnements. Mais la Chine obscurcit, dites-vous, et je réponds: La Chine obscurcit, mais il y a clarté à trouver; cherchez-la. . . . Il faut donc voir cela en détail; il faut mettre les papiers sur la table." The two English translations I consulted are M. Turnell in his edition of the *Pensées* (London, 1962), p. 229, and W. F. Trotter in his *Pascal's Pensées*.

[17] Pascal, p. 172.

[18] Pascal, p. 173.

universelle des historiens (1708) concluded that "The Phoenicians have
nothing elder than the Deluge," and "The Chinese pretend to Annals for
forty-nine thousand years before Fohi; but most of them agree that the
Memoirs are fabulous. ... "[19] Frank E. Manuel has remarked that Sir Isaac
Newton, like Pascal and Du Pin, attempted to demolish "the inflated claims
of Greeks, Romans, Egyptians, Chaldeans, Persians, and Chinese." Manuel
says that Newton found these claims to have been "sparked by diverse purposes, among them a simple desire to establish truth." Manuel goes on:

> But by all odds, the most deep-rooted of ... [Newton's] motives
> was a defense of the Hebrew scriptural tradition and Jewish anti-
> quities against the new libertines who were extolling the pagan
> ancients at Israel's expense. Not only was the Bible the most authen-
> tic history in the world, but the Kingdom of Israel was the first
> large-scale political society with all the attributes of civilization.
> Newton used Solomon's reign as the chronological divide; nations
> pretending that their forebears had organized empires before the
> tenth century were liars.[20]

In a sustained effort to refute the chronologies of the Greeks and Chinese,
Newton made a study of chronology. Indeed he became an ardent student of
the subject throughout the last thirty years of his life. According to Manuel's
research on the topic of Newton's library:

> Of the eighteen hundred or more volumes in the Huggins list, by far
> the majority are on the history of the ancient world, the history of
> pagan religions and mythology, the history of Israel, the history of
> the Christian Church and its doctrines, especially in the early ages,
> Biblical criticism and commentaries (particularly on the works of
> prophecy), and contemporary English theological disputations.
> There is a respectable sampling of modern European histories,
> though not of the great Renaissance Italians. Geography is well
> represented and there are a number of histories of non-European
> peoples, the Saracens, the Mongols, the Ethiopians, and the Chi-
> nese.[21]

Newton, in his posthumous *Chronology of Ancient Kingdoms Amended*,
criticized the pagans for only "boasting their antiquity, and not knowing

---

[19] Du Pin, *Bibliothèque universelle des historiens* (1708), p. 135.
[20] Frank E. Manuel, *Isaac Newton, Historian* (Cambridge: The Belknap Press of Harvard University Press, 1963), p. 89.
[21] Manuel, p. 43.

faith. . . ." As the conclusion of his 376-page *Chronology*, he wrote:

> And whilst all these nations have magnified their Antiquities so exceedingly, we need not wonder that the Greeks and Latines have made their first Kings a little older than the truth.[22]

As evident from material in the manuscripts of Newton's *Chronology* at New College and not in the published version, among "a few folios devoted to the history of China,"[23] Newton tried to reduce Chinese history from "Hoan ti [Huang Ti 黃帝] who founded the monarchy of China 1697 years before Christ" to the first emperor of the Ch'in dynasty, as "the same king gave the name of Hoan ti [Huang Ti 皇帝] . . . about 230 years before the birth of Christ."[24] Newton did not understand that 黃 [huang] and 皇 [huang] are different characters of Chinese—and, thus, denoted different emperors, when he declared all Chinese history before 230 B.C. to be

---

[22] Isaac Newton, *The Chronology of Ancient Kingdoms Amended* (London: Printed for J. Tonson in the Strand, and J. Osborn and T. Longman in Pater-noster Row, 1728), p. 376.

[23] Manuel, p. 136.

[24] Manuel's notes (pp. 284-285) read:

> The full text of Newton's discussion of Chinese chronology, New College MSS. I, fol. 80v, reads: "A book of Confucius called Scientia Sinensis was published at Paris A.C. 1657 [sic] & at the end of it is added a Chronological Table of the Monarchy of China. By this Table China is represented divided into many kingdoms above 1100 years before the birth of Christ & that these kingdoms continued warring with one another & conquering one another near 800 years together & at length when they were reduced into seven great great kingdoms Xi Hoan ti the king of one of them conquered the other six & founded the Monarchy of China and divided it into Provinces & this was about 230 years before the birth of Christ. The same king gave the name of Hoan ti to the succeeding kings of this monarchy a name wch remains to this day, & built the great wall of China against the Tartars & commanded all his people upon pain of death to burn all the books in China except those wch related to medicine & were judicial. And there are now no histories in China but what were written above 72 years after this conflagration. And therefore the story that Hoan ti founded the monarchy of China 2697 years before Christ is a fable invented to make that Monarchy look ancient. The way of writing used by the Chinese was not fully invented before the days of Confucius the Chinese Philosopher & he was born but 551 years before Christ & flourished only in one of the six old kingdoms into wch China was then divided. The histories wch were written before the conflagration of the books to the wars & leagues of that kingdom with its neighbors & therefore China being then divided into many kingdoms it is not likely that there could be any history of all China before that conflagration.

> Newton owned *Confucius, Sinarum philosophus, sive Scientia Sinensis Latine exposita . . . Adjecta est Tabula chronologica Sinicae monarchiae ab huius exordioad haec usque tempora*, 5 parts in 1 vol. (Paris, 1686-1687). Philippe Couplet, who prepared the chronological table, began with "Hoan ti primus

myth. Thus, Newton, in his way, had "solved" the problems of Chinese chronology according to his own belief "that mankind could not be much older than is represented in Scripture."[25]

As it turns out, neither Pascal nor Newton resolved the dichotomy between Mosaic and Confucian chronologies with respect to the date of the Biblical Deluge. Du Halde noted that if the Deluge were universal as the orthodox interpretation held, then there would have sufficient time for the Chinese, the descendants of Noah,[26] to grow populous and develop into a civilized Empire that kept accurate historical records. Couplet, in the "Chronological Table" appended to the *Confucius Sinarum Philosophus* (1687), attempted to minimize the problem by simultaneously using the Septuagint chronology, thus casting doubt on all dates before Huang Ti. This Chinese chronology went back nearly to 3000 B.C., and it discarded the Latin Vulgate text of the Bible translated in A.D. 397 by Jerome, which had been declared authoritative—or Canonical in the Roman Catholic Church—ever since the Council of Trent (1545-1563). Jerome's Latin translation of Eusebisus's *Chronicon* also dominated the Chronology of Western Europe without rival until the sixteenth century.

Instead of the shorter Vulgate chronology, the Jesuits suggested the longer Greek Septuagint (LXX) chronology, which places the creation in 5199 B.C.—rather than 4004 B.C.—and the date of the Deluge at around 2950 B.C., instead of 2349 B.C. Thus, the Chinese chronology discredited the Vulgate text.

Since the Jesuits attempted to interpret the Confucian *Five Classics* according to the dates of the Pentateuch of Moses, they arrived at the position that references to the Christian Creation and the worldwide flood could be found, albeit concealed, in the Chinese Classics. Ricci, along with the majority of the Jesuits, did not wish to discuss the metaphysical or mythological elements in the Chinese Classics, whereas the Figurists were interested in the correspondence between the "figures" of the Chinese Classics and Old Testament. Among these Figurists, Bouvet was the most authoritative. Bouvet

---

Imperator, a quo perpetua haec series genealogica trium familiarum Parincipum ducit exordium. Coepit imperare an. ante Christum 2697. imperavit an. 100" (p. 3) In the *Tabula Chronologica* Couplet noted under Xi Hoan ti, Annus ante Chr. 237: "Anno 25. libros omnes praeter medicos & judiciarios cremari jubet. Anno 26. plurimos litteratos vivos sepeliri mandat" (p. 17).

[25] Newton, p. 190.

[26] Jean Baptise Du Halde, S. J., *Description géographique, historique, chronologique, politique, et physique de l'empire de la Chine et de la Tartarie chinoise: Enrichie des cartes générales et particulieres du Thibet, & de la Corée, ornée d'un grand nombre de figures & de vignettes gravées en taille-douce.* (Paris: P. G. Lemercier, 1735), III, p. 2.

Sinica [*The Most Recent News from China*] (1697), and the *Discourse on the Natural Theology of the Chinese.* Bouvet himself stated that the *pa-kua* [hexagrams] of the *I-ching* alluded to the ideas of the "Creation"[27] and the "Trinity."[28]

At Bouvet's recommendation, the Chinese Emperor K'ang Hsi invited Jean-François Foucquet to Peking in 1711 to study the *I-ching.* Foucquet's only work printed during his lifetime, apart from a letter published in the *Lettres édifiantes* (1720), was the *Chronological Table of Chinese History*, published in Rome in 1729.[29] Another Figurist, Joseph Henri Prémare, also advanced the premise that a primitive revelation was transmitted through the Chinese Classics. Several of his works were published in Europe, notably his *Recherches sur les temps antérieurs a ceus dont parle le "Chou-king,"* which appeared as an introduction to De Guignes's edition of his fellow-Jesuit Gaubil's translation of the *Shu-ching* [*Book of Historical Records* 書經], one of the earliest Confucian *Five Classics.* Claude Visdelou, another Figurist, in "Description abrégée de l'Empire de la Chine . . . sur l'antiquité" (1728), mentioned that:

> L'Histoire populaire de cette Monarchie est hors de toute vraisemblance, pour ne pas dire manifestement fausse, puisqu'elle compte plus de quarante mille ans, depuis sa fondation . . . . car le temps le plus reculé, marqué dans la Vulgate, suffit a peine pour fixer la chronologie des Chinois: . . . C'est donc par une étude recherchée des Historiens Chinois & de leurs anciennes Chroniques qu'on a pu apprendre que le Roi *Jectan*, appellé dans leur langue *Yao* ou *Yao-tang*, [Chinese called Tang Yao instead of Yao-tung], a été le fondateur de ce grand Empire. Ils disent que ce Prince partit l'an 171 après le Déluge, du camp de *Sennaar*, où avoit été la Tour de Babel, . . . D'où il résulte que l'Empire de la Chine ayant commencé 230 après le Déluge, le 1886 du monde selon la Vulgate, a jusques à présent, 3845 années d'antiquité, comme on le voit par cetre supputation.[30]

These significant Jesuit studies of the Confucian *Five Classics* were

---

[27]Bouvet to Le Gobien, 8 November 1700, in Leibniz, *Opéra Omnia*, ed. Dutens, IV, 149.

[28]Bouvet to Leibniz, 4 November 1701. Paris: B. N. Fr. 17240.

[29]It was re-published in English translation in the *Philosophical Transactions of the Royal Society* 36 (London, 1919-1930), 394-424.

[30]"Description Abregée de l'Empire de la Chine, En forme d'une Lettre écrite à S. A. S. le prince Eugene de Savoye." *Sur l'Antiquité, l'Empire de la Chine* . . . écrite en 1728, p. 191.

50   David Wei-yang Dai

generally neglected during the European Enlightenment. In eighteenth-century Europe, only a few European scholars, including Leibniz and Matthew Tindal, paid any attention to their mythological interpretations.[31] Although Du Halde himself was not a Figurist, he accepted some of the Figurist theories—that Confucius had prophesied the Messiah[32] and that the son of Noah had founded the Chinese Empire.[33] Du Halde, in his *Description*, stated regarding the mythical accounts of Chinese antiquity, that Chinese history began with the reign of the Emperor Yao:

> ...C'est que les Historiens Chinois paroissent sincères, & ne chercher que la verité: qu'on ne voit pas qu'ils soient persuadez que la gloire d'une Nation consiste dans son ancienneté, & que comme d'autres Nations, ils n'ont point eu de raison prises du côte de l'intéret ou de la jalousie des Peuples voisins, pour altérer, ou falsifier leur Histoire, qui n'est qu'une simple exposition des principaux événemens, propres à servir d'instruction ou modele à la posterité.[34]

The existence of an oral tradition in China that traces the earliest epochs of Chinese history to a time before the Deluge and that retold a legend concerning the Creation was known to Du Halde but did not disturb his admiration for Chinese antiquity. The European intellectuals, however, were disturbed. The doubts that they raised as to the historical characters of the events recorded in the Pentateuch had a lasting effect.

The theological position, *extra ecclesiam nulla salus* [No salvation outside the church] had been earlier challenged by François de la Mothe le Vayer (1588-1672), tutor of Louis XIV and historiographer of the state. In his "De Confutius, le Socrate de la Chine," he marshaled statements about Chinese antiquity ("Les Chinois au contraire n'ont de temps immemorial qu'un seul Dieu, qu'ils nommoient le Roy du Ciel; & l'on peut voir par leurs Annales de plus de quatre mille ans....) to challenge the sole authority of Scripture.[35] Later, Spinoza, following Isaac de La Peyrère's departure from an orthodox Biblical interpretation,[36] objected that it was impossible for such a wide dispersal of population to have occurred in the time allowed by short orthodox

---

[31] Arnold H. Rowbotham, "Jesuit Figurists and Eighteenth-Century Religious Thought," *Journal of the History of Ideas* 17 (1956), p. 480.

[32] *Description*, II, 387.

[33] *Description*, III, 2.

[34] *Description*, I, 5.

[35] François de la Mothe le Vayer, *Oeuvers de François de la Mothe le Vayer*, Third Edition (Paris: Augustin Courbe, 1662), p, 668.

[36] A. Owen Aldridge, "Voltaire and the Cult of China," *Tamkang Review* II:2 (October 1971); III:1 (April 1972), p. 3. After his concise list on the background of

chronology. Through Spinoza's writings, Diderot and Voltaire—in particular—disparaged the infallibility of the Bible as well as the authorship of Moses.[37]

Voltaire, in his article "Chronology" in the *Dictionaire philosophique*, praised the Chinese for their great respect for their ancestors. Voltaire remarked that the Chinese recorded their ancestral history up to "the reign of the Emperor Iao [Yao 堯], two thousand three hundred and fifty-seven years before our Vulgar era."[38] Voltaire went on to praise the Chinese chronology as having "considerable value, when compared with the Chronological labors of other nations."[39] The Chinese had better and more ancient chronological records than the Indians, the Persians, or even the ancient Egyptians. In the article "Chine" in *Dictionaire philosophique*, Voltaire, supported by the Jesuit Parennin, who had resided twenty-five years in China, ridiculed the hypothesis that the Chinese originated from the Egyptians, as "in comparison with this extensive work [Chinese Great Wall] the pyramids of Egypt are only puerile and useless masses."[40] Voltaire, in his *Lettres chinoises*, also mentioned his preference for "the Chinese who have worshipped a single god for 4000 years to the Egyptians, who worship cows, cats and crocodiles."[41]

Charles Bonnet noted that one of the reasons behind Voltaire's "passion for Chinese" was "A hundred times he has turned the Chronology of this nation against that of Moses. He pretended to show that the Chinese are anterior by six or seven hundred years to the Flood."[42] Voltaire attempted to make use of the Chinese Classics to disparage the Mosaic Pentateuch. He ridiculed not only the Vulgate text of the Bible but the Septuagint as well. Tongue in cheek, he said,

> We shall not here speak of the universal deluge of Noah. Let it suffice to read the Holy Scriptures with submission. Noah's flood was an incomprehensible miracle supernaturally worked by the

---

the controversy concerned the Age of the World, he stated La Peyrete's hypothesis as follows: "From this background emerged La Peyrer's *Praeadamitae*, 1655, an attempt to justify the Scriptures by asserting the existence of men of earth before Adam including the Chaldeans, Egyptians and the Chinese."

[37] Leo Strauss, *Spinoza's Critique of Religion* (New York: Schocken Books, 1965), pp. 64-65. Adopted from Rule's "Confucius," p. 395.

[38] Voltaire, *The Works of Voltaire*, trans. William Fleming (New York: Dingwall-Rock, Ltd., 1927), Vol. 4, p. 127.

[39] Voltaire, Vol. 18, p. 176.

[40] Voltaire, Vol. 18, p. 150.

[41] Voltaire, *Lettres chinoises*, Lettre VII, and *Works*, Vol. 29, p. 476.

[42] Voltaire, *Correspondence*, ed. Theodore Besterman (Genève: Institut et Musée, 1953-1965), Letter 7336.

justice and goodness of an ineffable Providence whose will it was to
destroy the whole guilty human race and form a new and innocent
race. If the new race was more wicked than the former, and became
more criminal from age to age, from reformation to reformation,
this is but another effect of the same Providence of which it is impossible for us to fathom the depths, the inconceivable mysteries
transmitted to the nations of the West for many ages, in the Latin
translation of the Septuagint. We shall never enter these awful
sanctuaries; our questions will be limited to simple nature.[43]

Diderot, in his *Encyclopédie*—following Voltaire's step—disparaged the
Vulgate chronology by reference to Fu Hsi, who reigned several centuries
before the Deluge: he then purposely posed the choice for readers between
the Mosaic sacred books or the Chinese Classics. With tongue in cheek, Diderot rejected the story of Fu Hsi, owing to the mythical conception of his
having come into existence in 2954 B.C. through a rainbow [*l'arc-en-ciel*]
instead of by human agency.[44] Implicitly, he questioned also the authenticity of the existence of God both from Chinese historical books and the
Biblical chronology. These *philosophes* did not believe anything mystical or
supernatural. Instead, they wanted to discuss concrete methods for living well
and happily. A modern writer, Barker, comments on the Chinese and Biblical
chronology:

> It is nevertheless true that enough work in natural history had
> already been done by Buffon and others to convince Diderot of the
> inadequacy of the ecclesiastical interpretation of the age of the
> world. This conviction, along with his contempt for revelation,
> explains the skeptical tone that underlies the simulated orthodoxy
> of the long article on "Chronology sacree." After mention of various
> pagan chronologies he rejects them all as either fabulous or derived
> from the chronology of the Bible, and states that reason and religion
> oblige one to accept only the latter as trustworthy. But the Biblical
> chronology is not one but three, he adds, varying according to the
> Hebrew, Samaritan, and the Septuagint texts of the Scriptures.[45]

Similarly, the practical spirit in English thinkers made it impossible for

---

[43] "Changes That Have Occurred in the Globe," *Dictionnaire Philosophique* in
Voltaire, *Works*, Vol. 18, p. 130.
[44] Diderot, "Des Philosophie Chinois," *Encyclopédie* (Paris: Briasson, 1751), Vol.
III, p. 341.
[45] Joseph E. Barker, *Diderot's Treatment of the Christian Religion in the "Encyclo-
dédie"* (New York: King's Crown Press, 1941), p. 55.

them to accept the findings of the Jesuit Fathers concerning the Creation and the Flood. Although Samuel Johnson wrote the dedication for and the concluding paragraph to John Kennedy's *A Complete System of Astronomical Chronology, unfolding the Scriptures* (1762),[46] in the *Rambler*, on the subject of "the stated and established method of computing time," he wondered "why we should be at so much trouble to count what we cannot keep."[47] Defoe's satire on the uselessness of the disputes of chronology was much more severe. In *The Political History of the Devil*, Defoe jokes that "Satan, no doubt, would make a very good Chronologist, [and] could settle every Epocha, correct every Kalendar, and bring all our Accounts of Time to a general Agreement: as well the *Grecian Olympiads*, the *Turkish Heghira*, the *Chinese* fictitious account of the world's Duration, as our blind *Julian* and *Gregorian* Accounts, which have put the world, to this Day, into such Confusion, that we neither agree in our Holy-days or working-days, Fasts or Feasts, nor keep the same Sabbaths in any Part of the same Globe."[48]

Once the scoffers like Diderot and Defoe had had their say, no one took the old questions of debate concerning the date of the Creation and the Flood with the same seriousness. The scientists and scholars of the nineteenth and twentieth centuries paid much less attention to the theological-moral-scientific side of the problems and put more emphasis on the historical aspects. Indeed, what Struchius had once referred to as the "two Eyes of History," "*Chronology* and *Geography*,"[49] had become monocular: most cared now about geography. Even Johnson in an opening line from *The Vanity of Human Wishes*—"Survey Mankind from China to Peru"—limited himself simply to the physical comprehensive places and dates. After 1800, one heard no more of a title like "Comprehensive View of Time, since the Creation of the World."[50] Moreover, the only absolute orthodox systems of

<hr />

[46] In 1751 Kennedy published *A New Method of Stating and Explaining the Scripture Chronology, upon Mosaic Astronomical Principles, Mediums, and Data, as Laid Down in the Pentateuch.*

[47] Samuel Johnson, *The Rambler*, ed. W. J. Bate and A. B. Strauss; in the Yale Edition of the *Works of Samuel Johnson*, Vols. III, IV, and V (New Haven: Yale University Press, 1969), IV, 204.

[48] Daniel Defoe, *The Political History of the Devil*, Fourth Edition (London, 1739), p. 12. I am indebted to Paul Alkon and his unpublished paper "Johnson & Chronology" for this citation.

[49] Aegidius Struchius, *Breviarium Chronologicum* (London, 1699), p. 3.

[50] James E. Weeks, *The Gentlemen's Hourglass, or an Introduction to Chronology: Being a Plain and Compendious Analysis of Time, and its Divisions . . . Containing a Brief Account of the Flux of Time; the Value of Lives, and Explanation of Stiles, Epochs, Area's Periods, Revolutions, &c For the Use of Schools and Universities* (Dublin, 1750), p. 10.

Hebraic chronologies according to the Pentateuch had been interrupted by the Chinese historical records. Alexander Pope, early in *An Essay on Criticism* (1711) suggested the possible differences in time scale of human evaluation:

> 'Tis with our Judgment as our Watches, none
> Go just alike, yet each believes his own.[51]

In addressing the troublesome historical questions, he promoted Confucius in *The Temple of Fame* (1715):

> Superior, and alone, *Confucius* stood,
> Who taught that useful Science, to be *good*.[51]

Like Confucius, the pragmatists paid less attention to the debate on the dates of God's Creation and the Flood but stressed only human nature and human ethics. Thus Pope, the prince of the pragmatic poets in the eighteenth century, promoted the practice of human affairs in daily life:

> Know then thyself, presume not God to scan;
> The proper study of Mankind is Man.[52]

National Taiwan Normal University, Taipei

---

[51] Alexander Pope, *The Poems of Alexander Pope*, ed. by John Butt (New Haven: Yale University Press, 1963), p. 176.

[52] Pope, p. 144.

[53] Pope, p. 516.

THE ACCOMMODATION OF SCIENCE FROM THE WEST AND A NEW COSMOLOGY IN LATE 19TH-CENTURY CHINA: THE CASE OF K'ANG YU-WEI

San - pao Li

Alexander Koyré argues that what seventeenth-century Europe went through was not merely a scientific revolution, but a philosophical revolution as well. This revolution, indeed, has often been called the "crisis of European consciousness." In the process of the destruction of the cosmos and the infinitization of the universe, the Europeans discarded, by applying scientific thought, certain considerations based upon value-concepts, such as perfection, harmony, meaning, and aim. Discovery of the laws of Nature provided grounds for constructing new systems of values and new cosmologies.[1] Thomas Kuhn, who successfully demonstrated the plurality of the Copernican Revolution, also argues that the Revolution was in fact a revolution in ideas. "Initiated as a narrowly technical, highly mathematical revision of classical astronomy," he wrote, "the Copernican theory became the focus for the tremendous controversies in religion, in philosophy, and in social theory."[2] Once men discovered that this terrestrial home of theirs was no longer the unique focus of God's creation, but rather one of the multitude of planets circulating about one of an infinity of stars, the very foundations of their traditional cosmic world-order began to be shaken. The cosmological order of the past was suddenly upset. They began to evaluate their place in the cosmic scheme quite differently from their predecessors. They questioned with newfound courage the traditional cosmological view with its hierarchical structure and qualitative opposition of the celestial realm of immutable being

---

[1] See Alexandre Koyré, *From the Closed World to the Infinite Universe* (Baltimore: The Johns Hopkins Press, 1957), Preface and Introduction.

[2] Thomas S. Kuhn, *The Copernican Revolution: Planetary Astronomy in the Development of Western Thought* (Cambridge, Mass.: Harvard University Press, 1957), p. 2.

and the terrestrial or sublunar region of change and decay. The previous differentiation of high and low, noble and mean, in the human realm consequently became meaningless. Old beliefs and values were subject to serious examination. We may very well say that the immediate effect of the Copernican Revolution was to spread skepticism, bewilderment, and free thinking. It produced vast consequences and ushered Europe into an intellectual transformation of unprecedented magnitude.

Cosmology, by definition, is the framework of concepts and relations which man erects, in satisfaction of some emotional or intellectual drive, for the purpose of bringing descriptive order into the world as a whole, including himself as one of its elements.[3] The cosmologies which man has developed at various times and in different localities necessarily reflect the physical as well as the intellectual environment in which he lived, including above all the interests and the culture of the particular society to which he belonged. For in attempting to bring order into the universe as a whole, he must hew to those lines of thought by which he has already brought order into that portion with which he is most familiar. The resulting cosmology inevitably reflects the sociological, philosophical, and scientific predilections of the individual and his group.

Order and harmony are perhaps the two predominant concepts encompassing the entire spectrum of Chinese philosophy. The cosmological order and harmony were explained in traditional China in terms of one's awareness of his right place in time and space. For the traditional Chinese, time was not an abstract parameter, a succession of homogeneous moments, or an abstract addition of quantitatively equal and qualitatively indistinguishable units, but was divided into concrete, separate seasons and their subdivisions. Like time, space was highly heterogeneous and hierarchical. Time and space became value-laden concepts in traditional Chinese cosmology. The hierarchical social order was in effect thought to be a part of, and parallel to, the cosmic order. Neo-Confucian cosmology developed during the Sung was itself both a cosmic system and a constellation of moral and ethical values. It assumed the fundamental unity of natural and moral truths which encompassed natural, ethical, and social principles in an interlocking and mutually interacting whole. Like medieval European philosophy, Neo-Confucian cosmology had a considerably limited physical basis. The cosmic order and the human social order were conceived to be bounded and essentially congruent with each other.

Under such circumstances, it is reasonable to suppose that once the

---

[3] For the definition of cosmology used in this article, see *Encyclopaedia Britannica*, 1971 edition, vol. 6, p. 582.

traditional Chinese belief in social hierarchy lost the support of cosmology it became more difficult to maintain. The validity of the traditional hierarchical social order began to be challenged, for it was incompatible with a view of nature which recognized the nonhierarchical interplay of forces. Joseph Levenson shrewdly observed that "it was the steady advance of a western tradition of science that furnished criteria for reappraisal of the Chinese intellectual past."[4] The introduction of western astronomy, mathematics, and other exact sciences into China was significant not merely in the history of Chinese science but in her intellectual history as well. One of the reasons may very well be that the majority of those who were first exposed to modern scientific ideas were, in fact, articulate intellectuals rather than scientists. They were able to transcend the confines of specific fields of science. They projected the modern scientific concepts that they had somehow acquired onto a much larger philosophical canvas, hence providing new perspectives for the development of a modern China. K'ang Yu-wei (1858-1927) stands out as the most remarkable of these intellectuals.

K'ang Yu-wei was a man of extreme versatility and complexity. He was concerned with the viability of Chinese civilization in general and of its humanistic and societal patterns in particular. He vehemently challenged some of the most basic values of Confucianism, endeavored to synthesize the value and ethical systems of East and West, and most significantly, demythologized Chinese stereotypes. Furthermore, he championed vigorously such notions as equality, the individual's right of autonomy, the possibility of linear human progress, the necessity of accommodation and change, and the value of the demonstrability of science, each of which was indispensable if China was to modernize itself. The sources of his intellectual radicalism are naturally numerous. However, had he not been exposed to western science during the early stage of his intellectual development and had he not accepted the post-Newtonian heliocentric system so matter-of-factly, his philosophical outlook would have been utterly different.[5]

According to his autobiography, K'ang purchased all the publications of the Kiangnan Arsenal, which published many of John Fryers's works, as well as all the available issues of *Wan-kuo kung-pao* in 1883. Evidence

---

[4] Joseph R. Levenson, *Confucian China and Its Modern Fate: A Trilogy* (Berkeley: University of California Press, 1968), I:13.

[5] For an excellent account of the introduction of Copernicanism to China, see Nathan Sivin, "Copernicus in China," in Comité Nicolas Copernic, Union Internationale D'Histoire et de Philosophie des Sciences, *Colloquia Copernicana II: Études sur l'Audience de la Théorie Héliocentrique, Conférences du Symposium de l'UIHPS* (Toruń, 1973), pp. 63-122.

suggests that he must have read the translated books and articles on western astronomy which he had in his possession.[6] K'ang was in fact curious enough to arrange the use of a telescope and a microscope soon thereafter. They opened for him an entirely new intellectual perspective. He began his nightly astronomical observations as early as 1884. His fascinating astronomical treatise *chu-t'ien chiang* 諸天講 [Lectures on the Heavens] was in all probability drafted in 1885.[7] His acquaintance with western science and his venture into astronomical observations must have helped to alter his cosmological perspective and, in consequence, broaden his philosophical and ethical visions.

While K'ang consciously adopted the strongest possible position defending and advocating the heliocentric theory of Copernicus in his *Chu-t'ien chiang*, he denounced all the traditional Chinese cosmological theories as nothing more than the "prattle of children." No vestiges of the geocentric view were discernible in this work. "My attitude toward Copernicus," K'ang admitted, "is one of worshipful admiration, singing his praise and offering him oblation."[8]

Recognizing the revolutionary significance of the post-Copernican cosmology, John Fryer rightly began the first issue of his influential *Ko-chih hui-pien* 格致彙編 [Chinese Scientific Magazine] in February 1876 with an essay on the immensity of universe and on the planetary position of the earth. Essays of similar nature are also found in several issues in the *Wan-kuo kung-pao* published in August, 1878. The earth is referred to by K'ang as merely a "speck of dust" [*wei-ch'en* 微塵]. In fact, the Heavens of the Prime-Prime [*Yüan-yüan t'ien* 元元天], the highest of all the heavens in K'ang's own cosmic scheme, is also regarded as no larger than a speck of dust. This sense of cosmological relativism was repeatedly emphasized in his *Chu-t'ien chiang*. The qualitative differentiation between heaven and earth was totally eliminated. He identified the terrestrial globe as one of the infinity of celestial bodies. Men were no longer thought to be sublunary beings. They were, instead, in K'ang's view, not dissimilar to celestial or empyreal beings [*t'ien-jen* 天人]. China consequently became a relatively unimpressive nation, and the monarch could no longer claim to be the absolute ruler as

---

[6] Among the most noteworthy books on astronomy were Alexander Wylie's rendition of Sir John Frederick William Herschel's *Outlines of Astronomy* or *T'an-t'ien* 談天 (1859) and two other books made available by John Fryer: an illustrated text on the heavenly bodies, *T'ien-wen t'u-shuo* 天文圖説 , and a handbook on astronomy, *T'ien-wen hsü-chuh* 天文須知 .

[7] For K'ang Yu-wei's venture into science, see Kung-chuan Hsiao, "K'ang Yu-wei's Excursion into Science: *Lectures on the Heavens*," in Jung-pang Lo, ed. & tr., *K'ang Yu-wei: A Biography and a Symposium* (Tucson: The University of Arizona Press, 1967), pp. 375-407.

[8] K'ang Yu-wei, *Chu-t'ien chiang*, 2:2b.

"son of heaven." In the face of the immensity of universe, a sense of humility developed in K'ang; and cultural parochialism became nothing but naive and childish prejudice to him.

In two of K'ang Yu-wei's earliest extant manuscripts, "*K'ang-tzu nei-wai p'ien* 康子內外篇 [Esoteric and exoteric essays of Master K'ang]" and "*Shih-il kung-fa chüan-shu* 實理公法全書 [A complete book of substantial truths and universal principles]," he endeavored to interpret some of the fundamental concepts in Confucianism or Neo-Confucianism with a fresh vision derived partially yet decidedly from his familiarity with Copernican astronomy.[9] The concept of *jen* 仁 was constantly reiterated in traditional Chinese philosophy. All Confucianists, ancient and modern, assert in unison that *jen* represents the totality of all virtues. This view was reasserted with much vigor by K'ang. His utopianism is inconceivable without actualizing in its entirety *jen*, the categorical imperative. In K'ang's concept of *jen*, however, the impulse of transcendence is strongly accentuated. He looked forward to a new, undifferentiated social-moral order, fully manifesting human compassion and benevolence.

But what approach should be adopted for the realization of the virtue of *jen*? Unlike most traditional Confucianists, K'ang was convinced that *jen* could be fully manifested only at the expense of hierarchical social relations. K'ang no longer believed that the latter was a *sine qua non* for the actualization of the former. In fact, he regarded the rigidly defined social distinctions of traditional China as a serious handicap for the realization of *jen*. To K'ang, the traditional hierarchical social relationships could be abused by certain individuals, and as a result, the right of autonomy [*tzu-chu chih ch'üan* 自主之權] to which other individuals are also entitled would be denied. What K'ang envisioned was a totally undifferentiated social-moral order in contrast to the minutely differentiated one which is usually implied in such concepts as *i* 義 [sense of obligation] and *li* 禮 [propriety]. For K'ang, utopia was unattainable unless it was first recognized that human beings are born not only with equal endowment but also with equal worth and dignity. He regarded equality and autonomy as human right and as instrumental in bringing forth the "Great-Sameness [*ta-t'ung* 大同]" utopia.

[9] For preliminary analyses of these two manuscripts written by K'ang Yu-wei during the 1884-1887 period, readers are referred to the new articles of mine: "*K'ang-tzu nei-wai p'ien* ch'u-pu fen-hsi: K'ang Nan-hai hsien-ts'un tsui-tsao tso-p'in 康子內外篇初步分析：康南海現存最早作品 (A preliminary analysis of K'ang Yu-wei's earliest extant essay, *K'ang-tzu nei-wai p'ien*)," *The Tsing Hua Journal of Chinese Studies*, New Series XI, Nos. 1 & 2 (December 1975), pp. 312-347 and "K'ang Yu-wei's *Shih-li kung fa ch'üan-shu* (A complete book of substantial truths and universal principles)," *Bulletin of the Institute of Modern History, Academia Sinica*, No. 7 (June 1978), pp. 683-725.

We may, in this connection, draw into our discussion the cosmological scheme developed by Nicholas of Cusa (1401-1464), a forerunner of Copernicus, in which the hierarchical structure of the universe is rejected. Indeed, in the infinitely diversified and organically linked-together universe of Nicholas of Cusa, there is no center of perfection with respect to which the rest of the universe plays a subservient role. On the contrary, it is by being themselves and asserting their own natures that the various components of the universe contribute to the perfection of the whole. This view was at first challenged and debated but gradually gained recognition. By the end of the seventeenth century, the age-honored conception of the world as a finite and well-ordered whole in which the spatial structure embodied a hierarchy of perfection and value was already replaced by an indefinite or even infinite universe no longer united by natural subordination, but unified only by the identity of its ultimate and basic components and laws. If, with the destruction of the old cosmos, the earth could lose its central and thus unique status, how, then, could any individual claim to possess greater worth than others? The eighteenth century *philosophes* were able to argue that there was absolutely no reason for God to create one particular kind of being in preference to another.

K'ang Yu-wei's argument was very much in this vein. He questioned the validity of the sacrosanct relationships of inequality that existed in Chinese society and maintained that individuals in various human relationships ought to enjoy their right to autonomy equally. Wife and husband, both possessing souls of equal worth, should be equally free to express their preferences, even though their preferences may harmonize.[10] Parents are not entitled to any inherent prerogative over their children.[11] A teacher cannot command respect from his students simply because he is the teacher.[12] Even the ruler's role should be similar to that of a mediator. A mediator is ordinarily selected by agreement of the two parties involved. His power to arbitrate is derived; it is invested in him by others and not inherent in his position. K'ang went so far as to say that every individual should be provided with equal opportunity to be ruler.[13] Moreover, K'ang thought that while virtue commands respect, age itself does not.[14] Obviously, K'ang rejected the idea that the arbitrarily established hierarchies of traditional China reflected any absolute or universal moral values. This assertion of every individual's equal right to be his or her own master underlies K'ang Yu-wei's utopian thought. Without the newly

---

[10] K'ang Yu-wei, *Shih-li kung-fa ch'üan-shu* (hereafter, SLKF): *Fu-fu men* 夫婦門.
[11] SLKF: *Fu-mu tzu-nü men* 父母子女門.
[12] SLKF: *Shih-ti men* 師弟門.
[13] SLKF: *Chün-ch'en men* 君臣門.
[14] SLKF: *Chang-yu men* 長幼門.

acquired cosmological insight, he could not have become so bold as to attack the very core of the Confucian ethics.

Furthermore, the Confucianists unanimously acknowledge the individual's possession of the naturally-endowed *chih* [faculty to know or "Reason"], which distinguishes human beings from other animals. K'ang, however, felt that this *chih* should by no means be regarded as unlimited and having absolute validity. Human judgment is fallible. Ethical ideas as well as conventions are all socially determined, hence do not reflect absolute values. Indeed, there are many things that escape our sense and understanding. K'ang argued in the *Shih-li kung-fa ch'üan-shu*, although indirectly, that it is a grievous error to assert that perception and human understanding are the ultimate measures of things. No matter how reverently accepted and popularly practiced, institutions created by man should command no final authority. In fact, K'ang believed that should any institution or a certain teaching prove to be no longer adequate, it must be modified, updated, or even replaced with a new one, as what was witnessed in the cosmological transformation in Europe.

K'ang is one of the earliest modern Chinese intellectuals who campaigned assiduously against the notion "*an-yü ku-hsi* 安於故習 " or "being content with old practices." He argued forcefully in *K'ang-tzu nei-wei p'ien* that the traditional Chinese scholars, whether sophisticated or unsophisticated, accomplished or unaccomplished, must free themselves from their self-imposed *cul-de-sac*.[15] People must liberate themselves from ignorance and extend their mental horizons far and wide. The old traditions are to be scrutinized and whatever is obsolete discarded. Consequently, the point of departure should be the cultivation of each person's innate faculty to evaluate, the development of his or her conceptual apparatus, the intellect, and the formation of the habit of a perpetual search for truth and knowledge.

Although K'ang recognized that the attainment of the absolute truth is beyond human possibility, man is capable of discovering "axioms of geometry," which to K'ang represented the closest approximation of the absolute truth. the laws that proceed from the axioms of geometry were regarded by K'ang as "necessary truths /必然之實" or "eternal truths 永遠之實 " whereas those arbitrarily established by man are plainly "equivocal truths 兩可之實 ."[16] This very fact suggests that K'ang had more than a merely superficial appreciation of western science and regarded it both as a value in itself and as an approach to truth. His attachment to and deep admiration for science was already demonstrated in his *K'ang-tzu nei-wai p'ien*, where he criticized the arrogance and presumptuousness of the Ch'ing scholars. In

---

[15] K'ang Yu-wei, *K'ang-tzu nei-wai p'ien, Chüeh-shih p'ien* 覺識篇 , p. 13b.
[16] SLKF: *Shih-tzu chieh* 實字解.

order to convince them he asked these scholars to "fetch a telescope and ask them to see with their own eyes."[17]

Beneath the monochromatic appearance of the landscape of Chinese intellectual history was an undercurrent of discontent with and protest against Confucian ethics and conventional obligations. All such earlier protests voiced in different ways and at different times found eloquent and vigorous articulation in K'ang. A confluence of factors, internal as well as external, contributed to the shaping of the mind which anticipated and eventually succeeded in bringing forth a totalistic intellectual emancipation. K'ang Yu-wei challenged some of the most basic values of Confucianism and, with sincerity, attempted to disenthrall China from outdated concepts and to encourage the traditionally-minded Chinese to try to outgrow the psychological limitations imposed by their culture.

The intellectual breakthrough of the late nineteenth century is one of the central episodes in Chinese history. K'ang ushered in a new era during which the first steps toward modernity were made possible. He found new and powerful cosmological justifications for his ruthless attack against traditional Confucian ethics. He posed some important questions so sharply that thereafter they could no longer be neglected. We find in K'ang the beginnings of a new Chinese cosmology, a new ethics, and a new philosophy, which possessed great transforming potential. This new cosmology consequently exerted a great impact upon K'ang's disciples and in time upon the traditional Chinese society and its values and morality. It contributed to the emergence of a new awareness and a new mentality embraced by Chinese in their effort to bring China up to par with other modern countries.

California State University, Long Beach

---

[17]K'ang Yu-wei, *K'ang-tzu nei-wai p'ien, Chüeh-shih p'ien*, p. 14.

THE POWER OF THE OTHER: EDWARD S. MORSE
AND THE CHALLENGE OF JAPAN

Robert A. Rosenstone

The purpose of all interpretation is to conquer a remoteness, a distance between the past cultural epoch and the interpreter himself. By overcoming this distance . . . the exegete can appropriate its meaning to himself; foreign, he makes it familiar, that is, he makes it his own. It is thus the growth of his own understanding of himself that he pursues through his understanding of the other. Every hermeneutics is thus, explicitly or implicitly, self-understanding by means of understanding others.

$\qquad\qquad$ —Paul Ricoeur

The study of the West's Journey to the East is a study of the West; it is of the soul of the West that one learns, rather than that of the East.

$\qquad\qquad$ —Robert S. Ellwood[1]

An air of ethnocentrism or off beat Orientalism has always pervaded studies describing the role of Americans in the modernization of Japan. In broad historical works the old double stereotype has by now been banished: no longer do scholars treat nineteenth-century Japan as feminine and passive, a kind of inert and helpless body ready to be activated and given direction by a masculine, purposeful West. But when it comes to individuals such a view lingers, and we are still captive to notions of how Ernest F. Fenollosa taught the Japanese the value of their ancient art or how Lafcadio Hearn helped to save their tradition of folk tales. Perhaps this is understandable. Works on these topics are usually written by Americanists who lack both extensive

---

[1] Paul Ricoeur, *The Conflict of Interpretations* (Evanston, Ill.: Northwestern Univ. Press, 1974), 16-17; Robert S. Ellwood, "Percival Lowell's Journey to the East," *The Sewanee Review*, 78 (1970), 285.

exposure to Japanese culture and the language skills necessary to deal with native sources. Besides, to write of individuals is to see them as active agents, to stress their accomplishments. Yet this strategy has ignored a most important reciprocal aspect of America's encounter with Japan. The careers of the several hundred United States missionaries, teachers, technical experts and scientists who in the Meiji period went to bring the "advanced" civilization of the West to the natives were no simple one-way street. Americans who resided in Japan learned as well as taught, and some were considerably altered in belief and value system. It is no exaggeration to say that while they were consciously attempting to Westernize Japan, Americans in turn were unconsciously being Japanized.

To see this subtle but significant process at work, let us examine the career of a single, important figure, Edward S. Morse, a well-known natural scientist who became one of our first experts on Japan. As a popular lecturer, author of three books (including the influential *Japanese Homes and Their Surroundings*) and more than a hundred articles on Japan, curator of Japanese pottery at the Boston Museum of Fine Arts, and Director of Salem's Peabody Museum (which contained the extensive collection of Japanese folk art that he had made), Morse had a hand in shaping American views of Japan. He is an especially good subject because he seems the quintessential Yankee, self-made, practical, down-to-earth, democratic and little interested in matters aesthetic, historical, or philosophical. Having shed the Calvinism of his ancestors at an early age, Morse always remained captive of a secular Puritanism. Work was clearly the center of his existence. Family, love, idle pleasure, and friendship were all less important to him than the pursuit of his profession. In the realm of science he was no dreamer, no theoretician. Morse was content to believe in things he could see, touch, smell, dissect, and sketch. Everything which would not be described by such activities—and this came to include God—was of no interest to him. There was no pleasure or gain to be taken in the unseen and unknowable. To be interested in such matters was to waste time, and for the unreligious Morse, time-wasting was a cardinal sin.[2]

---

[2] For the basic outline but not the interpretation of Morse's life, this article follows Dorothy Wayman, *Edward Sylvester Morse* (Cambridge, Mass.; 1942). Though admiring and uncritical, the work can be trusted for the overall picture; it also contains significant extracts from his unpublished journals. Other biographical accounts include the following: J. S. Kingsley, "Edward Sylvester Morse," *Proceedings of the American Academy of Arts and Sciences*, Vol. 61 (Boston, 1926), 549-555; Leland O. Howard, "Biographical Memoir of Edward Sylvester Morse," *Biographical Memoires, National Academy of Sciences*, Vol. 17 (Washington, D.C., 1937), 3-29; Merrill E. Champion, "Edward Sylvester Morse, With a Bibliography and a Catalogue of His Species," *Occasional Papers on*

All this was true before Morse arrived in Japan at the age of forty and was almost as true afterwards. But one must stress the word "almost." Something in the experience of the Orient served to alter both Morse's career and his mentality. The former is easier to see. Three years of living there made Morse so interested in the culture that during the second half of his life studies of Japan took precedence over scientific pursuits. At the same time this alien social order, full of veiled invitations towards other ways of being, upset his lifelong beliefs. To combat its strong and subtle pull he was forced to cling tightly to previously established intellectual patterns. This meant that Morse's Japan scholarship was more than a way of explaining that nation: it was also a process of warding off its attractions, of reaffirming his old self by neatly separating subject and object and reducing the strangeness of experience by confirming it to familiar categories.

Were this Morse's response alone, it might be no more than an interesting historical footnote to the encounter of East and West. But extensive investigation of the careers of Americans who resided in Meiji Japan shows that he was hardly unique. Many of those who left written records—and this is especially true of that first generation of Japan experts, men such as William E. Griffis, Percival Lowell, John H. DeForest, W. Sturgis Bigelow, Fenollosa and Hearn—show significant signs of disturbance to their psychological, philosophical and social equilibrium.[3] As in Morse, such shifts are not confronted directly, but combatted by reliance on categories—analytic, taxonomic, theoretical—imported from home. This pattern suggests that there was something more to the experience than could be encompassed in words. Japan as a totality remained unknown and uncapturable; it was glimpsed only in bits and pieces, in fragments, in flashes and momentary illuminations. Good nineteenth-century positivists, these Americans were as unconscious of this partiality as of the unconscious itself. To us today the notion of the limitation of words seems more familiar. There is even a concept to suggest the power over us of that which cannot be fully conceptualized: we call it the Other.

To claim that, for nineteenth-century Americans, Japan was the Other, is

---

Mollusks, (Harvard University Museum of Comparative Zoology) 1 (Sept. 20, 1947), 129-144.

[3] Evidence of this disturbance is shown in my article "Learning from Those Imitative Japanese: Another Side of the American Experience in the Mikado's Empire," *American Historical Review*, 85 (June, 1980), 572-95. It is a theme which I expect to explore more fully in future articles dealing with such figures as William E. Griffis, Percival Lowell, S. W. Sturgis Bigelow and Ernest F. Fenollosa, and also in a book-length volume.

to grow neither poetic nor mystical. It is merely to make an attempt to label all those elements of the culture which eluded words and yet impinged upon and helped to shape discourse. It is to see that Morse and the other early Japan experts were faced with a broad if obscure challenge that they could experience but never define. How they met this challenge is one of the untold parts of the confrontation between the United States and Japan. To investigate it is to expand not only our knowledge of history but also to open a window on a problem which still endures—that is, how to understand and deal with that which is alien. For this purpose, Edward S. Morse is a perfect subject. Of all his contemporaries, none went ot the Orient with a mind so uncluttered by racial stereotypes and cultural prejudgments. Successful, stable and mature, not given to easy whim or sudden passion, he may serve as a tentative touchstone. That Morse was significantly altered by exposure to Japan suggests that in his experience we may find a path towards understanding that culture's perennial effect upon Americans.

I

Little in Edward S. Morse's life prepared him to appreciate the culture of Japan, but some factors made him unusually receptive to it. Basically he was an open-minded man who had few social, religious, or political reservations about alien societies. This attitude sprang from Morse's most enduring passion, his major way of relating to reality. From an early age his deepest love was to collect, classify, and compare things. Pursued with single-minded fervor, such activity helped to turn him into a scientist and brought him to the Orient in 1877. There he continued to act in the same manner he had at home, observing things carefully, sketching their shape and contour, noting their salient characteristics in words. In theory, this process involved no judgment of the behavior of what was being studied. What was necessary was to distance oneself from reality enough so that emotional reactions did not color one's observations.

It would not be accurate to say that Morse was a man without feelings, but only that he managed to keep them under tight control. Few flights of imagination ever disturbed his consciousness, and any sense of romance or adventure was channeled into a single-minded pursuit of accuracy in the world of natural history. This was true from his earliest days. In 1850, at the age of twelve, he was already a collector, on the hunt for tiny, shelled creatures in the woods and river banks and at the seashore near his home town of Portland, Maine. Other young people, or even adults, might lust after the shimmering beauty of those large, colorful shells found off the coast of Latin America or in the South Seas and brought back by sailors to the wharves, but Ned did not respond to them. His dreams were more mundane; his aim was to make a complete collection of local land shells. These tended to be tiny, unattractive, and of little value to stores, but Ned's interests were neither aesthetic nor monetary. Satisfaction came from the process itself, from studying shells through a three-dollar microscope, drawing them, arranging them neatly in the drawers of his cabinet.

This was a democratic kind of science, well suited to nineteenth-century America where, as De Tocqueville had claimed in the forties, there was not the kind of leisure class necessary to produce men of genius. Natural history, in fact, was the only scientific discipline in which Americans of that era excelled. No doubt this was because the abundant plant and animal life of the continent, even in long-settled regions like New England, was still dimly known. An amateur like Morse could make a mark in such a realm. All that was necessary was intelligence, persistence, energy, and a good set of eyes. Ned possessed all of these. At the age of seventeen he was overseer of the scientific collection of the Portland Society of Natural History. By the time he reached twenty his name had been listed three times in the *Proceedings* of the Boston Society of Natural History as discoverer of a new species.

The road from Portland to recognition as a scientist was shorter than one might imagine. Morse lived a version of the national myth which Benjamin Franklin had made of his own life, that rags-to-riches—in his case obscurity to fame—story which so fixated the consciousness of the nineteenth-century American middle class. Normally the tale was one of diligence flavored with a little luck. The first characteristic Morse had in abundance; the second he knew how to capitalize upon. Luck in his case was inseparable from talent and hard work. That early recognition by the BSNH was the springboard to success. In 1859 he came to the attention of Swiss-born Louis Agassiz, then considered by many to be the leading natural scientist in the world. Publicist and promoter as well as researcher, Agassiz was just on the eve of his greatest triumph, building at Harvard the largest Museum of Comparative Zoology in the world. Morse impressed him enough to be taken on as one of a dozen student assistants to aid in that undertaking; he was the only one of them not to have completed a secondary education.

Two years with Agassiz provided training and contacts enough to last a lifetime. When Morse left the Museum in 1861, he had some theory and an immense amount of practical experience under his belt. As the assistant in charge of mollusks—one of the four branches of living creatures according to the classification system of the time—he had not only sorted 30,000 specimens into 4,000 species in a single year, but had also started on the track of what would be his most important scientific contribution. His focus was brachiopods, tiny shelled creatures considered mollusks because, like clams and oysters, they were bivalves. Morse was not so sure, and for a decade he tracked brachiopods, living, dead, and fossilized. On dredging expeditions he sought them from the coast of North Carolina to the St. Lawrence River. Back to his home laboratory he brought specimens for dissection and study. Years of poring over shells and internal organs of creatures often only one-eighth of an inch in length led to the conclusion published in 1870 that brachiopods were not mollusks, but worms.[4] This conclusion put Morse on the scientific map, drew praise from scientists at home and abroad, and brought a complimentary letter from the giant in the field, Charles Darwin. For a naturalist of the time there could be no sweeter sign of recognition.

That Morse's major achievement should be the result of such routine, pedestrian, even dull labor, the product less of brilliance than of sheer doggedness, says much about the man and his age. Certainly this kind of science suited an ideology of egalitarianism. If Morse himself was an instinctive democrat, the attitude also brought financial reward. In the years after leaving the Museum it was one thing to be elected to the National Academy of Sciences and the American Association for the Advancement of Science, to receive an honorary Ph.D. from Bowdoin, to give an occasional course at Harvard or to deliver the Lowell Lectures in Boston, but daily bread and butter came from more popular activities. The bulk of Morse's income derived from writing for popular journals and delivering lectures to general audiences on topics like "Flowers and their Friends," "Glimpses of Insect Life" and "Glaciers." Beyond mere livelihood, such activity also partook of the American faith in the common people; it was part of a national belief in both the possibility of self-improvement and in science as a practical pursuit. In the introduction to the *American Naturalist*, a magazine which Morse helped to found, this was expressed with the suggestion that all scientific theories should be "subordinated to the practical advantage as well as to the intellectual and moral elevation of man . . . our science will be ennobled by publishing those facts and principles which interest alike the philosopher and the day laborer."[5]

To describe Morse's life primarily in terms of career is to see it through his own eyes. He possessed the mentality of a culture taught to believe the surfaces of the outer world are more important, more real than the experiences of the inner one. Unlike natural phenomena, which could be neatly categorized, emotions were messy and uncontrollable and best avoided. Morse knew this as early as his teenage years. His single-minded pursuit of shells

---

[4] Morse's findings were first reported as "The Brachiopoda: A Division of Annelida," *The American Journal of Science and Arts*, 50 (July, 1870), 1-5. The full research paper was "On the Systematic Position of the Brachiopods," *Proceedings of the Boston Society of Natural History*, 15 (March 19, 1873), and reprinted with the same title as a separate volume (Boston, 1873). Darwin's letter is quoted in Wayman, pp. 222-223.
[5] *The American Naturalist*, 1 (1868), 2.

made for a stormy relationship with his father. Johnathan Kimball Morse, deacon of the Baptist Church and a partner in a small business, was a wrathful man who never approved of his son's impractical aims. So disturbed was young Ned by Johnathan's repeated assaults with violent words, and even more violent prayers, that once he was driven to the edge of suicide. Momentarily that could seem preferable to abandoning shells which, as he confided to his diary, were "the only thing I care to live for. . . . "[6]

The chilliness of that remark touched all his human relationships. Even his worshipful biographer admits that Morse's heart "burned for science and humanity, rather than for those of his immediate circle."[7] To desert the ways of a harsh, narrow-minded father in favor of one's own desires may be to act in a manner common to generations of young American males, but Morse took the pattern one step farther: literally or symbolically he was always deserting those closest to him. His mother, a lively woman of intellectual bent, provided love and support to counterbalance the influence of his father in those sensitive adolescent years, but Ned was unable to repay her devotion in kind. Nor was he caring with his siblings. After his father's death in 1860, Morse allowed his older brother to shoulder the entire burden of supporting their mother and three sisters. His one lifelong friend, John Gould, received slightly better treatment. They had begun by sharing an enthusiasm for shells, but, responding to the call of practicality, Gould had gone to work in a bank. A cynical observer might suggest that Morse well knew how to choose friends because for years he would shamelessly borrow money from John—to study with Agassiz, to finance scientific ventures, to go to Japan. Gould's reward was a stream of letters full of Morse's latest accomplishments and explanations as to why he could not yet meet his financial obligations.

Indifference to intimacy and more than a hint of exploitation also marked his fifty-year relationship with Ellen Owen. At twenty Morse had worried that he would never love a woman; for the rest of his life his actions seemed to indicate that he never did. When he met Nellie in 1860, Ned felt himself unworthy and up she went on a pedestal: "She is the one to whom I will look for advice, one who will lead me to a higher scale of thought, and one I shall love to please by good behavior." So moved was he by some unaccustomed feeling in the heart that for a few weeks he did attempt to share his usual passion with her, hauling Nellie off to the Zoology Museum in Cambridge for private lectures on the animal kingdom, especially mollusks. In theory, marriage for Morse was a two-way street, a matter of sharing with someone

---

[6] Entry for April 27, 1858, quoted in Wayman, pp. 24-25.
[7] Wayman, p. 427.

"who will strive for my happiness in the same way I shall strive for hers."[8]
The reality ran in only one direction. Married life was foreshadowed when,
on the eve of the wedding in 1863, Morse invited John Gould to come along
and help turn the honeymoon into a snail-collecting expedition, exclaiming:
"What a delightful time we should have!"[9] In the long years after the ceremony, Nellie's role was to raise the children, take care of the household, and
stay out of his way. On many of his extended trips Morse left her and the
two children at home.

It was easier to leave human beings behind than to desert the Lord. God
the Father was closely linked to Johnathan the father, who insisted that his
children follow a devout path. Torn as a teenager by a religious crisis, Ned
ended it after attending a revival meeting where the doleful cadences of the
minister's gloomy sermon were intoned in a voice that seemed to issue from
a coffin. Finally and emphatically he rejected all notions of hellfire and
damnation, but he did not abandon the Almighty. When the controversy
over *Origin of Species* erupted in the early sixties, Morse—under the sway of
Agassiz, who never did accept Darwin's theory—rejected natural selection
because it meant the world was the product of mere "chance." More unusual
and telling was his complaint that "Darwin's chapter on the struggle for
existence smacks too strongly of Calvinism, and . . . Darwin's picture looks
a good deal like Calvin's drawing of us poor worms. . . ."[10] By 1873 Morse
had reversed his position, but no more than Darwin himself did he renounce
"the wisdom and goodness of the Creator." Still, the theory could be used
further to free himself intellectually from the church of his father, for man's
"origin from lower forms of life knocks in the head Adam and Eve, hence
Original Sin, hence the necessity for vicarious atonement, hence everything
that savors of the bad place. . . ."[11]

The shift on Darwin shows off two of Morse's most winning traits; he was
both fearless and open-minded. After a decade full of careful study and contacts with other scientists had served to convince him that Darwin was right,
he did not hesitate to speak out on what was still a touchy issue. To John
Gould's suggestion that he tone down such remarks rather than endanger
public support for his lectures, Morse answered sharply: "I should rather
come down to one meal a day and lumber along in debt than follow so humiliating a path. . . ." Not only did the American people need to learn the truth,
but he needed to speak it: "My chief care must be to avoid that 'rigidity of
mind' that prevents one from remodeling his opinions; there is nothing

[8] Diary entries Oct. 31 and Dec. 31, 1869, quoted in Wayman, pp. 145, 155.
[9] Letter to John Gould, March 29, 1863, quoted in Wayman, p. 201.
[10] Letter to John Gould, March 11, 1869, quoted in Wayman, p. 226.
[11] Letter to John Gould, Oct. 25, 1873, quoted in Wayman, p. 225.

[more] glorious to my mind than the graceful abandoning of one's position if it be false. . . . "[12]

This admirable attitude extended no farther than the realms of science and religion. Nowhere is there any indication that before going to Japan Morse ever questioned or displayed any curiosity about the premises of the social order in which he had been raised. His opinions in the realms of art, politics, history and general culture largely remain a blank. Up to the age of forty such matters rarely impinge upon his detailed diary, and what few entries exist indicate a mentality wholly conventional. This is hardly surprising. He was, after all, a largely self-educated small-town product who, according to his biographer "had never read a book on history, or philosophy, or art. Architecture, music, and sculpture were terra incognita to him."[13] He had resided in Cambridge but was ignorant of the politics and literary works of even such local figures as Nathaniel Hawthorne, Ralph Waldo Emerson, Henry David Thoreau, Henry Wadsworth Longfellow, Oliver Wendell Holmes, Bronson Alcott, Charles Eliot Norton or Julia Ward Howe. In the troubled political times leading up to the Civil War, Morse never expressed an opinion on either slavery or abolitionism, though when the call to arms came in 1861 he did respond like a good patriot and then was temporarily in despair when poor health barred him from the ranks.

To characterize Morse at the time he left for the Orient as a typical American is to do him, more than his homeland, a disservice. If in personal tastes and priorities he seems to express a national pattern, clearly in talents, energy, and professional interests he was unusual. The path from obscurity to fame might be a cultural ideal, but Morse followed it in his own way. Wealth meant nothing to him, though it is easy enough to see the incessant collecting of shells as an odd parallel to an obsession with piling up material possessions. In a small, offbeat sort of way, Morse was a kind of adventurer. The first of Agassiz's students to go out on his own, he for the most part avoided institutional or long-term commitments. His place of residence for sixty years was Salem, Massachusetts, but he was a restless sort, one who liked movement and diversity. More than once he quit good positions. After helping to found the *American Naturalist*, he left its editorial board; secure as curator of mollusks at the Peabody Academy, he then left the post. His writings included everything from newspaper articles to textbooks.[14] Briefly he served on the faculty of Maine State, Bowdoin, and Harvard Colleges. He

[12]Wayman, p. 225.
[13]Wayman, p. 104.
[14]Albert P. Morse, "Bibliography of Edward Sylvester Morse" (unpublished typescript, in possession of Peabody Museum, Salem, Mass.), is the only full bibliography of Morse material. Of its 558 items, 150 were published before his trip to Japan.

lectured all over the country, from Maine to Mississippi, from New York to California. In 1874 he had a first taste of Oriental culture in San Francisco's Chinatown; on the same trip he learned that the waters of Japan were loaded with dozens of varieties of brachiopods unknown in the United States. Seized by an immediate and overwhelming desire to study them, he spent three years of hard work attempting to raise the money and arrange the free time for an expedition there. For Morse no price was ever too high nor any distance too great when it was a matter of learning more about creatures who lived in shells.

II

There was a standard way to land in nineteenth-century Japan. From the slightly rolling deck of a ship one's eyes would take in the sunny morning splendors of Tokyo Bay, the Yokohama Bluff full of Western-style residences, the quaint roof shapes of the native quarters, the jutting line of terraced rice paddies and then, floating above all like a cloud, the peerless, snowy shape of Mount Fuji, whose perfection would be declared uncapturable in reams of words that captured little but cliché. Edward S. Morse was considerably more honest and less romantic than the normal traveller. His ship dropped anchor in the dark. On the boat taking passengers to shore he became interested enough in the odd native oarlocks to make them the subject of his first of many thousands of drawings of Japan.[15] This action may be taken as symbolic. For most Americans, the Japan of that era was nothing if not exotic, a land of strange people, architecture and art, of startling landscapes, mysterious religions, and outlandish customs like mixed nude bathing. Morse normally did not dwell upon such things. His daily journal rarely describes the "picturesque" and never makes any attempt to capture the poetry and romance of a feudal order only ten years in the past. When Japan's religions, history, or art impinge upon his pages, they always do so in terms of the daily and the commonplace.

The story of his career in Japan is quickly told. Arriving in June 1877 with the aim of doing marine research for a month, Morse was quickly offered a job as the first professor of zoology at the newly-founded Imperial University in Tokyo at a salary so high that even a man uninterested in money could not

---

[15] The sketch may be seen in Edward S. Morse, *Japan Day by Day*, 2 vols. (Boston and New York, 1917), I:2.

resist.[16] His first stint lasted until November, then he went home, collected his family and returned in April, 1878. He departed after two school years but came back for five months in 1882 on a trip largely devoted to buying pottery for his own collection and artifacts for the ethnographic section of the Peabody Museum in Salem. During his residency Morse was responsible for a significant number of firsts: At Enoshima he founded the first Japanese marine laboratory; in Tokyo, set up the first Museum of Natural History; at Omori, began the first archaeological excavation. He also initiated the first university press and was instrumental in training Japan's first generation of life scientists.[17]

These accomplishments encompass only the most obvious aspects of Morse's years in the Orient; they provide evidence of what he did for Japan but give little indication of what it did for and to him. There Morse underwent major changes of two sorts, public and private. If from the early eighties onward he devoted far more time to Japan than to zoology, he also underwent a series of alterations at once psychological and philosophical. Exposure to Japan compelled Morse to look for the first time at the United States with the eyes of an outsider or critic; it also raised deep and unanswerable questions about the values and practices of American culture. Unused to dealing with such troubling and elusive matters, Morse rarely confronted them directly and never systematically. But a close reading of his articles and books, journals, letters and diaries, shows just how Japan not only disturbed Morse but also served both to define and alter permanently his attitudes on matters political, social, cultural and aesthetic.

A major reason Japan could have such an effect is that life there was for an American such an odd combination of the familiar and the exotic. From the first days, Morse liked all those beliefs and ways that reminded him of home. Clearly the Japanese were a progressive people, in the process of abandoning superstitions—such as Chinese medicine—and embracing the latest scientific theories and technological methods in an effort to march

---

[16]The salary was $5000 in gold a year, plus a house and stable and transportation both ways for Morse and his family. See letter to John Gould, July 11, 1877, in Wayman, p. 238.

[17]Robert S. Schwantes, *Japanese and Americans: A Century of Cultural Relations* (New York: Harpers, 1955), p. 157; Chitoshi Yanaga, *Japan Since Perry* (New York: McGraw-Hill, 1949), p. 85; H. J. Jones, *Live Machines: Hired Foreigners and Meiji Japan* (Vancouver, 1980), p. 92. The first publication of Tokyo University Press was Morse, *Shell Mounds of Omori* (Tokyo, 1879), a report on the first archaeological dig in Japan.

Japan Day by Day, a nine-hundred page selection from his journals, is the most important source for Morse's time in Japan. Also useful are *Japanese Homes and Their Surroundings* (Portland, 1885), and, by way of contrast with an Oriental culture he did not like, *Glimpses of China and Chinese Homes* (Boston, 1903).

forward into the camp of advanced nations. They seemed a practical people who cared little for metaphysics or idle speculation, but who knew how to design and utilize superb tools, build functional houses, construct clean and hygenic toilets and work hard and efficiently. As part of both the practical and the progressive, the Japanese were highly committed to schooling at all levels. In the classroom, as in adult life, they exhibited the virtues of diligence, self-control, and seriousness. This flowed from a larger value system which surprised anyone who thought himself there to help civilize the natives. As Morse put it:

> A foreigner, after remaining a few months in Japan, slowly begins to realize that, whereas he thought he could teach the Japanese everything, he finds, to his amazement and chagrin, that those virtues or attributes which, under the name of humanity are the burden of our moral teaching at home, the Japanese seem to be born with.[18]

Native morality could appear to be Judeo-Christian, but, like all the other apparently familiar aspects of the society, it carried special Japanese flavor. To Morse, the relationship between precept and behavior was the difference. His observations led to a startling conclusion: the Japanese actually practiced what Americans largely preached. Cleanliness of person and household, simplicity, courtesy, and consideration were all part of daily life. So were a number of the Ten Commandments. Parents were highly honored and crime was at a minimum. Houses had no locks and owners could leave stores unattended, confident that customers would pay for what they took. A traveller like Morse could leave a gold watch and eighty dollars on a tray at an inn and return a week later to find nothing missing. So safe was the land, so law-abiding the people and so rare the existence of "hoodlums," that one could journey to the most remote districts with no pistol for protection. Once Morse noted that in Tokyo eleven murders had been committed in a decade, while in the state of Michigan—with a smaller population— eighty-seven had occurred in a single year. Such facts made him assert that "A man is safer in the wilder regions of Japan at any hour, night or day, than in the quiet streets of Salem, or any other city in our country."[19]

The familiar helped to make the culture comfortable for an American; the unusual made it interesting. Morse was not a seeker of the exotic; rather, he was won by some of the most characteristic native beliefs and behavior patterns. Take the matter of religion. To someone who had battled free of

[18] Morse, *Japan Day by Day*, I: 44.
[19] Morse, *Japan Day by Day*, II: 112.

the exclusive, narrow doctrines of Calvinism and who had experienced the sombre, traditional New England Sunday, Japanese attitudes were refreshing in their breadth and tolerance. Here were two religions, Shinto and Buddhism, living together in harmony and mutual respect. People might show little deep faith in either, but they flocked to shrines and temples for colorful festivals that featured food and drink and playful, tipsy behavior. Most happy was the fact that their doctrines in no way ran counter to the findings of science. Darwinism blended nicely into the traditional respect for natural life and reverence for ancestors. This meant that when Morse delivered a public lecture on natural selection, the audience listened with an open mind and no opposition to the theory was raised in the name of dogma.[20]

Far more important than religion was the widespread influence of the aesthetic. Untutored in art Morse might be, but he could not help succumbing to the beauty of line, color, texture and form that suffused the culture. At home he had considered science a kind of democratic pursuit; in Japan he encountered a democracy of the artistic. Not only did people throughout the land—aristocrats and farmers, villagers and residents of Tokyo—share a deep appreciation for "artistic designs and the proper execution of them," but the humblest items—bowls, stone lanterns, utensils, towels, roof tiles, kettles, umbrellas, toys—were graced by an exquisite level of design and ornamentation.[21] That the Japanese aesthetic was simple, restrained and asymmetrical made it all the more appealing. Homes might be bare and almost spartan, but rooms possessed a harmony of dimension and a refinement of color that Morse had never before encountered. The same held true for gardens which, in the smallest of areas, could convey significant feelings with only a minimum of plants, trees, rocks or sand. A general reverence for nature also partook of the artistic. The national love affair with seasonable changes, with blossoming plum and cherry trees, flowering lotus and frozen pines, helped push Morse to the judgment that the Japanese "were the greatest lovers of nature and the greatest artists in the world."[22]

They were also the best-mannered of people. Indeed, to a good democrat, raised in a land where self-assertion and pushiness were honored in myth and rewarded in life, the elaborate courtesy of the Japanese could seem like a caricature of all that was effete in the abandoned aristocratic traditions of Europe. Yet Morse loved it all, the ceremonial bowing, ritual gift-giving, and formal patterns of speech. Perhaps this was because here, too, Japan was a

---

[20] Morse, "Science Lectures in Japan," *Popular Science*, 14 (Jan., 1879), 388-389; Robert S. Schwantes, "Christianity *Versus* Science: A Conflict of Ideas in Meiji Japan," *Far Eastern Quarterly*, 12 (Feb. 1953), 125.

[21] Morse, *Japanese Homes*, p. 173.

[22] Morse, *Japan Day by Day*, I: 253.

kind of democracy. Class distinctions there were, but good manners were the possession of rich and poor alike. Ex-samurai, rickshaw men, shopkeepers, laborers, artists, professors and tea house girls all struck him as polite, orderly, modest, and self-effacing in speech and action. This was a revelation. It indicated that mass behavior did not have to sink to some low common denominator but might in fact level upwards to patterns of high refinement.

A nation is ultimately people, and if Morse had never displayed much interest in the topic, Japan forced him to consider the varieties of human behavior and social roles. Like all Westerners he was smitten by the charms of Japanese women. The perpetual public cheerfulness, grace, and reticence of the young ones made them delightful company, and as caring, devoted wives and mothers they were without equal. Nor were they immodest, as some foreigners claimed. Touring a series of public baths with thermometer in hand to measure the average temperature of the scalding water, he reported that the Japanese did not stare at each other, but if an outsider hazarded a peek, the women quickly covered their nakedness. Even *geisha* did not draw his disapproval. Morse reported, with a kind of calculated innocence, that these women who entertained at parties were no more than the counterpart of young ladies at home, invited to dinner as a kind of social lubricant, "for the purpose of having things go off pleasantly."[23] The difference here was that *geisha* were professionals, and thus "far more entertaining than the usual run of girls and women. . . ."[24]

With his background as someone who neither cared nor thought much about women, it is hardly surprising to find Morse more disturbed by the behavior of Japanese males. To American eyes, this could seem odd in the extreme. As youngsters they shared the characteristics of girls, being polite, neat, well-behaved, and yet playful. An appreciative Morse never tired of expressing wonder that in the classroom from elementary school through college they could be so orderly and attentive. But such good behavior also made him suspicious. More than once he was moved to raise the ominous question, "Are they effeminate?"[25] The same could be asked about adults. After all, they wore robes, moved with grace, were soft-spoken and courteous, had difficulty saying "No" to a direct question, enjoyed playing apparently childish games, and displayed an inordinate passion for matters artistic. Japanese men wrote poetry, arranged flowers, performed tea ceremony, painted pictures, dwarfed trees, and were capable of going into raptures of joy over the perfection of a single cherry blossom. To combat the

[23] Morse, *Japan Day by Day*, I: 97-100.
[24] Morse, *Japan Day by Day*, II: 353.
[25] See, for example, *Japan Day by Day*, I: 297, II: 277.

disturbing implications of all this, Morse had to continually remind himself that they were also intrepid warriors, men who in battle displayed "the fiercest courage and fighting valor."[26]

Not everything in Japan pleased Morse, and a few native practices drew his criticism. Like so many foreigners baffled by the complexity of the language, especially its written form, he longed for the Japanese to abandon it in favor of English, arguing that this "would add greatly to their development along our lines."[27] He also found the use of nightsoil to fertilize crops unhygienic, the kneeling of servants undemocratic, the lack of chivalry towards women unromantic, and the persistence of popular superstition unmodern. But he did not judge such practices harshly. Obvious remnants of an earlier age, they might be expected to vanish as the nation continued to modernize. Only two aspects of the culture struck him as hopelessly beyond redemption; traditional music and the attitude towards time. The combined sounds of koto, samisen, and Japanese voice sounded so dismal and monotonous that he was led to ask, "Is this music?"[28] As for the propensity to mix work and pleasure, to drink endless cups of tea and discuss everything but the business at hand, he found this practice horrendous. Free of the Yankee concern with dollars and the Puritan fear of God, Morse was still enough of his culture to think that if time was neither money nor the Lord's, it was still something best filled up with work, not play.

III

That Japan intrigued and pleased Edward S. Morse was only the beginning point for the disturbance which changed his view of the world. The most significant evidence of this alteration is his drastic career shift. In the forty-four years following his third trip to the Orient, Morse became widely known as a Japan expert. Much of his lecturing, many of his writings, both popular and scholarly—including all his important publications—and the major institutional positions he enjoyed—curator of Oriental pottery at the Boston Museum of Fine Arts and Director of the Peabody Museum in Salem—were all the result of his experience there.[29] Were it not for Japan, Morse would be no more than the most minor of footnotes in the annals of American natural history.

[26] Morse, *Japan Day by Day*, I: 297.
[27] Morse, *Japan Day by Day*, II: 115.
[28] Morse, *Japan Day by Day*, I: 401-402.
[29] Of 558 items in Albert P. Morse's bibliography (see note 14), more than 200 are connected to the Japan experience.

Inklings of the shift came during Morse's first visit, but the flowering of his passion for Japan occurred during the second and longest sojourn, when he travelled extensively, traversing the country from Hokkaido to Kagoshima. It began when his attention was drawn to shell heaps at Omori, initially spied from a railway car between Yokohama and Tokyo. Having seen fellow scientists investigate such sites in New England, he correctly guessed them to be kitchen middens of a prehistoric people. The excavation that he directed at Omori put Morse in touch for the first time with artifacts of a primitive people. From this it was but a short step to an interest in other still little known aspects of the Japanese tradition such as early burial tombs, roof tiles, customs of the Ainu, methods of arrow release, latrines, and forms of architecture.[30]

Such topics may have diverted Morse from his pursuit of shelled creatures, but the place in his heart reserved for brachiopods was filled by something only the Japanese consider a high art form: stoneware pottery. Six months into the second stay he began to take an interest in this common ware, then virtually unknown outside the island empire, and soon he was involved in collecting it. Acquaintances introduced him to more serious examples of such work and shared their knowledge of the tea ceremony aesthetic that for almost three centuries had guided the native potter's hand. If the words *wabi, sabi* and *shibui*, which represent the pinnacle to which such pottery aspires, cannot satisfactorily be rendered into English, Morse could certainly see that restraint, severity and minimal decoration were its overriding characteristics.[31] That was part of the appeal. It is not surprising that the boy and man who had spent decades investigating the most unadorned of shell creatures gravitated to this humble ware rather than to Japan's more famous, brightly-colored porcelains.

A later generation may see that tea ceremony pottery exhibits a kind of exquisite, reverse snobbism, an aesthetic that approaches decadence in its adulation of the accidental, the deformed, the simple. Morse never acknowledged this. His principles of collecting harked back to an earlier period of life, and were different from that of any Japanese. Natives might collect pottery for beauty, but Morse's aim was completeness of kiln, lineage, region. Here his natural history background was crucial. An eye trained to

---

[30] Some of his works prompted by Japan are "Latrines of the East," *American Architect*, 42 (March 18, 1893), 1-18; "On the So-called Bow-Pullers of Antiquity," *Bulletin of the Essex Institute*, 24 (1894), 141-166; "Terra-Cotta Roofing Tiles," *Bulletin of the Essex Institute*, 24 (1892), 1-72; "Old Satsuma," *Harper's New Monthly Magazine*, 77 (September 1888), 512-529; "Was Middle America Peopled from Asia?" *Appleton's Popular Science Monthly*, 54 (November 1898), 1-16.

[31] Morse, *Japan Day by Day*, II: 399.

see marginal differentiations of shells quickly came to recognize the marks of hundreds of potters and the clay, glazes and styles of many traditions. Before the end of his second stay a proud Morse could report that in contests with connoisseurs, he could more than hold his own identifying the origin of previously unseen pieces. When he sold the collection to the Boston Museum of Fine Arts in the mid-nineties it was considered one of the most complete in the world. The two-volume catalogue he published as a guide to the collection splendidly classified the production of the Japanese potters, but, characteristically enough, wholly avoided making any aesthetic judgments.[32]

This passion for pottery marked more than a career shift; it was also a way of coming to grips with the lure of Japan, with Japan as the Other. Collecting stoneware was for years neither useful nor profitable, personally, financially or intellectually. It occupied much time and energy, drew Morse away from his major field of expertise, did nothing to enhance his reputation or income as a lecturer and writer, wiped out the profits he had hoped to make from teaching in Japan and caused him to disappoint his wife by absorbing money he had promised would go for redecorating their dilapidated, threadbare home. That it satisfied a lifelong impulse to collect, compare and classify is only a partial explanation of his behavior. More important was the fact that pottery offered him a means of dealing with perhaps mastering the strong pull of this alien social order. To collect stoneware was to approach the unfamiliar in a familiar way, to ward off attraction by simultaneously drawing close to and yet separating himself from the Other. By classifying such apparently humble objects scientifically, one could be aesthetic without giving in to aestheticism; it meant that Morse could spend hours enjoying the subtle beauty of a crackled, hairline glaze on a three-hundred-year old teabowl without having to face the accusation—either from others or oneself—that to do so was to indulge in a love for the sensuous and a taste for the delicacy, even effeminacy, of high art.

Collecting pottery was not enough wholly to contain the attractions of Japan. When after two years Morse refused a contract renewal and returned to the United States, he was hoping both to capitalize on the Oriental experience and return to natural history. But his former life soon proved to be too routine, colorless, boring. For the first time in his life Morse simply could not settle down to work. Long-planned projects—a further study of brachiopods, a book on evolution, another zoology text or even a volume on Japan—remained in abeyance. Two years of unproductive restlessness

---

[32] *Catalogue of the Morse Collection of Japanese Pottery*, 2 vols. (Cambridge, Mass., 1901).

led to a decision to return to the Orient. The ostensible reasons were a need
to fill out the pottery collection and to gather ethnographic materials for the
Peabody Museum.[33] Certainly these were the most important professional
activities during five months of travel, for but Morse they were not enough.
Japan had created a deep dissatisfaction in him, one not easily banished. To
deal with it he now undertook a most uncharacteristic approach. The man
who had all his life kept reality separated from the self by a wall of concepts
now made a brief attempt to become Japanese.

The activities which provide evidence of this significant move are his study
of two traditional art forms: tea ceremony and Noh drama singing. Not only
are these, especially the latter, a trifle esoteric even to natives, but they also
run directly against Morse's prior judgments and values. Tea ceremony, an
elaborate, meticulous ritual in the service of the simplest of tasks, may be said
to have as its chief aim a way of artistically wasting time. Nowhere did a hint
of this pass Morse's pen when he bragged of being the "first foreigner" ever
to undertake its study and practice. Noh singing, full of sounds that Morse
had once refused even to consider music, now provided deep pleasure as he
sat on his knees for hours and tried unsuccessfully to imitate his teacher's
"rich and sonorous" voice. In such a short time he could not hope to master
either of these difficult forms. But his aim was something different: "It is by
taking actual lessons in tea ceremony and in singing that I may learn many
things from the Japanese standpoint."[34]

Coming from a man who liked the Japanese for being progressive and
practical, who cheered their abandonment of ancient ways, who disliked
their attitudes towards time, and who believed it would be a good thing if
they forsook their native language in favor of English, these are significant
words indeed. They show how much Morse was touched by the ineffable
side of this culture. The wish to see and feel the world from the Japanese
standpoint was an attempt to narrow a gap between what he was and what
he wished to feel, to become that which was so appealing. His words and
actions may be seen as no less than an act of love towards a nation that had
disturbed and enriched him in ways he could neither fully understand nor
express. They represent the farthest Morse could go towards narrowing an
unbridgeable gap, the closest he could get towards denying his heritage and
self in an effort to share the consciousness of the Other.

For Morse—perhaps for anybody who makes one—this kind of move was
doomed to failure. When he departed Japan in November, 1882, it was for
the last time. During the next forty-four years he would publish extensively

[33] Wayman, *Morse*, p. 271.
[34] Morse, *Japan Day by Day*, II: 344, 401-402.

on Japanese culture, become an acknowledged expert on its pottery and twice be decorated by the Emperor for meritorious service to the nation.[35] In this period he undertook several trips to Europe, whose society and art were less pleasing to him than those of Japan. Seeing Paris through eyes accustomed to Tokyo, he could comment disdainfully. "The lavish appeal to the senses shows how far the Parisian has departed from enjoyment of simple things." After viewing the art collections in Dresden, he flatly stated, "Japanese pictorial art has ruined my appreciation for this stuff."[36] Given his growing fame, the Japanese propensity to honor foreigners who have aided them and his increased financial security after selling the pottery collection to the BMFA for $73,000, there is little reason to suppose Morse could not have easily undertaken another journey to the Far East. That he did not do so, that after 1882 he chose to view Japan from afar and only through a study of her artifacts, surely says something about the pain—sweet though it might be—of his last venture there.

Morse might not be able to return to the Orient, but the entire second half of his life was colored by his experience there. Japan drove him back to his native land with a different mindset; the Other provided a new perspective on himself and his homeland. The man who had never voiced an opinion on social or aesthetic matters now became a critic of American practices. To read Morse's works on Japan is to be faced with an endless series of contrasts between two civilizations. So many of the attractive aspects of Japan raised doubts about things at home. Their politeness highlighted American coarseness and crudity; their honesty and self-control, American theft, disorderliness and random violence; their well-behaved youngsters, America's ill-mannered ones; their simplicity and elegance of taste in home and garden, America's ugly, dreadfully crowded counterparts. Japan even suggested a lesson that surely was strange to any American raised on a diet of republicanism and economic opportunity; this was that one could judge a civilization by its manners. Here Morse was moved to call on Edmund Burke to express what he felt: "Manners are more important than laws . . . they vex or soothe, corrupt or purify, exalt or debase, barbarize or refine. . ."[37]

---

[35] Emperor Meiji awarded Morse the Third Class of the Order of the Rising Sun, and his successor, Emperor Taisho, added the Second Class of the Order of the Sacred Treasure. See Wayman, *Morse*, pp. 381, 429.

[36] Diary entries May 19, 1889, and October 17, 1887, quoted in Wayman, *Morse*, pp. 353, 344.

[37] Morse quotes Burke in *On the Importance of Good Manners* (Boston, 1894), pp. 23-24. This was a published version of a Founder's Day address delivered at Vassar College.

The alterations of mindset did not only concern social phenomena; they also included the self. Japan provided a broader definition of human potential, of masculine and feminine behavior. It encouraged Morse to indulge impulses stifled at home, to allow the aesthetic, the feminine, the unpractical become part of life. If this could only be temporary, if the support systems for tea ceremony or Noh singing did not exist in America, if most of the time such impulses were hidden by the preoccupation with analysis and classification of pottery, one must still imagine that in the realm of experience where no payoff can accurately be measured, even a temporary or partial indulgence allowed Morse to feel a larger and more complete sense of selfhood. No doubt this underlay the broadened sphere of American topics on which he could write. In the post-Oriental years Morse did not hesitate to speak out on matters artistic, literary, social and political.[38]

Frustration was also part of the legacy from Japan. Take the matter of all those delightful practices that Morse so admired. It was natural enough for him to assert "We have much to learn from Japanese life," and to write on the need for better manners or a heightened sensitivity to the aesthetic, but it was virtually impossible to be specific about how Americans might incorporate such things into the national life. This was also a problem on the personal level. After coming home Morse little altered his way of living or his habits. Always he had been brusque, slovenly, informal, and outspoken, and the polished society of Japan did nothing to alter these characteristics. Nor did he attempt to make either his home or working space become more like the spare, simple rooms he had admired. Morse's study remained a crowded mess, his tables heaped with shells, papers, books and ashtrays overflowing with half-smoked cigars. For years after returning home from the Orient thousands of pieces of pottery were stacked on sagging shelves built along the walls in a manner that would have horrified any Japanese. But to keep the collection hidden away and to display it one piece at a time, as a native would have done, would have run counter to the deepest of his lifetime patterns.

The tension between ideal and reality that such conflicts embody says something larger about the Japan experience. That culture seemed to hold out a promise—perhaps a series of promises—that could never be fulfilled.

---

[38] Much of this was in newspaper articles, letters to the editor and public lectures. Clippings detailing his views can be found in the Peabody Museum archives. More easily obtainable are such works as *Museums of Art and Their Influence* (n.p., n.d.); "If Public Libraries, Why Not Public Museums?" *Atlantic Monthly* 72 (July 1893), 112-119; *Can City Life be Made Endurable* (Worcester, Mass., 1900); "Natural Selection and Crime," *Appleton's Popular Science Monthly* 41 (August 1892), 433-436; *The Steam Whistle a Menace to Public Health* (Salem, Mass., 1905).

If Morse could never again view his homeland with the eyes of innocence that had been his before the age of forty, he could also never fully banish the new feelings which had been raised. Ultimately Japan left him in a state of discomfort that could fade but never wholly vanish. It had showed him the attractions of the Other, provided ways of sharing the feelings of the Other, but finally frustrated any desire to blend with the Other. The experience was like that of an unconsummated love affair in which Morse was perpetually on the brink of possessing that which finally cannot be possessed. Or perhaps it would be more correct to say that, except for those religious few whose lives are a successful quest to blend with the One, consummation is never more than temporary, and that when the fires of passion grow dim we are larger for having had the experience of the Other but nonetheless remain separate and alone with ourselves.

Such an experience of Japan was not Morse's alone. Similar hopes and conflicts pervade the lives of many Americans who lived there either in the nineteenth century or in later periods, including today. To encounter Japan is not only to be reminded of the strength and continuity of culture, tradition and history, it is to learn that as human beings we can expand ourselves ineffably by touching the Other and letting it touch us. Of course one need not journey to the Orient to find the Other; it is available daily in those unknown and unknowable aspects of acquaintances, friends, lovers and mates. The difference is that Japan has been capable of penetrating defenses designed to deny the alien aspects that underlie everyday life. By upsetting the common definitions of reality it drives us back to reexamine our own ways, which is to say ourselves. This was the importance of the Other in the life of Edward S. Morse. Insofar as his values remain part of us, we may share and learn from his experience. Insofar as the passing of a century has made him alien, Morse is now Other to us. Looking into a mirror that reveals, however dimly, images of both another culture and the past, may help us to shed our too-easy ethnocentrism, see better who we are and catch a glimpse of that perennial cultural challenge which seems to issue from Japan.

California Institute of Technology

III

EAST ASIAN WRITERS AND THE WEST

THE AMERICAN EXPERIENCE
IN MODERN CHINESE POETRY

Dominic C. N. Cheung

I

The American experience in modern Chinese poetry refers specifically to the personal experiences and fragmentary impressions of America of modern Chinese poets. The works of Wen I-to, a poet-artist from Peking, who came to Chicago in 1922 when he was twenty-four years of age, mark the early stage of the American experience and are characterized by both his aesthetic appreciation of sojourn in a foreign environment and bitter protests of humiliating experiences in the foreign land.

Socialist poets including Ai Ch'ing in Mainland China clearly evaluate the American phenomenon in the context of Marxist dialectics. In particular, when America was intensely involved with the Korean War in the early 1950s, and later with the Vietnam War in the 1960s, these poets criticized United States expansion in Southeast Asia and the unjust conditions of the immigrant Chinese in America.

In Taiwan, on the other hand, American literature exerted a significant influence during the process of westernization in modern Chinese poetry. This is understandable considering the close political and economic ties between Taiwan and the United States since 1949, ties which remain intact even today despite the inevitable severance of formal political and diplomatic ties between the two countries. Early literary journals such as *Wen-hsüeh tsa-chih* [Literature], edited by the late Hsia Chih-an, an English professor at National Taiwan University, who later lived in Seattle and Berkeley; and *Hsien-tai wen-hsüeh* [Modern Literature], headed by Pai Hsien-yung, a prominent novelist now teaching at the University of California, Santa Barbara, displayed a strong European-oriented modern consciousness. American literature, in particular that of the modern period, was enthusiastically introduced in these journals to the Chinese audience. "The Love Song of J. Alfred Prufrock" and "The Waste Land," for example, were widely read and appreciated. Such American poets as Eliot, Pound, Frost, Cummings were often mentioned and quoted in creative works and literary criticism. In addition, Chinese poets and writers, returning from the Writers Workshop or the International Writing Program at the University of Iowa, exerted an enormous influence in the shaping of modern literature in Taiwan.

Since literature of the 1930s remains a taboo in Taiwan, there appeared an abrupt discontinuity in the modern tradition of Chinese literature, particularly in poetry. In fact, the Taiwan government considered most of the literature of the Thirties not only to have exposed the horrors bred by the social system but also to have instigated rebellions among workers and students. Indeed, the Republican government attributed its downfall on the mainland in part to the influence of leftist writers. Once you have been bitten by a snake, a Chinese saying has it, rope and string will scare you for the next ten years. This is just the post-traumatic mentality manifested by the Taiwanese government. When a cultural continuity reaches an abrupt end and finds itself in a vacuum, for writers to turn to foreign sources to fill the void seems inevitable. A flood of western influences which covered the post-1949 era was due exactly to the almost complete rejection of the writings of the Thirties. Indeed, the "modernization" of literature in Taiwan can easily be termed "Americanization."

II

Wen I-to graduated from the Ch'ing-hua School in Peking and later studied in the Chicago Arts Institute in 1922. When he first came to Chicago, the "imposing beauty" (in Wen's own words) of the city immediately attracted his attention. His initial impression of America was that "Americans have a far better sense of aesthetics than we."[1] These remarks were made probably in reference to the social circle of Chicago literary elites, including

---

[1] There are two parts, or stages to be found in Wen I-to's American experience. The first stage begins with his enrollment at the Art Institute of Chicago, where "Autumn Colors" was written. The second stage includes his transfer to Colorado College in Colorado Springs, and his short stay in New York where he joined the Art Students' League. Wen wanted to leave for Colorado to join his writer friend Liang Shih-ch'iu, who was an English student at Colorado College at that time. Nevertheless, Wen's dislike of America also contributed to his leaving Chicago. In one of his letters, he writes, "Oh, I have just come to Chicago for a week, but already am bored with the life here." For details, see "Chronology," *Wen I-to ch'üan chi* 聞一多全集 [The Complete Works of Wen I-to] edited by Chu Tzu-ch'ing 朱自清, (Hong Kong, 1972), reprint of 1948 edition published by 開明書店, Shanghai, pp. 38-42.

Carl Sandburg, Amy Lowell, and Harriet Monroe, with whom Wen was closely associated. On the other hand, living in a foreign environment gave Wen a deep feeling of nostalgia. He wrote to his friend that "without leaving one's country, one will not know what homesickness is." After he finished writing "Autumn Colors" and "The Laundry Song," two poems which marked the earliest American experience of the Chinese poets, he again wrote, "I hope after you have finished reading these poems, you will not misunderstand that I am thinking of a private 'home.' No! I am thinking of China's mountains and rivers, woods and plants, birds and beasts, houses and mansions, and the people too."[2]

"Autumn Colors" and "The Laundry Song" represent two types of American experience, one leading to further appreciation of American beauty and the other scorning on the injustice of the American society. Shortly before "Autumn Colors" was written, Wen mentioned to a friend that he was deeply impressed by John Fletcher's use of color imagery in his "Chinese Poet Among Barbarians," and that in reading the poem, Wen's happiness "scorched his own heart." Wen's poem was originally entitled "Autumn Woods" but later was changed to "Autumn Colors" because the new title alluded to the famous classical couplet of Lu Yu in which the Sung poet talks of his poetic feelings, sharp as a blade of knife, clipping the autumnal scene into the colorful patterns of his poems. Furthermore, according to Wen's letter written to Liang Shih-ch'iu, a life-long friend of Wen and at that time a student at Colorado College, Flether's poem evoked in Wen "the feeling of colors, I am now writing a long poem entitled 'Autumn Colors'—a study of colors."[3]

"Autumn Colors" is indeed a study of colors, presenting an intellectual and emotional complex in an instant of time.

> Water in the creek
> As purple as ripe grapes
> Rolls out golden carp's scales
> Layer upon layer
>
> Several scissor-shaped maple leaves
> Like crimson swallows
> Whirling and turning, rising and dipping
> On the water.

[2] *The Complete Works of Wen I-to*, Vol. 1, p. 38.
[3] *The Complete Works of Wen I-to*, Vol. 1, p. 39.

Thick and fat like bears' paws,
Those dark brown leaves
Scattered on the green.
Busy, timid squirrels
Scurry out and in among the leaves,
Gathering food for the approaching winter.

Chestnut tree leaves, now of age,
Complained to the western wind all night long,
Finally win their freedom.
With a deep blush on their dry faces,
They giggle and bid farewell to the ancient branches.

White pigeons, multi-colored pigeons,
Red-eyed silver gray pigeons,
Raven-like black pigeons,
With a golden sheen of purple and green on their backs—

So many of them, tired of flying
Assemble beneath the steps.,
Their beaks buried in their wings,
Quietly they take their afternoon nap.

Crystalline air, like pure water, fills the world:
Three or four pert children
(In orange, yellow and black sweaters)
Dart through the clove bushes,
Like goldfish cavorting among the seaweeds.[4]

Although the poem contains sixteen stanzas altogether, the above six stanzas present a wide spectrum of colors and the poet's exultation in his world of colors. While his feelings are revealed through the vividness of colorful patterns, the poet's romanticism is well checked by using colors as "objective correlatives." In the case of the pigeons, for example, seven different colors are used in describing the dozen pigeons on the steps—a picture completely static, yet with a full array of emotional colors.

---

[4] *The Complete Works of Wen I-to*, Vol. 3, under the section "Poetry and Criticism," p. 106. I have adopted the partial English version of the poem from Kai-yu Hsu's English translation in his *Twentieth Century Chinese Poetry: An Anthology* (Ithaca, N.Y.: Cornell University Press, 1970), pp. 52-53. Hai-yu Hsu also has a full account of Wen I-to's life and works in his new book *Wen I-to* (Boston: Twayne Publishers, 1980).

Indulgence in the enjoyment of exotic scenery did not last long, for soon Wen came to realize his incurable homesickness for China. In Wen's poems, the Chinese setting is replaced by the western environment, yet Wen's description of his miserable American autumn in "Autumn Is Deep Now," iterating his close attachment to the country where he belongs, presents the same tone of sentimentalism often found in the poems of nostalgia. In one of the stanzas, he says:

> Holding a thick blanket all day long
> And lying like a cat close to a stove,
> I curled myself in a rocking chair,
> Rocking, rocking,
> Thinking of my country,
> Of my family,
> Of my school,
> My old friends,
> And the good old days, forever gone. [5]

Sentimentalism, however, was not the only reason prompting Wen's desire to return to China. Wen encountered the hostility and injustice imposed upon minorities in a white society, and for a Chinese intellectual, the insults were too painful to swallow in silence. In 1923, when Wen I-to was twenty-five years old, he wrote a letter home from Chicago, telling of his plan for an early departure for China. Part of the letter reads:

> As an educated Chinese youth, staying and living in America is beyond imagination. Let us wait until my return to China year after next, and I will tell my family all the stories by the stove. I will weep bitterly to release my anger. Since I have five thousand years of history and culture, in what way am I incompetent to the Americans? Would you say my countrymen cannot make good weapons and kill people openly? All in all, it is too hard to describe how they despise and discriminate against our people here. After my return to China, I will even advocate Sino-Japanese friendship against the Americans, rather than advocating Sino-American friendship to ward off the Japanese. [6]

The same Byronic anger and cynicism can be found naturally in Wen's poems written about the American experience. "The Laundry Song" is an

---

[5] *The Complete Works of Wen I-to*, Vol. 3, p. 220.
[6] *The Complete Works of Wen I-to*, Vol. 1, p. 40.

outstanding example. Speaking in a scornful tone, Wen reiterates the tragic
and wretched lives of the Chinese laborers in America, using the laundryman
as a metaphor. The laundryman works by taking off the dirt from his cus-
tomer's clothes. Consequently, when people have made their clothes dirty,
realistically or symbolically, they have no need to clean them because they
can leave them all to the Chinese laundryman:

> (One piece, two pieces, three pieces,)
> Washing must be clean.
> (Four pieces, five pieces, six pieces,)
> Ironing must be smooth.
>
> I can wash handkerchiefs wet with sad tears;
> I can wash shirts soiled in sinful crimes.
> The grease of greed, the dirt of desire . . .
> And all the filthy things at your house,
> Give them to me to wash, give them to me.
>
> Brass stinks so; blood smells evil.
> Dirty things you have to wash.
> Once washed, they will again be soiled.
> How can you, men of patience, ignore them!
> Wash them (for the Americans), wash them![7]

Apparently, America creates more questions in Wen's mind than answers.
He continues to ask in his poem: "You say the laundry business is too base./
Only Chinamen are willing to stoop so low?" and "Washing the others'
sweat with your own blood and sweat?/ (But) do you want to do it? Do you
want it?" Wen's anger is understandable. In the past hundred years, thousands of Chinese came to America and worked at the railroads, mines, farms
and in various odd jobs, dedicating their efforts and lives to further solidifi-
cation of the American dream. And yet a hundred years later, they are still
"invisible," still being looked upon as menial laborers:

> Year in year out a drop of homesick tears;
> Midnight, in the depth of night, a laundry lamp . . .
> Menial or not, you need not bother,
> Just see what is not clean, what is not smooth,
> And ask the Chinaman, ask the Chinaman.[8]

---

[7] *The Complete Works of Wen I-to*, Vol. 3. Kai-yu Hsu's translation is used. See Hsu,
Twentieth Century Chinese Poetry, p. 55.
[8] *The Complete Works of Wen I-to*, Vol. 3. See Hsu, *Twentieth Century Chinese
Poetry*, p. 56.

Unfortunately, Wen's protest in his poems of American experience was little noticed by the modern poets in the early stage of modern Taiwanese poetry. These poets, who were influenced by the French symbolists or the American modernists, were more interested in detecting the incubus of mechanical culture and the consequent disillusionment of the modern mind than observing the bitterness of the Chinese in America. Ya Hsien, an early modernist poet in Taiwan, accuses the coming of dominance of the machine age in "Chicago." He first quotes Carl Sandburg's famous lines—"City of the Big Shoulders:/ They tell me you are wicked," then proceeds with his own description of the modern city:

> In Chicago we will love by push button, hike by machine
>   bird
> Pick daisies from ad billboards, and under the trestles
> We will rail a cold, lonely culture
> From the Seventh Street south
> I know there an equation concealed in your hair
> As the taxicabs prey on the stars of our Lord
> I stretch my arms to breathe the aroma of mathematics.

Although the "equation" and the "aroma of mathematics" are in part metaphors referring to his personal experiences, they convey an image of the mechanical or mathematical culture which poses an immediate threat to the natural beauty and human intellects:

> Sometimes in the early evening
> Timid angels carefully flutter around
> But their tender arms are broken, still, by electric cables
> Among the chimneys.

There is, in Ya Hsien's poem, a strong tone of protest, yet his argument is aimed more at the conflict between the romantic "I" and his deformed, mechanical nature. Using his personal images and metaphors, the poet places the romantic "I" or the poet's own self in the center of the lyrical experiences, in which the "I" struggles with the mechanical civilization:

> Thus, you were mind that night
> Just like a butterfly turned lost in the cinders
> Right in Chicago
> Only butterflies are not steel
>
> But when the steam screams in such hurry-scurry
> Underneath the park's artificial pines

Whose satin scarf is it
That saves this coarse, illiterate city with bliss . . . [9]

Ya Hsien did not visit America until 1966 and "Chicago" was written in 1958. In fact, other poems like "Babylon," "Arabia," "Jerusalem," "Greece," "Rome," "Paris," "London," "Naples," "Florence," and "Spain" in his collection of poems called *The Abyss* were written before the poet had a chance to visit any of these cities or countries. In his "Poetic Notes," Ya Hsien wrote:

> A Poet without a wife can still write about a bride in his poem. Compared to life, poetry is sometimes better and sometimes worse. As for me, I tend to the latter. I think the task of a poet is "to collect the unfortunate incidents." When one feels unfortunate and holds on to this feeling, he has his existence. Existence, after all, is a bliss.[10]

If we follow logic of Ya Hsien's statement, a poet can certainly write about Chicago without coming to America, just as a poet can write about a bride without having a wife.

In Ya Hsien's poem, the physical presence of the poet is not an essential factor in determining the authenticity of his American experience. In the process of his narration, the poet moves in and out of his exotic landscape. Consequently, foreign objects, or names of places, are not indicators of things or locations but become "objective correlatives" which link up the poet's intricate experiences, past and present.

In Yang Mu's "The Lake Boulevard," a poem on Chicago, the poet's description of the "leaf" and the "face" is transcendent of all geographical factors, but once they are put in connection with "Lake Michigan" and "Chicago Sun Times Building," they present immediately an American experience.[11] Within this context, the metaphors of the leaf and the face become

---

[9] See Ya Hsien's *Shen Yüan* 深淵 [The Abyss] (Taipei: 晨鐘出版社, 1970), pp. 111-112. I have obtained the English translation of this poem from Wang Chinghsien's guest edition of Taiwan issue in *Micromegas*, Vol. V, No. 3 (Amherst, Mass., n.d.), p. 26.

[10] *The Abyss*, p. 233. Ya Hsien's statement, of course, was not aimed at the logic I have derived, but is rather a proclamation of his surrealist poetics.

[11] According to the "Prolegomena" of Chang Mo and Ya Hsien, eds., 六十年代詩選 [Poetry of the Sixties] (Kaohsiung: 大業書店, 1961), p. vi, one of the two major functions of modern poetry is: "Through introspection and association, the poet links broken and disparate experiences together, presenting to his audience a more complete cognition of the world." Thus to Yang Mu, the whole conglomeration of his foreign experience should be termed Chinese-American rather than just American experience.

significant, juxtaposing the "I" and the "you" or the poet and his love, in the following stanzas.

What is it that sinks gradually?
Sinking gradually into Lake Michigan,
Like a large leaf, after corrosion by the autumn wind,
A leaf, sick with nostalgia.
Sunlight, birds' chirpings, and
The sudden falling of a purple scarf in the tree shades

. . . .
. . . .

Suddenly I raise my head,
Between the sky and the Chicago Sun Times Building,
There is a face,
Once cried over, loved, and thought about,
Withering now in the chilly gust. [12]

Yang Mu's American experience includes his wandering from the Midwestern States to the West Coast and finally his permanent residence in Seattle, the pattern shared by other modern Chinese poets. Many of his poems are about America, but some of his prose also deals with America. In fact, the reading of the poem "The Lake Boulevard" should accompany the reading of his prose "Remnants of Chicago" which tells of his awareness of Wen I-to's stay in the city and Jackson Park in Wen's "Autumn Colors." Yang's prose style is highly lyrical, with the intensity indigenous to his poetry:

> . . . poetry and prose grow together with plants and trees, and art stays on forever. As for human lives, they are forever feeble and pitiful. I always think, when autumn comes to Jackson Park, will the red leaves feel lonelier and lonelier? Will the disappearance of an oriental poet from the bench affect the transcendent beauty of nature? [13]

Yü Kuang-chung represents still another way of treating American experience in poetry. He was the first Chinese poet from Taiwan to come to the Writers Workshop at the University of Iowa in 1958. In the following year, he returned to Taiwan. In 1964, on invitation of the United States State

---

[12] See Yang Mu,楊牧詩集[Collected Works](Taipei: 洪範書店,1987), pp. 331-332.
[13] See Yeh Shan (former pen-name of Yang Mu), 葉珊散文集 [The Prose Works of Yeh Shan] (Taipei:洪範書店,1977), p. 171.

Department, he lectured in America for a year, staying mainly in Illinois, Michigan, Pennsylvania, and New York. He returned to Taiwan again in 1966. Three years later, he taught at Temple Bell College in Colorado as a visiting professor for two years. In 1971, he returned to Taiwan. During these thirteen years from 1958 to 1971, Yü came to the United States three times and stayed there for more than four years altogether. His journeys in America covered a vast area of the country. In 1964, he was described as having driven more than thirty thousand miles, his trips covering twenty States. Contemporary poets in America, such as Ferlinghetti and Ginsberg, excited him.[14] The impact of the Beat culture on Yü becomes apparent. The beatniks, hippies, and the "San Francisco Renaissance" lead Yü to a more anti-conventional consciousness. His poems have become longer, his syntax more colloquial, and his imagery more bold and sensual. The poem "Music Percussive" (otherwise translated as "Beat Music") is a good example of Yü's new direction:

> . . .
> Chianti, and tea bags,
> Cold drinks and hot dogs,
> Pizza, ravioli, macaroni, cheese,
> Steel the city, cement the road,
> After 70-miles per hour still unhappy,
> After a dinner, unappetizing, cold,
> You are an undigested plum,
> China O China you are a queue,
> Trademark-like trailing behind you.
>
> . . . .
> . . . .
> Out of the barber's you come, no happier than when you
>   entered.
> China O China you just won't cut or shave away,
> . . . .
> . . . .
> Spacious is the bread basket that feeds most of the States,
> Where once troubadoured Whitman, Sandburg and Mark
>   Twain.
> Here once I chanted, in my age of anxiety,
> On Eliot's dying waste land I once breathed drought.
>   Now the Old Possum's dead,

---

[14] See "Author" in 七 十 年 代 詩選 [Poetry of the Seventies] (Kaohsiung, 大業書店, 1969, p. 105.

The grass greens again with the green of youth,
        green from here to the Rockies' foot,
And youthful ears inebriate have turned to the Westcoast,
In the mesmeric rhythm of Bob Dylan have turned to
        Ginsberg and Ferlinghetti,
        From Wichita to Berkeley,
        Down comes T.S.E.
Up files Whitman, and Frisco takes all Muses as his brides. [15]

The style of the above stanzas is reminiscent of Allen Ginsberg's "America," and indeed, during the anti-Vietnamese War days in the sixties, the quest for love and peace is deeply embedded in Yü's poetic mission. This can be seen readily in the "Double Bed":

Let war rage on beyond the double bed
As I lie on the length of your slope
And hear the straying bullets,
Like a swarm of whistling will-o'-the wisps
Whisk by over your head and mine
And through your hair and through my beard,
On all sides let revolutions growl,
Love at least is on our side.
We'll be safe at least before the dawn.
When nothing is there to rely upon,
On your supple warmth I can still depend,
Tonight, let mountains topple and earth quake,
The worst is but a fall down your lowly vale.
Let banners and bugles rise high on the hills,
Six feet of rhythm at least are ours,
Before sunrise at least you still are mine,
To kindle a wildness pure and fine.
Let Night and Death on the border of darkness
Launch the thousandth siege of eternity
As we plunge whirling down, Heaven beneath,
Into the maelstrom of your limbs. [16]

---

[15] *Poetry of the Seventies*, pp. 106-107.

[16] See Chang Mo, et al., eds., 中國當代十大詩人選集 [Contemporary Chinese Poetry: Ten Major Poets] (Taipei: 源成出版社, 1977), p. 117. I have obtained the English version of both of these poems, "Music Percussive" and "Double Bed" in 中國當代文學選集 [An Anthology of Contemporary Chinese Literature, Volume 1: Poetry], ed., Chi Pang-yuan, et al (Taipei: 國立編譯館, 1975), pp. 108-113 and 115.

Despite the fact that these poets revolutionalized modern Chinese poetry both in syntax and ideas, strengthening Chinese poetic uniqueness, their poetic as well as physical experiences of America remain congenial to their Chinese identity, without imposing any threat or causing bitterness or anger in them. It is true that their treatments of the western environment, particularly that of America, reveal their strong affinity to western civilization. To the Chinese audience, America as found in Wen I-to's "Autumn Colors" or Yü Kuang-chung's "Double Bed" is a land of wonders.

III

The concern for the immigrant Chinese in America, which inspired Wen I-to to write "The Laundry Song," is absent in modern Taiwanese poetry. This concern, however, is found in the poetry in Mainland China. The overseas Chinese experience was treated together with the poet's strong protest against American military and economic involvement in Southeast Asia. Ai Ch'ing's long poem "The Atlantic" is strong evidence of protest. The poem was written on the airplane when the poet was leaving West Africa for South America. On his way across the Atlantic Ocean, he says,

> Oh! Atlantic,
> For how many years
> Have you become the home of great pirates,
> The origin of colonialism
> And the warm-bed of world wars!

> In those faraway seaports,
> We can see
> Innumerable fleets at anchor,
> From faraway, they look like cities at sea;
> Every warship is waiting
> For the crucial moment
> To leave the seaport,
> And take off the cannon covers.

> . . .

> And on both coasts of the North Atlantic
> Inside the skyscrapers of some
> Clamorous cities,
> Many people busy calculating
> The selling of loads and loads of arms . . .

At night, in a lighted conference room
Of a certain building,
People hold secret meetings,
On how to invade a young republic,
And whether to arm a battalion
For Ngo Dinh Diem's troops
Is more economical
Than to arm a battalion
Of Chicago's jobless workers. [17]

In Ya Hsien's "Chicago," the city is scorned and condemned as a great Moloch threatening the ultimate existence of the intellect. Yet Chicago is a different city in Ai Ch'ing's eyes. Like many big cities in the United States, Chicago is a place full of warmongers and politicans, making secret deals to destroy the peace of the world. To Ai Ch'ing Chicago is utterly deplorable. The city is a hotbed for warlords and financial magnates who are symbols of world disasters:

They want to start a war at any time,
Like lighting a fire-cracker;
They want to take the fates of other nations
To start a large-scale game,
And they proclaim, "This is the will of the Lord,"
In their happy minds, they themselves are the Lord. [18]

Ai Ch'ing's condemnation of America is strongly colored by his ideology and may not be convincing to those who do not share that ideology. Yet his political consciousness commands him to make his language powerful and his message clear. The alternate uses of metaphors and symbols also prevent the poem from being overtly didactic, showing clearly Ai Ch'ing's poetic talent.

In the area of reflecting the life of the suffering Chinese in America, modern Chinese poetry in Mainland China tends to be openly political, placing a rather abstract anti-capitalist stance in the center of the poems. Consequently, many poems simply fail to move the reader, lacking the persuasive power which we find in Wen I-to's "The Laundry Song." A poem called "An Overseas Chinese in America," written by Wang Nan-shan, was published in the September issue of the *Jen-min wen-hsüeh* [People's Literature] in 1956. [19] The story of the poem is as follows: There was once a boy named Chang Hsing who was a wanderer since he was seven years old.

---

[17]1956 詩選 [Poems in 1956] (Peking: 人民文學社 , 1958), p. 348.
[18]*Poems in 1956*, p. 349.
[19]*Poems in 1956*, pp. 372-393.

When he turned seventeen, he was lucky enough to be picked up by an old Chinese sailor in Hong Kong, who sneaked him off to America. After many hardships and almost losing his life, Chang Hsing finally landed on the American continent. He worked at odd jobs for three years before he finally became a cook for an American named Johnson:

> And he started making friends
> With onions, tomatoes, and potatoes . . .
> Working as a cook,
> He also scrubbed the floor,
> Cleaned the silverware, bowed to people,
> Opened the door for Johnson;
> Chang Hsing was quite satisfied.

After he worked for Johnson for thirteen years, he managed to save enough money to return to China. Johnson, on the other hand, became rich by finding a coal mine. All these years, he had treated Chang Hsing badly, beating and kicking him all the time. One day, Johnson's business went broke and he ran everywhere asking for loans. He gathered almost enough money for a comeback except for a few hundred dollars more. Finally, he turned to Chang for help—

> He said to Chang:
> "If you lend me the money, my good friend,
> I will share with you my whole fortune in the future.
>
> After I become rich,
> Gold and jewelry, whatever you choose,
> Ships and airplanes, whatever you wish to travel,
> I will bow and salute you
> And send you back to China."

As the reader could expect, poor Chang lent Johnson all the money and the American became rich once again. In order to save his face and fame, he kicked Chang out of his house forever. Change was left alone in America, penniless and heartbroken. He became a madman.

The poem undoubtedly presents a tragic vision of the Chinese in America, depicting Chang Hsing as a symbolic victim for thousands of immigrant Chinese in America. However, the poem more strongly shows a vindictive intent, arousing hatred between Chinese and Americans, than to any socio-historical perspective. In addition, the poet fails to see the realism in the submission of the immigrant Chinese in America behind the act of lending money and being cheated; instead, he tries to instigate more anger and violence. Despite the shortcomings, the poem presents one distinct example of treating Chinese-American experience as a tragedy of class exploitation, racism, and cultural oppression. Many stories and events about early Chinese settlers in America are worthy of poetic portrayal and of being eulogized. There are also unnamed heroes in America who can trace their heritage back to Chinese origins.

IV

In the recent thirty years, the split of the two Chinas, and their differing relationships with America, have resulted in different portrayals of the American experience. In Taiwan, the American influence has turned the poets' attentions to a rather sweet side of life in America, and this sweetness has caused them to forget, at least temporarily, the bitterness of the early immigrants and settlers in America.

On the other hand, after the long confrontation between America and China, with the two wars in Korea and Vietnam as climaxes, a hostile attitude toward the American experience has developed. The long history of Chinese suffering overseas was chosen not for the purpose of tracing the ethnic identity of these unnamed heroes, but rather as a case of capitalistic oppression of the Third World. After the recent establishment of cultural ties between China and America, more poems about America will be written. Will Mainland China turn its attention to the sweet side of American experience, and will Taiwan to the bitter side? The answer should be irrelevant to the policies of the two governments, but should depend upon the future experience of Chinese in America. A poet should praise and criticize his experience according to his social conscience, a factor independent of and transcendent to political interference.

University of Southern California

TANIZAKI'S WEST:
A FABLE OF THE OCCIDENT

Saralyn R. Daly

> We first spread a parasol to throw
> a shadow on the earth, and in the
> shadow we put together a house.
>
> Tanizaki, *In Praise of Shadows*

Only in ignorance of Tanizaki's aesthetic preferences could one fabricate a clarity to define intent or meaning in his fiction. Four novels examined in translation[1] suggest the range of his achievement of fifty-five years, though Tanizaki's shadows deepen for the reader who cannot respond to the social specificity and allusive depth of the original Japanese.

Selective chronology[2] provides a moment of security in fact:

1886	Born
1910	"The Tattooer" ("Shisei")
1915	First marriage
1917	Mother died
1922	"Aguri" ("Aoi hana")

---

[1] Translations of Tanizaki's writing are referred to in the text by abbreviations, as follows: *DMOM: Diary of a Mad Old Man*, tr. Howard Hibbett (Tokyo: Charles E. Tuttle, n.d.); *Key: The Key*, tr. Howard Hibbett (London: Panther Books, 1964); *PoS:* "In Praise of Shadows," tr. Edward Seidensticker, in *Japan Quarterly*, 1 (1954), 46-52; *Sisters: The Makioka Sisters*, tr. Edward G. Seidensticker (N.Y.: Grosset & Dunlap, 1966); *SJT: Seven Japanese Tales*, tr. Howard Hibbett (Tokyo: Charles E. Tuttle, n.d.); *SPN: Some Prefer Nettles*, tr. Edward G. Seidensticker (Tokyo: Charles E. Tuttle, 1967).

[2] Precise details of serial, book, and English translation publication may be found in Hisaaki Yamanouchi, *The Search for Authenticity in Modern Japanese Literature* (Cambridge: Cambridge University Press, 1978), pp. 200-201. Translations into European languages are listed in Armando M. Janeira, *Japanese and Western Literature: A Comparative Study* (Rutland, Vt.: Charles E. Tuttle, 1970), pp. 378-379.

1923	September 1, the Great Earthquake in Tokyo and Yoko-
	hama, moved to Okamoto (between Kobe and Osaka,
1928-29	*Some Prefer Nettles* (*Tadekuu Mushi*)
1930	Divorced first wife
1931	Second marriage
1933-34	"In Praise of Shadows" ("In'ei Raisan")
1934	Divorced second wife
1935	Third marriage
1935-38	Translating *The Tale of Genji* (*Genji Monogatari*)
1939-41	*Genji* published
1943	*The Makioka Sisters* (*Sasame-yuki*), Part I
	publication suspended by military censors
1946-48	Publication of Parts II and III
1956	*The Key* (*Kagi*)
1961-62	*The Diary of a Mad Old Man* (*Fūten Rōjin Nikki*)
1965	Died

It is customary to regard Tanizaki's change of residence from modern, though earthquake-razed, Yokohama to the Kansai area as pinpointing his turn from the influence of "decadent" Western writers (typically and repetitively named are Poe, Baudelaire, and Wilde) back to his traditional Japanese roots, particularly manifest in work of the thirties and forties.[3] I believe, however, that it took no earthquake or change of dwelling to return the writer to beginnings he never left.

"The Tattooer," written while he was still attending the University of Tokyo, reveals Tanizaki immersed in the recent past; the short story is laden with such accurate cultural, geographical, and historical detail as will later characterize the chronologically precise *Makioka Sisters*.[4] Seikichi, the tattoo-artist, lives in the Fukagawa district of Edo, near the Hirasei Restaurant, convenient to the "gay quarters." He works in an eight-mat studio and has a bamboo-floored veranda where he admires *omoto* lilies until the arrival of an apprentice-geisha from the Tatsumi quarter. The tattooer was formerly an "ukiyoye painter of the school of Toyokuni and Kunisada." (*SJT*, 161)

---

[3]This routinely repeated statement appears in Nakamura Mitsuo, *Contemporary Japanese Fiction: 1926-1968* (Tokyo: Kokusai Bunka Shinkokai, 1969), p. 10; modified in J. Thomas Rimer, *Modern Japanese Fiction and Its Traditions: An Introduction* (Princeton: Princeton University Press, 1978), p. 22; Makoto Ueda, *Modern Japanese Writers and the Nature of Literature* (Stanford: Stanford University Press, 1976), pp. 62 and 75, alludes to the change, but reviews (pp. 55-60, 81) Tanizaki's comments on Tolstoy, Dostoyevsky, Goethe, Shakespeare, Zola, Flaubert, Radiguet, Stendhal, and George Moore, as well as his quotation of Oscar Wilde. Donald Keene, *Landscapes and Portraits: Appreciations of Japanese Culture* (Tokyo and Palo Alto: Kodansha International, 1972), pp. 179-180, provides more biographical detail.

[4]Ueda, pp. 59-60.

The latent sadism of the young girl is stimulated by two traditional pictures (*SJT*, 165-6).
Even the central action, the tattooing of the girl, originates in reality. Though Tanizaki increases the extraordinary quality of the event by suggesting at the beginning of his tale that only men were tattooed at that time, the seventeenth century *Great Mirror of the Art of Love* (*Shikidō Ōkagami*) by Fujimoto Kizan reveals that one of the highest pledges of love from a courtesan to her lover was displayed by tattooing an inscription, usually an abbreviation of his name and *inochi*, with sometimes lines of verse, upon her body.[5] In Tsuruya Namboku's erotic Kabuki play *Lady Sakura* (1817), such a tattoo upon the arm of the lady reveals her love for Gonsuke.[6]

Another seventeenth century document, *The Authoritative Summary of the Rules of Japanese Painting* (*Honchō Gahō Taiden*) by Tosa Mitsuoki begins my chain of speculation. Of *ukiyo-e* painters, Mitsuoki wrote, "They only think of exact resemblance to the actual object. They paint too much detail. The result is a lowly style."[7] Would young Tanizaki, so knowledgeable about the Edo period, not know the status of the *ukiyo-e* creations? Would he, moreover, an aspiring writer of fiction specializing in Japanese literature at the university, be unaware of the prefatory remarks of Tsubouchi Shōyō in *The Essence of the Novel* (*Shōsetsu Shinzui*), published in the year before Tanizaki's birth?

> Everywhere historical romances and tales are being published. . . . a staggering production of books, all of them extremely bad.

Having described the "framework of morality into which [these writers] attempt to force their plots," Tsubouchi continues

> In actual practice, however, only stories of bloodthirsty cruelty or else of pornography are welcomed. . . . popular writers have no choice but to be devoid of self-respect and in all things slaves to public fancy and the lackeys of fashion . . . pandering to the tastes of the time.[8]

Of course, "The Tattooer" lacks moral purpose, but clearly no Japanese

---

[5] Keene, p. 248.

[6] Donald Keene, *World within Walls: Japanese Literature of the Pre-Modern Era, 1600-1867* (N.Y.: Holt, Rinehart and Winston, 1976), p. 460.

[7] Makoto Ueda, *Literary and Art Theories in Japan* (Cleveland: The Press of Western Reserve University, 1967), p. 141.

[8] Donald Keene, ed. *Modern Japanese Literature* (N.Y.: Grove Press, 1960), pp. 55-57.

writer needed to seek in Western Europe models for this well established sadomasochistic tradition.

Allusion carries immense suggestive significance, basic throughout the structuring of meaning in traditional Japanese literature. If my guess is correct, Tanizaki expects his title to recall for his reader not only the old custom of the geisha tattoo but also the striking "tattoo" recognition scene in act one of *Lady Sakura*. Describing the play as Namboku's finest work, Donald Keene writes

> Sakura is a new and startling creation. Unlike the delicate princesses of most Kabuki plays, she lusts after the burglar who raped her, is ready to take a priest as lover when that seems advisable, and raises no objection to being sold to a brothel. . . . No matter how brutally Gonsuke behaves, she loves him all the more. . . . she is by no means the conventional evil woman of Kabuki; her depravity even gives her allure.[9]

These are the erotic overtones which model the future brought upon the young apprentice geisha by the gift of Seikichi's tattoo.

Tanizaki thus begins his career deeply rooted in the traditions of the nineteenth-century Edo he portrays. He is, moreover, writing a tale of the sort which the clients of Edo's Yoshiwara, the licensed quarter, always loved; perhaps as part of his repugnance for the European "naturalism" favored by Tsubouchi, Tanizaki may have deliberately challenged the literary critic and professor of an earlier generation by creating a modern *ninjōbon*, precisely the kind of erotic tale about love in the licensed quarters which became popular in Edo around 1820.[10] He has imagined his way into the genre appropriate to the setting he describes.

The gauntlet, if thrown, lies before us with precise disclosure of the artist's intent and simultaneously of his modesty. With its opening description of the time of the story—

> In the illustrated romantic novels of the day, in the Kabuki theatre, where rough masculine heroes like Sadakuro and Jiraiya were transformed into women—everywhere beauty and strength were one.
> (*SJT*, 160)

---

[9] Keene, *World within Walls*, p. 465. Keene, pp. 424, 429-30 describes the career of Toyokuni, a "celebrated artist," who flourished from 1790 to 1816.
[10] Keene, p. 416.

Tanizaki announces his method, the mode of his imagery, and—surprisingly prescient—an essential theme of his future work. The time and again the source of his fictive vision are reenforced by the information that

> Seikichi had formerly earned his living as an ukiyoye [*sic*] painter of the school of Toyokuni and Kunisada, a background which, in spite of his decline to the status of a tattooer, was evident from his artistic conscience and sensitivity. (*SJT*, 161)

Kunisada was the indispensable illustrator of Ryūtei Tanehiko's books from 1815 until the death of the author. From 1825 till 1842 they collaborated on the forty volumes of *The False Murasaki and the Rustic Genji* (*Nise Murasaki Inaka Genji*), a kabuki-ized version of Genji Monogatari. The student specializing in Japanese literature, who in his maturity will translate the mediaeval classic three times,[11] surely is already exploring versions of the work which will most inform his writing. And in "The Tattooer" he reflects the tone reported by Donald Keene, who comments on the *Rustic Genji*'s progress through the licensed quarters in pursuit of three lost treasures:

> ... there is something unpleasantly cold and deliberate about Mitsuuji's systematic use of the women he sleeps with to further his investigation.[12]

Compare this with Tanizaki's story. After the young girl has recognized her latent sadism in the two picture scrolls, she pleads with Seikichi to take the paintings away.

> "Don't talk like a coward," Seikichi told her, with his malicious smile. "Look at it more closely. You won't be squeamish long."
> But the girl refused to lift her head. Still prostrate, her face buried in her sleeves, she repeated over and over that she was afraid and wanted to leave.
> "No, you must stay—I will make you a real beauty," he said, moving closer to her. Under his kimono was a vial of anesthetic. . . .
> (*SJT*, 166)

From the time of his morning encounter, relentlessly, until the "full light of the spring dawn" following, Seikichi tattoos "a huge blackwidow spider"

[11] Ueda, *Modern Japanese Writers*, p. 80.
[12] Keene, p. 433.

until it "stretched its great legs to embrace the whole of the girl's back."
(*SJT*, 167-8)

This manipulation of a helpless, drugged woman through the night cannot
but remind us of Ikuko and her professorial husband in *The Key*. During the
forty-six years which intervened, Tanizaki, by attendance at performances
of his beloved Kabuki and Bunraku, could regularly renew his ambivalent
image of the dynamic female victim.

Even the foot-fetish recurs notably. Seikichi recognizes the object of his
attentions by the reappearance of her desirable foot:

> This one was sheer perfection. Exquisitely chiseled toes, nails like
> the iridescent shells along the shore at Enoshima, a pearl-like round-
> ed heel, skin so lustrous that it seemed bathed in the limpid waters
> of a mountain spring—this, indeed, was a foot to be nourished by
> men's blood, a foot to trample on their bodies. (*SJT*, 163)

Greeting the girl, he says, "This is the first time I have seen your face, but I
remember your foot." (*SJT*, 164) In the opening entry of his diary the aging
professor describes his taste:

> Moreover, she knows that I am something of a foot-fetishist and that
> I admire her extraordinarily shapely feet. . . . If I want to kiss her
> instep, she says "How filthy!" or "You shouldn't touch a place like
> that!" (*Key*, 12)

Returning to Kabuki, we find in Chikamatsu Monzaemon's *Love Suicides
at Sonezaki* (*Sonezaki Shinjū*, 1703), as Donald Keene tells us,

> The most dramatic moment . . . occurs when Tokubei, hiding under
> the porch of a brothel, hears Ohatsu ask for a sign that he is ready to
> die with her. He takes her foot, which hangs over the edge of the
> porch, and passes it across his throat. . . . [13]

Both foot-fetishists perish of their exertions. "You are my first victim," the
transformed girl tells Seikichi, who begs only to see the tattoo, his masterpiece, once more. (*SJT*, 169) The devious professor, who "loses" his key,
dies of a stroke brought on by his wife's deliberate intensification of his
sexual excitement. After his death she reviews the diaries through which,
each pretending not to read the other's, they manipulated one another. From
April 10 she admits,

---

[13] Keene, p. 256.

I was trying to lure him into the shadow of death. . . . From then on my diary was written solely for that purpose. . . . I did every thing I could to excite him, to keep him agitated, to drive his blood pressure higher and higher. (Even after his first stroke I kept on playing little tricks to make him jealous.) (*Key*, 126-7)

The mocking exaggeration of these motifs—reluctantly manipulated women who eventually are empowered to destroy the obsessive admirers of their feet—culminates in *The Diary of a Mad Old Man*.[14] The old man, Utsugi Tokusuki, whose voyeuristic advances toward his daughter-in-law, Satsuko, began with a look at her foot sticking out of the shower, ends paralyzed. He is brought to this crisis by over-zealous efforts to make a rubbing of her feet, adequate for carving on his tombstone. His diary entry of November 17 exposes consciousness that his emotional and physical abasement is absurd. To establish the tone of the entry, he acknowledges that Satsuko will "call it the craziest thing she ever heard of. . . . " and later will think "That crazy old man is lying under these beautiful feet of mine. . . . I'm trampling on the buried bones of the poor old fellow." (*DMOM*, 154) His imaginings of her future experience rise to extravagance, which foreshadows the coming scene:

. . . Satsuko will be aware of the presence of my spirit, joyfully enduring her weight. Perhaps she may even hear my charred bones rattling together, chucking, moaning, creaking . . . she would hear my bones wailing under the stone. Between sobs I would scream: "It hurts! It hurts! . . . I've never been more happy. . . . Trample harder! Harder!" (*DMOM*, 155)

This masochism is reflected in the postures he assumes as he attempts to make a clear rubbing. First he kneels at her feet while she lies, by his request, on a bed in a Japanese-style hotel room, i.e., on the floor. Then he asks her to sit in a chair while he lies on his back "in a cramped position." For nearly two hours the process continues as he ruins twenty squares of specially ordered paper and must send to the stationer for forty more. (*DMOM*, 156-7)

The attitude toward this extravagant endeavor is expressed in events involving Utsugi's daughter Itsuko. Unexpectedly she and his nurse return to the hotel and interrupt the rubbing session. Understatement expresses their view and thus directs the reader's appraisal of the scene:

[14]Howard Hibbett, "Fantasy in the Fiction of Tanizaki Jun'ichirō," in Saburō Ōto and Rikutarō Fukuda, eds., *Studies in Japanese Culture* (Tokyo: Japan P.E.N. Club, 1973), p. 163, describes *DMOM* as a "satirical portrait."

Satsuko promptly disappeared into the bathroom. Innumerable splotches of red on white were scattered about the Japanese room. Itsuko and Miss Sasaki exchanged bewildered glances. Miss Sasaki silently went about measuring my blood pressure.
"It's 232," she announced gravely. . . .
(*DMOM*, 158. Translator's elipsis)

Within four days Utsugi has returned to Tokyo and suffered a stroke, followed by repeated attacks of *angina pectoris*. Extracts from the nurse's report and the doctor's clinical record detail his extensive and unpleasant physical decay and treatment, as well as his hospitalization from December 16 to February 7. After his return home, the old man requests Itsuko to retrieve the rubbings in Kyoto and ask a stonecutter to "carve them on a tomb-stone in the manner of the Buddha's Footprint Stone." Itsuko's account continues:

He said that Chinese records describe the footprints of the Buddha as twenty-one inches long and seven inches wide, with wheel markings on both feet. The wheels needn't be inscribed, but he wanted the design from Satsuko's feet expanded, without distorting it, to the same length. He told me to be sure it was done exactly that way.
(*DMOM*, 176)

If doubt remains on how one should respond to the meticulous detail of this obsessive desire, Itsuko's conclusion is definitive: "I couldn't possibly make such a ridiculous request. . . . " (*DMOM*, 176)

Confirmation that the work is intended as a satirical comedy may be found in another look at Tanizaki's traditional roots. Circling back to the earlier ukioy-e training of our tattooer, Saikichi, and his "floating world," we find as well, in an earlier parody of *Genji*, both a tale and a woodblock scene that provide interpretative depth for Utsugi's interest in Satsuko's bathing, a concern which begins early and ends the novel.

Very much like *Some Prefer Nettles*, *The Diary of a Mad Old Man* opens at a theatrical performance, as the old connoisseur introduces his son and daughter-in-law to a play they have never seen. The diary entries of June 16 through 18 introduce as well the efforts of the old man to corrupt Satsuko. On June 20 an entry reveals him caressing her toes for the first time. By June 26 the themes of his impotent perversity, the unpleasantness of his aged infirmities, and his preoccupation with his anticipated funeral and burial are established. On July 23 he records a detailed floor plan of his house in order to explain the convenience (for the plot) of his newly-built, tiled bathroom with shower. This swift exposition prepares the reader for July 23, when Satsuko, reclining on a rattan chaise lounge in order to take her turn at nursing duty for the diseased old man (she assists in bathing him as well, because the tiles are slippery), remarks that her presence excites her father-in-law. He records in his diary, "It was the first time Satsuko had been so coquettish, which *did* excite me." (*DMOM*, 40, translator's italics) The next afternoon she "excites" him even more by looking in upon him from the adjoining bathroom while she is taking a shower: "Only her head—I couldn't see the rest of her." She appears to extend an invitation:

> "Even when I'm in the shower I never lock this door! It can be opened any time!" (*DMOM*, 42)

Utsugi's excited speculation follows:

> Did she say that because I invariably take my own bath in the evening, or because she trusts me? Or was she saying "Come on in and look, if you want!"? Or: "A silly old man doesn't bother me in the least"? I have no idea why she made a point of saying such a thing. (*DMOM*, 42)

However, he soon confirms his hopeful suspicions. On July 26 he tries the door when Satsuko is showering. Upon her invitation he enters, towels her back, gives "her a tongue-kiss on the soft curve of her neck at the right shoulder," and is rewarded with a satisfactorily stinging slap. (*DMOM*, 48) Two days later he is allowed to kiss her below the knee, that much of her leg being exposed for his delight while she showers. Not allowed to use his tongue, he finds the experience disappointing: "It tasted like a drink of water instead of a kiss." (*DMOM*, 51) An improvement occurs on August 11, when Satsuko not only turns off the shower, but says she will allow him to use his tongue. The entry details Utsugi's pleasures:

> I crouched over just as I had on the twenty-eighth of July, glued my lips to the same place on her calf, and slowly savoured her flesh with my tongue. It tasted like a real kiss. My mouth kept slipping lower and lower, down toward her heel. . . . My tongue came to her instep, then to the tip of her big toe. Kneeling, I crammed her first three toes into my mouth. I pressed my lips to the wet sole of her foot, a foot that seemed as alluringly expressive as her face. (*DMOM*, 66)

At this point Satsuko terminates his efforts by turning on the shower, dousing his head and face. When the novel ends in the following April, the old man, convalescent from his latest stroke and heart trouble, has had the lawn dug up and construction begun on a swimming pool. His son's comment that

Moronobu: Picture-book edition of *The Man Who Spent His Life in Love.*

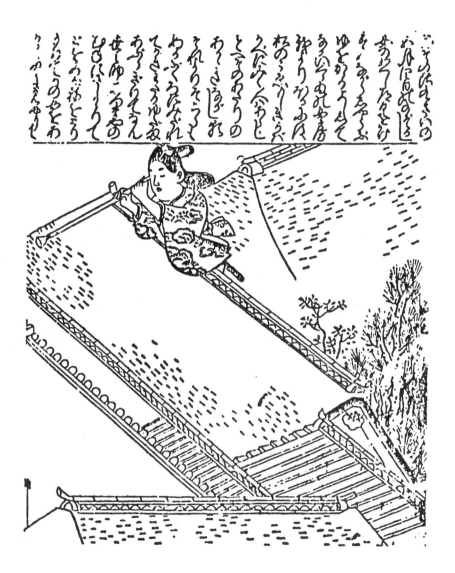

"'The old man's head is full of daydreams, just watching them work on that pool'" (*DMOM*, 177) suggests, perhaps naively, his imaginings of Satsuko bathing again and visually more available.

An informing traditional context, I suggest, is the work of two seventeenth century giants of popular *genroku* fiction and the associated woodblock illustration, respectively Ihara Saikaku and Hishikawa Moronobu. They come together brilliantly in Saikaku's "erotic picaresque" *The Man Who Spent His Life in Love* (1682), the first *ukiyo-zōshi*, an account of "a rake's progress from precocious childhood to lecherous old age" and, equally appropriate to Tanizaki's lifelong interests, a burlesque of *Genji*.[15] Both wittily illustrate the epitome of voyeurism with the picture for Chapter 3, in which the hero Yonosuke, at the age of nine, uses a telescope to spy on a lady in her bath. The response of the bathing lady to Yonosuke's amorous invitation recalls the repulsion-attraction subtleties of Satsuko:

> "When things are quiet tonight open this back-gate and listen to what I have to say to you!" "Certainly not!" she answered—but she did it.[16]

Utsugi's voyeurism extends, as in many Tanizaki fictions, to arranging for his manipulated and manipulating young woman to have an extra-marital affair with Haruhisa, a man he has chosen. Candidly the old man explains his motive:

> "Now that I can't enjoy the thrill myself anymore, I can at least have the pleasure of watching someone else risk a love affair." (*DMOM*, 58)

Like the earlier lady in the bath, though Satsuko refuses in the entry of August 5, the affair appears to be in progress (at least in Utsugi's view) three days later, and continues to the end of the novel. In the final "Abstract from Notes" by Utsugi's daughter the selected suitor is behaving much like Genji himself: Satsuko, no longer sharing her husband's bedroom, has "moved into the guest room. And I also hear that Haruhisa steals upstairs now and then." (*DMOM*, 176)

---

[15] Howard Hibbett, *The Floating World in Japanese Fiction* (N.Y.: Oxford University Press, 1959, repr. Freeport, N.Y.: Books for Libraries Press, 1970), p. 42. In Chapters 3 and 5 he provides an extended account of the book and its several illustrated versions.

[16] Hibbett, *Floating World*, p. 87. On p. 79 Hibbett suggests that the scene parodies *Genji*.

How many variants on this theme has Tanizaki composed? The tattooer creates as his masterpiece a woman who will erotically win and destroy innumerable unnamed males. The professor in *The Key* begins the corruption of his wife by exposing her, unconscious and naked, to Kimura, his daughter's fiancé. By the time the professor has died of erotic exertions, both daughter and wife are complying with his intent. Kimura will marry the daughter "for the sake of appearances; and the three . . . will live . . . together." (*The Key*, 127) *Some Prefer Nettles* provides a more complex, less conclusive and, perhaps for that reason, more sympathetic account.

Not at all a caricature, the treatment in this mid-career novel counters willful male lust with mature concern for family obligations and cultural continuity. As the novel begins, Kaname, no longer sexually attracted to his wife Misako, believes that he wants to divorce her. His hesitation, marked partly by a vague, unengaged debate between feeling and reason and more clearly presented as that between Japanese and European culture, continues to the end of the book. He seems to encourage his wife to have an affair with and eventually to marry her friend Aso, though at the time, contemplating them together, he is jealous. He appears to desire Louise, an Eurasian prostitute, and yet wishes to abandon her permanently. He thinks of himself in the beginning as Westernized, but during his reluctant visit to a Bunraku play at the invitation of Misako's aging, traditional father, he is quickly moved first to envy and soon to imagine himself becoming like the older man, even with a traditional geisha mistress like the old man's O-hisa. At the end of Chapter 2 he ruminates as he watches a scene from *Love Suicide at Amijima*:

> A pair of conflicting emotions pressed themsleves on him: old age brought its own pleasures and was not really to be dreaded; and yet that very thought, a symptom of approaching old age, was something he must resist, if only because of the advantage it might give Misako. The reason for their decision to separate, after all, was that they did not want to grow old, that they wanted to be free to live their youth again. (*SPN*, 26)

Detail after detail in the rest of the novel suggests that neither husband nor wife are the Western moderns they pretend to be. In the end, the old father says of his daughter, " . . . this modernness of hers is a pretty thin veneer," and Kaname acknowledges, " 'Mine is thin too'." (*SPN*, 189)

Until this scene Misako's father has been presented to the reader, from Kaname's scoffing "Western" viewpoint, as a dilettante dwelling in his willfully recreated fantasy of old Japan, cultivating refined tastes and training his doll-puppet mistress to provide traditional comfort and pleasures. Suddenly the situation is reversed. Tradition, in the actions of the old man, emerges as mature, practical, realistic. The father calls upon his son-in-law to recognize his responsibility as a husband. He describes the sexual incompatibility of the couple as a realistic, everyday occurrence, something to accept, to live with. In the course of his argument he indicates his awareness that O-hisa is *not* the puppet Kaname has imagined:

> If the two of you aren't suited for each other, though, if you think you're not compatible, don't worry too much about it. Time will pass and you'll find that you are very much suited for each other after all. O-hisa's far younger than I, and we aren't what you could call well-matched, but when two people live together, an affection does develop, and somehow they get by while they're waiting for it to. Can't you say after all that that's what a marriage is? (*SPN*, 189)

Every action of the novel evidences the victory of the old man, hence the substance of traditional views and ways as opposed to what turns out to be the frivolous, insubstantial modernity of Kaname and Misako. When the story begins, the couple reluctantly accepts his invitation to a Bunraku play. At the end they have with equal reluctance obeyed his summons to his home to discuss their plans for divorce. Pressured by his insistence, they do everything they had agreed with each other not to do: Misako dines alone with her father in order to submit to the private interview she has feared; both will spend the night side by side in the father's cottage, "a novel arrangement for Kaname and Misako." (*SPN*, 201) As he looks around the bedroom, Kaname realizes the old man's intent:

> He suspected that tonight, however, the old man hoped for great changes to come from throwing them together. This benevolent scheming was a little disconcerting, but not enough so that Kaname felt pressed to try for an escape. He was sure that the time had passed when one night could make a difference. (*SPN*, 198-199)

He still thinks he is resisting, but this has been the pattern from the beginning.

As Tanizaki argued, in the traditional Japanese manner by implication, for the values which preclude divorce, he was probably contemplating his wish to divorce his own wife of about eighteen years, for whom, like Kaname, he had chosen a lover and arranged a second marriage. It is as if in imagination Tanizaki worked out a future by exploring the possibility of a decision that the divorce would not be possible. With that imagined knowledge, he could experience his response to such a circumstance. The tattoo artist projected himself with such enthusiasm into the capacities of his work of art that he became his own, or its, first victim. Did Tanizaki now enter into the being of his character Kaname with such feeling that he could not tolerate a decision against his own divorce? But the circumstances were fortunately a little different. The candidate selected was willing to marry Tanizaki Chiyoko so, presumably with a clear conscience as all was well arranged, the writer divorced her in the year following publication of the novel.

Thinking about the matter in *Some Prefer Nettles* had led Tanizaki to portray women of varied types and in a variety of relationships with those upon whom they are more or less dependent. The extent of that dependency in the cases of Misako and Louise delineates the pressures which Kaname wishes to disregard by his intended escapes, neither of which seems very likely at the end of the story. Misako's father, on the other hand, has chosen responsibility for his mistress O-hisa and, like an artist, hopes to shape her more nearly to his traditional ideal. Perhaps because the problem was crucial to the writer's future life, this novel signals the beginning of a rich middle period in which his writing will summon humane and serious insight to deal with complex interpersonal relationships.

Within six years of the publication of *Some Prefer Nettles* Tanizaki had divorced his first wife, married and divorced another, and married again. With the third marriage, which lasted until his death, he began translating *Genji*, an undertaking he would also complete three times.

Both experiences laid the ground for his most extended and selfless study of human relations and particularly of female character, *The Makioka Sisters*. Here he displays his greatest range and depth of understanding in the treatment not only of the four sisters but of a wide variety of minor figures. In his sensitive account of the affairs of an Osaka family during 1936-41, years immediately preceding the war with the United States and its allies, his scope has expanded to encompass a novel of extensive social and historical awareness.

Though a novel of contemporary history, Tanizaki's old motifs are still present in accounts of attendance at Kabuki plays and performances of traditional dances and songs. Even "Snow," the song which had evoked for Kaname a Proustian passage of memory (*SPN*, 115-119),[17] is twice danced and sung by Taeko, the least traditional of the sisters. Classic are the several extended descriptions of cherry blossom viewing at Kyoto, the differences on each occasion reflecting changes in relationships among family members (*Sisters*, 19, 86-87, 150, 296). Again, the "firefly hunt on the Uji" scene from the play *Morning-Glory Diary*, which Kaname has viewed in the Awaji puppet theater (*SPN*, 138, 144), is fully realized as an outing of three of the

---

[17]The Proustian comparison has been discussed in Wayne Falke, "Tanizaki: Opponent of Naturalism," *Critique*, 18 (1966), 22.

sisters (*Sisters*, Book III, Chapter 4). These "set pieces," as well as the epi-
sodic structure of the novel, provide many opportunities for moments of
feeling such as *aware* and *sabi*, so dear to Japanese aesthetic tradition.

At last Tanizaki treats his basic subject, the manipulation of a woman,
within a conventional "real" world rather than as the result of male caprice
or erotic fantasy. The many benevolent attempts of the family to arrange a
good marriage for Yukiko, the retiring third sister, constitute the main plot
of the book. This concern has become a way to record sensitively the myriad
motions of the Japanese mentality considering modes of rapprochement and
conciliation as a means of effecting social action. Mistrust of motives, self
doubt, and deep caring to understand others conflict especially in Sachiko,
the responsible second sister, whose mind, examining and reexamining the
words of her sisters and others, Tanizaki has opened to the reader. Loving
and faithful, she moves from hope to anxiety, and finally to sadness as she
frequently reviews their utterances and gestures. Gradually, with the assistance of her poet husband, she recognizes the increasing distance from her
oldest sister, Tsuruko, and experiences the sorrow of that alienation. She
observes the moral deterioration of the youngest, Taeko, who also wills a
parting from her family but sorrows at her own design. In contrast, Sachiko
perceives the unspoken reluctance of Yukiko to leave her second sister's
home and must eventually act, with regret, against that subtle resistance
to the proposed marriages which repeatedly threaten to take Yukiko away.

Through this emotional process, suggested in accounts of Sachiko's mental
questioning, Tanizaki moves the plot forward, enacted within a traditional
cultural framework. Sachiko's experience of the novel's action remains as
non-judgmental as the author's account of which it partakes. In episode
after episode the Japanese sense of finish is implicit in openendedness which
to the Westerner seems incomplete. The reader is left with images as either
Sachiko or Tanizaki has seen them—images that the traditions of *Genji*,
ukiyo-e painting, kabuki, and the other arts and pleasures of old Japan
inform but which the author does not intend to bring into too full a light.

Inevitably lacking in all translations are the precisions and implications of
the Japanese language and the styles so carefully selected and shaped by the
writer. His virtuoso work in employing dialect for characterization and
authenticity began as early as *Manji* (still not translated). Serialized in 1928,
the work appeared for six months in the standard dialect of Tokyo, but then
Tanizaki hired assistants to "translate" his language into Osakan.[18] In a
review of the translation of *Some Prefer Nettles* Ishikawa Kin-ichi regrets

---

[18] Details and the aesthetic effects are discussed in Keene, *Landscapes*, pp. 180-181,
and Hibbert, "Fantasy," p. 162.

that the differences between Kyoto and Tokyo speech cannot be evident.[19] He also reveals to the reader who does not experience Tanizaki in Japanese that in *The Makioka Sisters* the dialects of Tokyo, Osaka, Kyoto, and Kobe and an Ashiya *patois* are spoken.[20] Even visual nuances are lost in the English version of *The Key*; the Japanese printing distinguishes clearly between the two diaries: one is written in *hiragana* and the other in *katakana* characters,[21] styles which convey distinct differences in degrees of formality, status, and even sexual identity. Sensitivity to the usefulness for fiction of a language so morphemically and graphemically specific in its implications could not be a novelty. Donald Keene's account of Shikitei Samba's novel, *The Up-to-date Bathhouse* (*Ukiyoburo*, 1809-13) provides a possible model for Tanizaki's natural exploitation of the richness of Japanese:

> Samba never attempted to create individual characters . . . but he could reproduce exactly the manner of speech of the Edo merchant who cannot refrain from advertising his wares even when in the bath; or the Confucian scholar who gives Chinese names to even the most plebian Japanese objects; or the housewife who speculates about the kind of husband her daughter will marry; or the young lady who exhibits her literary pretensions; or the servant who complains about an unreasonable master. Samba's readers laughed not at the antics of a favorite character . . . but an anonymous people whose speech, recorded with diabolical accuracy, revealed common human weaknesses.[22]

The structure of Japanese morphology and syntax, with its specifications of gender, social position, intent, and even degree of certainty and politeness expressed, provides the writer with an enviable medium. In a language which not only accommodates but mandates such effects, it would hardly seem possible that one might write a "Western" novel. But Tanizaki's cultural preferences are certainly implicit as early as his 1922 short story "Aguri." In an account of the young man Okada's excursion to the foreign shops of Yokohama to outfit his mistress Aguri in Western clothing which will "accentuate every curve and hollow, give her body a brilliant surface and lively flowing lines . . . ," an undertaking that "ought to be like a dream come true," the "massive Western-style buildings" are unnerving. Okada wonders

---

[19] *"Some Prefer Nettles* by Tanizaki Jun'ichirō," *Japan Quarterly*, 2 (1955), 532.
[20] Ishikawa, p. 531.
[21] Yamanouchi, p. 120.
[22] Keene, *World within Walls*, p. 415.

> Could anyone be alive in these silent buildings, with their thick gray
> walls where the window glass glittered like fish eyes . . . ? It seemed
> more like a museum gallery than a street. (*SJT*, 199)

Sensually he anticipates dressing Aguri to reveal every detail of her body:

> European women's clothes weren't "things to wear"—they were a
> second layer of skin. They weren't merely wrapped over and around
> the body but dyed into its very surface like a kind of tattooed deco-
> ration. When he looked again, all the goods in the show windows
> seemed to be so many layers of Aguri's skin, flecked with color,
> with drops of blood. (*SJT*, 200-201)

Images that recall the Kabuki-like sadism of "The Tattooer" acclaim the
clinging clothing—"blue, purple, crimson skins . . . formed to [Aguri's]
body" in opposition to "that baggy, shapeless kimono," which conceals the
details of her beauty. (*SJT*, 201) Though when fully dressed in the new
clothes, Aguri will display a "radiant smile," throughout the process of shop-
ping, measuring, and fitting she remains "glum." Her ambivalence is a small
reflection of the author's. Surely the store clerk's explanation, "a little
rough-spoken," of how to wear women's underwear, as well as his measuring
of Aguri's arms and legs, suggest brash crudity.

> It seemed to Okada that he was having a price set on Aguri, that he
> was putting her on sale in a slave market. (*SJT*, 204)

Okada is pleased to dress (or symbolically tattoo) the naked woman, but has
earlier expressed intense revulsion toward the stifling Western dress he wears.
The most dynamic segment of the story denounces such clothing in pains-
taking detail:

> First of all, his feet were cramped by these tan box-calf shoes that
> compressed them in a narrow mold. Western clothes were intended
> for healthy robust men: to anyone in a weakened condition they
> were quite insupportable. Around the waist, over the shoulders,
> under the arms, around the neck—every part of the body was pressed
> and squeezed by clasps and buttons and rubber and leather, layer
> over layer, as if you were strapped to a cross. And of course you had
> to put on stockings before the shoes, stretching them carefully up on
> your legs by garters. Then you put on a shirt, and then trousers,
> cinching them in with a buckle at the back till they cut into your
> waist and hanging them from your shoulders with suspenders. Your
> neck was choked in a close-fitting collar, over which you fastened a

nooselike necktie, and stuck a pin in it. . . . The thought that he was wearing such appalling garments made Okada gasp for breath. . . . (*SJT*, 195)

When at the end of the story Okada dresses Aguri, "going round and round the white figure, tying ribbons, fastening buttons and hooks, is it not an implicit torture of his "slave"? Fantasizing upon his own clothes as "shackles," he has long since "imagined himself breaking down and sobbing."

> At last he begins to kick and struggle, tearing off his necktie and collar and throwing them down. . . . "I can't walk anymore . . . I'm sick . . . ," he mutters, half delirious. "Get me out of these clothes and put me in something soft!" (*SJT*, 196-7)

Thus even in this early story of the pursuit of Western modes Tanizaki recoils. He is on the way to the definitive credo of 1934, "In Praise of Shadows."

The rejection of the bright, glittering revelations[23] of Western clothing accords with his aesthetic preferences:

> In the mansion called literature I would have the eaves deep and the walls dark, I would push back into the shadows the things that come forward too clearly, I would strip away the useless decoration. (*PoS*, 52)

Perhaps for Tanizaki the turn from the West was simply a turn away from Tokyo and Yokohama toward Kyoto and Osaka in the Kansai area, where he lived in the traditional shadows and continued to write brilliantly after 1923.[24]

California State University, Los Angeles

---

[23]Wayne Falke, p. 24, describes the use of light in *The Key*, written thirty-four years later: "In anger, Tanizaki floods his literary world with light, and the resulting ugliness is a call for the aesthetic world of shadows." The presence of the motif in "Agura" evidences the consistency of Tanizaki's taste.

[24]This essay was written before publication of Gwenn Boardman Petersen's *The Moon in the Water: Understanding Tanizaki, Kawabata, and Mishima* (Honolulu: University Press of Hawaii, 1979), a work, like my own, intending to increase understanding of Japanese fiction through a knowledge of cultural backgrounds. With such kindred intent, it is not surprising that we substantially agree in interpreting Tanizaki.

AMERICA
IN POSTWAR JAPANESE LITERATURE

Noriko Mizuta Lippit

When Natsume Soseki returned from London in 1903 as a psychologically disturbed man, his confidence as a member of the Japanese elite miserably shattered by his struggle with the West, Japan was just about to celebrate a victory over Russia and to enjoy confidence in itself as a modern nation.
Although the victory in the Russo-Japanese War was received as the fulfillment of the Meiji goals of modernization, Soseki's mission of cultural modernization as a member of the Meiji elite was a miserable failure. Soseki's struggle, just like that of other Meiji intellectuals who stayed an extended period of time in foreign countries, was both personal and cultural.

Although conflict with foreign cultures had previously been a vital force in the development of Japanese culture, it was in the modern period beginning with the Meiji era, a period described precisely as that of *kaikoku* [the opening of the nation], that the search for personal and cultural identity generated by the nation's exposure to foreign cultures became a dynamic force in literary development. Kato Shuichi and Saeki Shoichi, two leading literary critics who themselves stayed in the United States for an extended period of time, insist on the importance of examining the development of modern literature and culture from the perspective of writers' and intellectuals' struggle with foreign cultures. [1]

Both Kato and Saeki point out that the geographical isolation of Japan created a psychological isolation, resulting in two quite typical attitudes toward foreign cultures: first, the attitude of trying to break down the isolation by opening oneself to the outside world and trying to learn as much as possible from foreign countries; and second, the attitude of trying to justify the feeling of isolation by insisting upon the uniqueness of Japan's culture

[1] Saiki Shoichi, *Uchi to soto kara no Nihon bungaku* [Japanese Literature from Inside and Out] (Tokyo: Shincho Sensho, 1969); and Kato Shuichi, *Nihon no uchi to soto* [Japan Inside and Out] (Tokyo: Bungei Shunju, 1969).

and the inevitability of isolation. This pattern of absorption and rejection, being open and closed, cosmopolitan and traditional, can be seen on both a cultural and a personal level.

After the first twenty years of enthusiastic learning from the West which Japan began with the start of the Meiji era, a period characterized by *Roku-meikan*, Japan entered a period of cultural nationalism represented by Miyake Setsurei, Shiga Juko, Ozaki Koyo, Kota Rohan, Higuchi Ichiyo and Takayama Chogyu. This cycle was completed, however, with a return to the phase of openness after the Russo-Japanese War, when the renewed cosmopolitanism was represented by naturalist writers and those of the Shirakaba group. The development from Taisho democracy to the Marxist movement, which can be understood in terms of intellectuals' attempt to transcend the national in their search for the universal, was followed in its turn by a phase of reaction marked on the one hand by rejection of the outside and the universal, and on the other by the insistence on Japan's uniqueness embodied in the nationalist movement.

This cultural cycle can also be seen in the personal development of artists and other individuals. Herbert Passin writes:

> Writers . . . start out passtionately pro-Western and then become passionately anti-Western. . . . For many who had lived or studied abroad, the greatest fruit of the experience was not so much their direct learning as the new insight it gave them into their own country. . . . In the best cases a higher, personal resolution was achieved, liberated from the chain of causation, autonomous cosmopolitan.[2]

The two leading Meiji novelists, Natsume Soseki and Mori Ogai, are the best examples of the cultural cycle experienced as a personal cycle. Both Soseki and Ogai held prestigious government fellowships for study abroad, and both had the ambition and sense of mission to contribute to building the nation. They returned to Japan, however, with a deep-seated skepticism about the compatibility of Japanese culture with that of the West and about the concept of the modern self. Despite his disillusionment, Mori Ogai continued to support the government's effort to modernize and to expand militarily, while Soseki abandoned his official position among the Meiji elite to become a titleless, individual writer. Remaining aloof from the nationalistic fever created by the victory in the Russo-Japanese War, Soseki was led by his struggle against the modern ego to the realm of oriental religion and nature.

[2] Herbert Passin, "Modernization and the Japanese Intellectual: Some Comparative Observationns," in *Changing Japanese Attitudes Toward Modernization*, ed. by Marius Jansen (Princeton: Princeton University Press, 1965), pp. 477-478.

Nagai Kafu, another major writer, one whose publications began in the late Meiji period, went to America and France and returned to Japan having learned much from Western works of naturalism and decadent literature. Subsequently, however, he immersed himself in the world of old Edo, isolating himself from the mainstream literary and intellectual activities of his contemporaries.

Noguchi Yonejiro, an influential poet of symbolism who came to the United States to establish himself as a "Western" poet, presents still another example of this cultural cycle manifested on a personal level. Although his English poems achieved considerable success, and although he was married to an American woman and had children, Yone gradually came to identify himself with his Japanese cultural heritage and returned to Japan, abandoning his American family. Finding himself disappointed with Japanese life and the Japanese literary cycle, he tried to develop the idea of a greater Asian cultural heritage, even while translating English and American poetry into Japanese and attempting to become an unofficial ambassador to an English-speaking country. Ultimately, however, his sense of alienation from both Japan and the West led him to turn his back on the West completely; basing his stance on his illusionary vision of a greater Asian cultural sphere, he fervently supported Japanese militarism at the end of his life.

Yokomitsu Riichi, a most outspoken writer of modernism in the early Showa period, also started his creative career with a strong sense of being a member of the international writers' circle and of participating in the world literary movement of modernism. His modernist writing led him to struggle with the Japanese language, and after traveling to Paris via China, he returned to the world of Shintoism. *Ryoshu* [Loneliness on a Journey], his last work and his masterpiece, reveals the agonizing struggle the intellectuals experienced in their attempt to create a modern identity.

It is not only those writers who stayed in foreign countries over an extended period of time who followed this pattern of *"Nihon kaiki* [return to Japan]," but many writers who never went abroad as well. Tanizaki and Kawabata are perhaps the two most prominent examples of this, while the writers of *Nihon Romanha* [Japanese Romantic Group] present examples of the most radical turn to nationalism; many of them were Marxists before becoming ultra-nationalists. The severe censorship and legal sanctions imposed against those who participated in leftist or anti-war activities of course played a crucial role in their turning to a nationalistic concept of cultural heritage, but the sense of the impending destruction of the cultural heritage these writers felt during the early Showa period also played a major role. The confrontation with what they perceived as aggressive and foreign forces turned even such cosmopolitan writers as Yokomitsu, Yone Noguchi, and Takami Jun to a defense of traditional culture and to nationalistic rhetoric.

This of course does not mean that all the writers who stayed in foreign countries committed themselves to *Nihon kaiki* in as radical a manner as those writers mentioned above. Such writers as Maedako Hiroichiro, Kaneko Kiichi and Suzuki Etsu, all of whom stayed in the United States in the twenties, remained proletarian socialist or anarchist writers. And poets like Kaneko Mitsuharu, even though prevented from publishing, continued to write anti-war poems during the war years and remained outside the intellectuals' struggle with the traditional culture.

If I may engage in an admitted oversimplification, Ogai's return to history, Soseki's exploration of religion and return to nature, and Kafu's retreat to an aesthetic world represent three typical patterns of writers' disillusionment with modernization and the paths they took in their search for identity. Before the Second World War, most of the government-sponsored students were sent to European countries, while the intellectuals who came to the United States came as individuals with ambitions and status not very different from those of immigrants. After the war, however, the emphasis shifted drastically from Erupe to the United States. Although only a few writers were able to travel abroad in the 1940s and 1950s, those who did went mainly to the United States under government-sponsored programs or with Fulbright fellowships.

In view of America's overwhelming importance in the postwar economic and political development of Japan, it is not surprising that American culture evoked a complex reaction in Japanese intellectuals and artists. On the one hand, they maintained a suspicious and critical attitude toward American culture, looking down on its materialism, vulgarity, and lack of sophistication, as represented by gum-chewing GIs. They lamented the Americanization of the younger generation, the worst of which was represented by the girls who gained their livelihood, materially and symbolically, from American bases. On the other hand, Japanese intellectuals also shared the reaction of the masses in perceiving the United States as being in many ways a symbol of an affluent, democratic nation which could stand as the symbol of a positive future for Japan. America became the most favored subject of studies, and American studies programs became firmly established in the universities. Those intellectuals and government officials who were sent to the United States to study enjoyed the privileged position of an elite in the 1940s and 1950s, while the younger generation, fostering its dreams of visiting the United States, studied American English.

The intellectuals' reaction to America was, however, predominantly critical, a reflection in considerable measure of their leftist orientation, and one of the severest criticisms of America appears in the literature of the atomic bomb,[3] a literature in which the image of America as victorious over a feudalistic, colonialist Japan clashes with the image of America as an aggressive destroyer of humanity. The fall of Stalinism, therefore, and the beginning of the Japanese economy's great leap forward around 1956 had a drastic impact on their attitude toward American culture.

From the late 1950s to the mid-1960s, many significant essays on America were written by leading writers and critics who visited the United States. In 1960, Oda Makoto's *Nandemo miteyaro* [Let Us See Everything] was published, becoming an instant best-seller.[4] Oda was a Fulbright exchange student and had studied at Harvard for a year in 1959. He was writing novels at that time, but his works had not been published and his primary reason for coming to the United States was to study. On his return to Japan he became an anti-Vietnamese war activist, a principal organizer of the famous Beheiren [Citizens Committee for Peace in Vietnam] and a spokesman for the Japanese new left and citizens' movements.

In *Nandemo miteyaro*, Oda presents his persona as a man who is always aware of himself as a Japanese, yet is completely free from any feeling of inferiority with regard to Western culture. The protagonist is an outsider to the American establishment as well as to the Japanese establishment. He is an intellectual observer who mixes freely with the blacks, beatniks, and others living on the periphery of society, sharing with them the sense of alienation, loneliness and the kind of freedom and aloofness which intellectual detachment from the mainstream of American life creates. In the protagonist's consciousness there is a cleavage not so much between East and West as between the capitalist ruling class and the new generation of intellectual youths who question the values of American society. Oda's America is that which was emerging from McCarthyism, the America of the civil rights movement and the New Left intellectuals, and the America whose antiestablishment lyricism had already been expressed in the poetry of the beat generation.

Oda identified himself as a product of the postwar age of economic development, an involved victim yet an intellectual observer whose detachment enabled him to attain the insight to grasp the human condition. Oda did not remain a detached observer, however, but started an active politico-cultural movement through which he tried to achieve concrete changes in society. Oda's new left movement presented one way of relating politics and literature, politics and intellectual activities, a relation which Japanese

---

[3] See, for example, Nihon Gendai Shinjinkai, ed., *Shi no hai shishu* [Poetry of the Ashes of Death] (Tokyo: Hobunkan, 1954).

[4] Oda Makoto, *Nandemo miteyaro* (Tokyo: Iwanami Shoten, 1964).

intellectuals have been desperately in search of since their disillusionment with the Communist Party.

Nandemo miteyaro presents a different kind of learning from the West, an understanding of the common fate which capitalist Japan shares with the United States and of the alienation of the individual in materialistc and machine-governed culture. A witness of the diseased America, Oda found his grotesque sense of yellow Japan's conspiring with the United States in oppressive exploitation heightened as he became more involved in protesting against the war in Vietnam and neo-colonialism in Asia. Oda's America is no longer a nation of progress and democracy, but a decadent nation whose creative energy has been dissipated.

Yet this America is not so different from the future image of Japan which Oda envisions. His strong sense of affinity with the habitués of Greenwich Village coffee houses who sip French coffee precisely because it is not American coffee echoes the optimism and sense of power of the new generation rather than desperation and cold criticism. *Nandemo miteyaro* presents one definite perspective which bridges the gap between the West and Japan; the United States is perceived as an internal condition which Japan must overcome in order to secure a humanistic society with justice to its citizens and the citizens of the world. Oda's major novel, *America*, deals with monopoly capitalism and multinational corporations. Despite its title, the novel is as much about Japan as it is about America; the America of the title is often no more than a symbol of Japan. Oda's understanding is one extension of that of the prewar leftist intellectuals, yet his cosmopolitanism, his search for universal justice, is clearly based on his own criticism of the intellectuals' defeat during Japan's involvement in Asia.

Around the same time that Oda was emerging as a writer with a clear sense of identity, Eto Jun, a leading literary critic, spent a few years at Princeton University studying F. Scott Fitzgerald. Eto made his literary debut with his brilliant work on Soseki around the same time that Oe Kenzaburo and Ishihara Shintaro made themselves spokesmen of the new age. The personal meaning of Eto Jun's experience in America is as significant as that of Oda Makoto in his later development as a writer. Eto Jun's *Amerika to watashi* [America and I][5] is a detailed, minute record of his experience in the United States. *Amerika to watashi* presents another kind of confidence Japanese intellectuals gained in their relation to the West: It is the sense of participation in the international community of scholars and writers, a sensible community which recognizes the significance of the cultural background of writers for their creativity. The work is filled with a somewhat naive sense of

---

[5] Eto Jun, *Amerika to watashi* (Tokyo: Iwanami Shoten, 1964).

joy brought by his success in this community and a reaffirmation of the continuity of the cultures both of Japan and of the West. It is an affirmation of
the culture of the establishment or, politically speaking, of capitalist society.
Eto's insistence on the significance of the universality and intercultural
compatibility of literary works and scholarship is an extension of what Soseki
unsuccessfully tried to achieve.

Another kind of confidence Japanese writers gained in relation to American culture is presented by Yasuoka Shotaro and Kojima Nobuo, both of
whom are usually classified among the "third new writers [*daisan no shinjin*]
and were contemporaries of Mishima Yukio. Yasuoka stayed in North Carolina in the late 1950s and early 1960s, and his *Amerika kanjo ryoko* [Ameri-
can Sentimental Journey][6] is considered a major work. Yasuoka's America
is a rural America where people live without cultural sophistication and with
a sense of isolation from world affairs. Like his other numerous essays on
America, the book is filled with his amazement over the backwardness of
American life, large segments of which he sees as fragmented, conservative,
and undynamic. What Yasuoka found abroad was not so much a sense of
superiority over Americans but a sense of the similarity of the common
people of both the East and the West. Under the superficial glamour of
American progress, he perceived a layer of the life of common people who
are slow in changing themselves and who live with the sense of themselves
created by their daily lives. On that level, Yasuoka sees both Japanese and
Americans as almost the same, both of them unable to articulate their relationship to their cultural heritage or to the modern age.

Yasuoka's United States is not seen through the eyes of outsider intellectuals and hippies, as in the case of Oda Makoto, nor is it seen through
the eyes of establishment writers and scholars, as in the case of Eto Jun, but
through the eyes of anonymous common people who have no channel for
expression in art or scholarship. America for Yasuoka is no longer an object
to criticize, attack, or transcend, nor is it a cosmopolitan community which
Japanese can aspire to join without losing their identity as Japanese; it is a
dull and unexciting local area, a corner of the world whose commonness
presents one universal condition of man in overtly middle-class society.

Kojima Nobuo's *Hoyo kazoku* [The Embracing Family][7] is possibly
the most widely praised novel of the 1960s among the works of the *daisan
no shinjin*. In this work, the aftermath of Japan's struggle with America is
treated. The middle-aged protagonist of the novel is a scholar and translator
who stayed at an American university without bringing his wife. The fact

[6] Yasuoka Shotaro, *Amerika kanjo ryoko* (Tokyo: Chuokoronsha, 1961).
[7] Kojima Nobuo, *Hoyo kazoku* (Tokyo: Kodansha, 1971).

that he went to America alone, a commonplace enough practice for Japanese people, created some tension in his married life and is referred to often as one of the sources of his wife's frustration.

The protagonist, Miwa Shunsuke, takes for granted his home life, which is composed of his wife, who is staying at home as the center of the family surrounded by children; he tries to take care of his wife's basic frustration in life by buying a new house, installing modern electric appliances, and constantly complying with his wife's desire to make their lives more comfortable and affluent. Although he is perfectly comfortable with outdated facilities and an old house, he finds himself seated in a shining modern house, constantly thinking about and planning the further modernization of their living environment.

The novel starts with his discovery of his wife's adultery with an American who stayed at their house as their son's English-speaking companion. It is at this time that he realizes that it is no longer possible to maintain the traditional position and power of a husband and father. Before Tokiko, his wife, who admits openly her sexual involvement with the American but dismisses her lover as a temporary infatuation, he is at a loss with regard to what he should do or feel. He feels that without his knowledge his wife has realized the epitome of the freedom to which Japan had aspired since the time of modernization, and finds himself hating that freedom. He questions on what grounds he can criticize the adultery and finds indeed no moral basis for his criticism. This modern man, a translator of foreign literature, feels that he still clings to the patriarchal values and yet is helpless in restoring those values.

Yet even with his patriarchal power fallen, he still has a responsibility to maintain the family. He finds that he has no way to escape the reality of his wife's adultery except to accept her as his wife. Here obviously the reference is to Shiga Naoya's *Anya Koro* [*The Dark Passage*] in which the protagonist, upon discovery of his wife's affair with her cousin, abandons the family, escaping into nature. In doing so, he abandons the effort to establish a modern ego, which he hitherto believed was the subject of his search. Kojima also refers to another significant novel, *Yoake mae* [*Before the Dawn*] by Shimazaki Toson, whose protagaonist fervently supports the ideal of the Meiji reforms and modernization, but who finds himself completely at odds with the reality of a modernized Meiji society and dies insane. Just as the protagonist of *Hoyo kazoku* states, he feels as if he were experiencing the second *kaikoku* [opening of the nation]; he is the Showa man who accepts the logic of modernization but whose sensibility longs for traditional Japanese life.

The protagonist of *Hoyo kazoku* embarks on a pathetic effort to maintain his family without any values that he can believe in with regard to the family, marriage, or love; he does so because he feels that he can cling to nothing other than the family. The miserable husband and wife embrace one another in a sea of nothingness, isolated and disillusioned yet holding on to the bond of the family. The protagonist accepts the fact that his feudal values are useless and about to be destroyed, yet he does not believe in love as the basis of marriage either, having been deeply disillusioned in marriage. He can fight against or defend nothing: all he feels is the need to secure his everyday life. When his wife falls ill with cancer, he realizes how important she was in maintaining that everyday life. The novel ends with her death and the protagonist's mad search for a new wife to take her place.

It is clear that America plays a symbolic role in this novel; it is America which had undermined traditional life to the point of its total destruction. It is actually America which concretely created the moment of revealing the chasm underlying the surface of modernity. America is clearly treated as a symbol of modernization.

The *Hoyo kazoku* makes it clear that the intellectuals' struggle with modernization was still a vital theme in the 1960s. Unlike his Meiji and Taisho precedessors, however, Kojima's protagonist has no place to turn when he is lost in the reality of modern Japan; nature, the traditional cultural heritage, and Zen Buddhism have already lost any meaning for him as a solid basis of value. He is a product of modernization, but he cannot find any identity as a modern self or any positive value in the concept of modernity. The novel suggests that there is no longer a conflict between the modern and the traditional, or between the West and the East, both of which had hitherto presented strong values incompatible with each other, for both values have lost the power to shape a positive image of modern life. America intruded into the family, collapsing it, but America is also dismissed as something unimportant, for it no longer presents any model for a positive and imaginative life.

The writers of a younger generation which began to write in the 1960s have still another experience of, and reaction to, America. Tomioka Taeko, one of the leading poets of the 1960s, has been writing poems in which her sense of loss in modern life is expressed through a deliberate distortion of language. Born in Osaka of parents who lived completely outside middle-class life (her father was an old-fashioned business gambler), Tomioka's sense of alienation from and antagonism to modern Tokyo culture had already formed the basis of her poetic imagination. Yet only when she lived in New York did she come to realize fully that her literary roots were in the life of pre-modern common people. This realization, however, came through her struggle with English rather than her cultural unease in the United States. Japan for her is as modern as America, if not more so, and her sense of herself

as an avant-garde poet had already extinguished the gap between modern
East and West. However, Tomioka felt lost in New York in a way similar to
the alienation she felt in modern Tokyo, yet more strongly so because her
language was more inadequate in expressing or understanding herself in New
York than in Tokyo. In her poem entitled "There is nothing to do in New
York," she writes:

> There is nothing to do in New York
>
> So
> I can think
> why she is not liked by people
> and can think what she was eating
> and can think in passing
> who
> grammar is passionate
> and why
> people do
> what is good for people
> and why Americans
> cook meat
> without salt and pepper.
>
> Since the summer
> our muscles have been slightly feverish
> we took off our clothes at the doctor's
> and always came back wearing only our jackets
> it was because we were lazy
> and had nothing to do with history or intention
> or suddenly we
> were at Times Square buying pictures of the naked
> like death
> or suddenly we were
> talking to a Jew
> in a toy store
> in a shabby building on the East Side
> or suddenly we were
> riding empty subways in broad daylight
> suddenly we were living
> never being murdered
> this too is
> irrelevant to anyone's joy
> to what are we irrelevant
> and to what are we relevant

if we talk about it
then
I am
in relation
to you
that is (to say)
your
cigarettes and the small change in your pocket
are scattered on the Bowery
every day
in order to be in relation to fear constantly
you believed so

Today too
a person visited a person
no incident occurred
only
the wind blew
in winter and in spring

In the scenery outside
there was a long line of their overcoats
they ate the still life
they made a purple stool
they are relative pronouns
they are slanted surfaces
they are still alive
English
does not shout like human beings
we timidly
enter a coffee shop
from outside
only to throw away a huge slice of lemon
floating in the cup
nothing happens
what is going on
is the progress
which continues
like a long long earring
hanging forever
from an old woman's circumsized earlobes
that is
brown women
drank brown coffee
became brown

pink women
drank pink cocktails
and became pink
they exist for a long time
in this world
I
from yesterday
had nothing to say
I had used up
all the examples
even if you die
it does not make any story
the only thing I know
is that nobody shouts
for the past few hundred years
no one has heard human voices.[8]

What she describes is the inadequacy of language in expressing her alienation from English. Language has become useless and reality turned into ominous objects devoid of any systematic meaning. Her struggle with language is centered not so much around her inability to perceive and understand reality as around her amazement that the Japanese language is incompatible with American reality. Since she perceives reality only through Japanese, which cannot make any sense out of American reality, America becomes the sum of incomprehensible objects, an unreal reality which poses a threat to her existence as a poet. The loss of language means directly the loss of reality for her. On her return to Japan, she embarked on a search for the "genuine" Japanese, delving deeply into Bunraku and her Osaka dialect in her effort to uncover the connection between the art of narration and the reality of daily life.

Subsequently she turned to novel-writing. In her major work, *Meido no kazoku* [*A Family of Hades*],[9] she deals with a young woman who watches the absorption of the indigenous culture by a new one and the destruction of those who embody it; but she has no empathy with, or aggressive defense of, the old culture of common citizens. The indigenous culture of her parents, Osaka's merchant culture, certainly presents a value in itself and the mark of one way of life, but it belongs to the past and does not offer any guidance for her own life. Tomioka, who sometimes becomes anachronistically involved in traditional culture, declaring in the fashion of Tanizaki

---

[8] Tomioka Taeko, *Tomioka Taeko Shishu* [Collected Works of Tomioka Taeko] (Tokyo: Shichosha, 1967), pp. 594-608. The translation is mine.

[9] Tomioka Taeko, *Meido no kazoku* (Tokyo: Kodansha, 1974).

that she aspires to be an "artisan" of the old type rather than a modern artist, is supported by her confidence that she will not confuse the elements of the indigenous culture with the elements of avant-garde art, that is, by her confidence in her ability to place the old culture correctly in history.

Tomioka's conscious turning away from intellectualism represents another kind of criticism of modernization. Tomioka criticizes the intellectual elitism in art and literature which accompanied the entire modernization process from the Meiji period on. She tries to make art compatible with the life of the common people in the age of mass culture by connecting modern art not with traditional high culture but with traditional low culture. In her turning from avant-garde poetry to the novel of colloquial language, her confrontation with English in New York played a decisive role.

Japanese exposure to American cultural reality in the postwar period, mainly in the 1950s and 1960s, inspired Japanese writers to reflect deeply upon their own cultural roots and identity. While all the writers dealt with in this essay strengthened their consciousness of their own cultural identity, their cultural confidence differed from that of their pre-war predecessors who made *Nihon kaiki*; Japanese traditional culture and social philosophy were no longer a place to which they could return. The alternatives open to Ogai, Soseki, and Kafu in the Meiji period had been already intellectually closed for them, and the nationalistic culturalism of the late Taisho and early Showa periods had no place in their intellectual endeavors. Although they were critical of the Meiji attitude toward modernization, they were keenly aware that Japan had already followed the Western path of modernization and that not only was there no way to turn back but also Japan must share the ills of modern society with the Western nations. Their discovery was that America was no longer a nation from which they could learn, but a nation whose illness Japan had to share.

In an age when people make honeymoon trips to the United States by Jalpak, it is certain that writers will no longer write essays on their American experiences. From the perspective of the present, the works of Oda, Eto Jun, and Yasuoka appear very naive, simply because the shock of recognition that the authors experienced by being exposed to American reality no longer inspires our self-reflection as Japanese. Japan has caught up with the United States materially and America has even become symbolic of modern Japan, an interchangeable image as in the case of Murakami Ryu's *Kagirinaku tomei na buru* [*Almost Transparent Blue*], a recent Akutagawa Prize-winning novel. In this context, writers have dismissed the United States as a subject of search or struggle.[10]

---

[10] In recent years, novels in which the search for Japanese cultural identity was inspired by the author's exposure to American society have continued to appear, including

Like the family of Miwa Shunsuki, the protagonist of *Hoyo kazoku*, are
we Japanese to turn to each other, the adulterous and cancerous wife and
the helpless and impotent husband embracing, trying desperately to maintain
a framework which will enable us to continue daily existence, or are we to
turn to some other source of cultural stimuli? If Saeki's and Kato's thesis
that Japan as a peripheral culture constantly requires vital contact with
another culture to maintain a sane balance in cultural development is correct,
then the recent travel boom to China must certainly be the sign of the beginning of another cycle.

University of Southern California

such works as Oba Minako's *Urashimaso* [*Manuscript of Urashima Grass*] (Tokyo,
1977) and Meio Masako's *Aru onna no gurimpusu* [*Glimpse of a Certain Woman*]
(Tokyo, 1979). These works, however, reflect the writer's experiences abroad in the
1960s, and thus share the consciousness of and search for cultural identity with the
writers discussed in the essay.

IV

WESTERN WRITERS AND THE EAST

VICTOR SEGALEN'S *STELES* AND CHINA

Jean-Luc Filoche

A doctor and a naval officer, Segalen was also a writer and a poet. His medical thesis, *Les Cliniciens-ès-Lettres*, dealt with mental illness in the literature of his time. Since writers may be concerned with medicine, he asks, why could not a doctor show an interest in literature, especially when it claims to be pathological?[1] Later, when his duties took him to Tahiti, he paid a last tribute to Gauguin, who had just died; on his way back to Europe, he took advantage of passing through Djibouti to follow Rimbaud's footsteps in Harrar. In 1909, he sailed to China.

At the beginning of the twentieth century, the Far East was no new attraction in Europe. As early as the seventeenth and eighteenth centuries, Europe's passion for China was obvious: Jesuits were founding missions in China, Leibnitz advocated a union between East and West in *Novissima Sinica*, and philosophers like Pascal, Montesquieu and Voltaire constantly referred to China. In the following century, the trend continued but the center of interest had changed. At first philosophical and religious, it became political and economical: in 1842, England obtained the Hong Kong concession and the right to trade in five ports; in 1860, other ports were opened to Europeans. Finally, in 1898, Russia, Germany, England, and France were given extra-territorial concessions. In short, after the colonization of Northern America and India, Europe launched the conquest of Africa, the Pacific Ocean, and the Far East. Needless to say, in such a context, Cathay had lost the magic halo it had had in the days of Marco Polo.

Segalen is aware of this. As early as *Les Immémoriaux*, a novel dealing with his trip to Polynesia, he could suggest that the Polynesian race was doomed by the corrupting influence of European Christianity. His disillusion is the same when he lands in China: on the one hand, he shows no great

---

[1] For further details on Segalen's life and works, see Henry Bouillier, *Victor Segalen* (Paris: Mercure de France, 1961), pp. 34-35.

enthusiasm for the Chinese revolutionaries whom he accuses of only trying to graft European usages and slogans on their own country; on the other hand, he sees in traditional China a people crushed by its history, condemned to perpetuate the gestures of an ancient civilization. In this respect, his position seems surprising because most Westerners consider China's past as the source of its prestige and the sure proof of its difference from the West; whereas Segalen disdains China's past as a prison of ritual where nature is choked by artificiality. Hence his lack of sympathy for the Chinese, whom he considers to have become the ugliest people in the world because of this artificiality, and whose character is either childish or senile.[2]

However shocking and even racist such attitudes might seem, it is nevertheless a healthy attitude, for Segalen's rejection is never an irrevocable condemnation of China; rather it expresses the will not to be caught in the traps of cheap exoticism and local color, for exoticism can hide ugly realities under flashy and attractive appearances. Therefore, Segalen's exploration of China will begin by unveiling these realities.

The exploration takes place on both geographical and poetic levels. From 1909 to 1910, he makes a tourist's reconnaissance of Central China and Japan; in 1911, he goes to fight the plague epidemic which broke out in Manchuria; later, in 1914, he organizes an archeological expedition to the upper Yangtzu. Thus, more than any other of his contemporaries who preferred to remain in the diplomatic circles of the capital, he travelled all over China: a strange attitude indeed for somebody who, on the surface, could appear not to like China. His geographical exploration will extend to the field of poetry: if he rejects the stifling aspect of ritual in Chinese culture, he shows sympathy for the Chinese reserve and secrecy; if he rejects both traditional and revolutionary China, he sides with "the admirable fiction of the emperor, Son of the Pure Sovereign-Sky" which "is not to be lost."[3]

Here lies Segalen's originality: his archeological investigation is allied with a literary and fictive conception of China. His letters are explicit:

> It's not a question of saying what I think of the Chinese (to tell the truth, I don't think anything of them) but what I imagine of them; and not through the colourless imitation of a "documentary" book but in the lively and real form beyond all reality, the work of art.

he writes in *Briques et Tuiles*: and again, to Debussy, in 1911:

[2] Bouillier, p. 155.
[3] Bouillier, p. 175.

After all, I didn't come here to look for Europe or for China, but for a vision of China. This China I hold and sink my teeth into.[4]

In 1912, just before the first edition of *Stèles*, he sums up his position when he writes:

> You see, the task is superhuman. To learn about an immense country and when one begins to grasp it, to realize that it exists no longer and that it has to be resurrected. . . .
>
> First the so-called modern, new, republican China must be deliberately suppressed.
>
> Frankly, it's not out of sheer prejudice that I hate China, but because of its essence and nonsense. It's caricature itself, pitiful Bovarysm, pettiness, cowardice, despicableness of all kinds, boredom, boredom above all. Ancient China remains beautiful but only when seen through the eyes of certain people; one must understand, redigest, remake.[5]

In other words, rejecting the myths, Segalen's approach will take the shape of a vision which will remake China in order to render its fictive nature and secret character key elements of China's allurement for the West.

Stèles is the story of this remaking and vision.

The remaking process begins in the very choice of the Chinese stone stela, whether considered as a monument or a historical writing.

Through the stela, Segalen makes contact with Chinese civilization and culture, since stelae go back as far as the Chou Dynasty, the last of the Royal Dynasties (1050-256 B.C.). By bearing more than three thousand years of history, the stelae fit Segalen's project, a portrait of Ancient China. They also explain why his *Stèles* are organized according to ancient China's cosmic conception of the world. According to it, the world is a square surrounded by the Four Seas, where Barbarians dwell, whereas the Interior of the Seas, China, is divided into five cardinal points: South, North, East, West, and the Middle, given that the Middle coincides with the capital, the center of the world, and the sacred place where the mysterious terrestrial influx can best be felt. Again, and in accordance with Chinese tradition, the cardinal orientation dictates the content of the inscription on Segalen's

---

[4] Bouillier, p. 188.

[5] Segalen, quoted by Victor P. Bol, *Lecture de Stèles* (Paris: Minard, 1972), p. 12.

Stèles. The South bears the imperial decrees, the North is devoted to friendship, the East to love, the West to war, and the Middle to mysticism.[6]

Deeply rooted in Chinese tradition, the text of *Stèles* is mainly inspired from the *Li Chi* or *Book of Rites*, translated by Father Couvreur, and Father Wieger's *Textes historiques*, an anthology of texts pertaining to the millenial history of China, from the mythical Five Sovereigns until the eve of the Chinese Republic. Thus, *Stèles* is impregnated with Chinese philosophy as revealed not only in the *Li Chi* but also in the other four Classics of the Confucian Canon: the *Shu Ching* [*Book of Documents*], the *Shih Ching* [*Books of Odes*], the *I Ching* [*Book of Changes*], the *Ch'un-Ch'iu* [*Spring and Autumn Annals*], without forgetting the *Lun Yü* [*Analects*]; in addition to this Confucian "Bible," *Textes historiques* also refers to Buddhism, Taoism, and Christianity via Nestorianism.

Once again, Segalen's literary attitude seems paradoxical. Just as he rejects China but explores it as an ethnologist, the writer remakes China by plunging deep into Chinese history and philosophy. In other words, he rejects China not out of ignorance but knowingly, for the remaking can only begin when he is filled with Chinese customs and literature; instead of substituting Western thoughts for Oriental thoughts, or even blindly accepting the latter, he becomes imbued with them in order to understand them better, to call them into question, and to bring out their specificity.

The calling into question is obvious and is seen in the composition of his work. True to the traditional five cardinal points, he adds a personal touch by supplementing them with a sixth one, "Roadside Stelae," to which we will return. Next, he accepts the principle of the Chinese stela but rejects its inscription: "The Chinese stone stelae contain the most boring literature: the praise of official virtues, a Buddhist ex-voto, the recall of a decree, an invitation to good manners."[7] This refusal is not surprising because, devoted to the rituals which constitute Chinese civilization, the text of the stone stela is a mere reflection of the pettiness and boredom Segalen deplores in the Chinese society of his time. Consequently, when he turns toward the past and relinquishes the present, he never favors the first over the second. Segalen is not a dupe. The present is what it is because of the past; therefore, the past will also have to be called into question. This is indicated by the bipartite construction of many *stèles*: the first part is a summary of the situation mentioned by the Chinese epigraph figuring in each of his poems, whereas the second part offers a personal view-point which runs counter or differs from

---

[6] For example, Marcel Granet, *La Pensée chinoise* (Paris: La Renaissance du Livre, 1934), pp. 96-96.

[7] Bouillier, p. 189.

the first part. Far from being a copy, each *stèle* remakes and reworks Chinese stelae and philosophy. Segalen's intention is clear from the first *stèle*, whose eloquent title, "With No Dynasty Mark," sets the tone of his poetry:

> To honor established Sages; number the Righteous;
> broadcast once more that such and such a one has lived,
> and was noble, and his countenance virtuous,
> All that is well. Though it is not my concern. . . .
> Focused on what has not been said; subjected to the unproclaimed;
> bowed down towards the uncreated,
> I devote my joy, my life, my piety to the annunciation of dateless
> reigns, dynasties without accessions, names without persons,
> persons without names,
> Everything that the Sovereign-Sky contains, unachieved by man.
> But of what unique era, undated, without end, whose characters are
> unutterable and which all men establish in themselves and revere,
> At dawn when they become Sage and Regent on their own hearts'
> thrones.[8]

Among the major Chinese literati aimed at in this *stèle*, Confucius (whose portrait, incidentally, remained in the door-way of almost every school till 1911) is a prime target. Confronted with the political, moral and cultural decadence of the end of the Chou Dynasty, Confucius claims to save the world with moral reform. Never metaphysical, his philosophy is above all an ethics in the service of politics; hence his compilation of the *Shu Ching* or his participation in the rewriting of the *Shih Ching*. In the *Four Books*, a collection of Confucian thoughts, it is clear that the Sage wants to provide all men with rules for an authentic and virtuous life whose model would be the Hsia or Shang-Yin civilizations. So to speak, Confucius shares with Segalen a feeling of disappointment regarding the present and a desire to find solutions in the past. But whereas Segalen intends to consider the past as fiction, Confucianism takes possession of the past, endows it with temporal and spatial dimensions, sets it as an historical reality in order to draw precepts used to establish an eternal moral human order; Confucianism institutes myths and rites which, under humanistic pretences, codify human behavior. The *Chung Yung* [Doctrine of the Mean] is explicit. A perfect mankind can only exist in an order based on Heaven, "the will of Heaven is named natural law. The observance of natural law is called the rule of our actions. . . . To depart

---

[8] Some *stèles* have been translated by Nathaniel Tarn in *Stelae* (Santa Barbara: Unicorn Press, 1969). The other *stèles* are my translation.

from the rule of our actions, even for a moment, is never permitted. . . ."[9] As a result, Heaven, the law and the rule will give Chinese society its mythical and hierarchical system, from the familial relationships to the relations between the Prince and the Supreme Ruler in Heaven.

Such a society leaves nothing aside. From a political standpoint, everything must be well ordered and first finds its place inside the "correct designations [*cheng ming*]," for they fix language and actions, as we are told in this passage from the *Analects*:

> Tzü-lu said (to Confucius): "The overlord of Wei is to entrust the government to you. What is the first thing to be done?" "The essential thing is to make the designations correct," the Master answered, and he added: "If designations are not correct, words cannot be consistent; if words are not consistent, state matters will fail; if they fail neither rites nor music will flourish."[10]

The repercussion is felt on a poetic level: everything must be said in order not to leave any room for interpretation. In his Preface to the *Shih Ching*, Father Couvreur comments upon Chinese allegory as follows:

> Allegory is a simile whose application is not expressed, it is like a fable whose moral must be guessed by the reader. The application thus left to the commentators' shrewdness is not always free from difficulty. More than once, after many a conjecture, allegory remains uncertain or obscure.[11]

Now uncertainty or obscurity are not allowed in a society where everything is strictly regulated. The body falls under the same condemnation, for senses are held in suspicion, in the *Chung Yung* for instance:

> This is why the Sage carefully observes what cannot be seen and fears what cannot be heard. For nothing is more real than that which cannot be seen and nothing is more certain that that which the senses cannot grasp. For this reason, the Sage shows great diligence in watching over his most secret thoughts.[12]

Unlike Segalen's Sage, the Confucian Sage recognizes that the invisible and

---

[9]Chow Yih-ching, *La Philosophie chinoise* (Paris: P.U.F., Collection "*Que sais-je*," 1956), p. 22.

[10]Granet, p. 445.

[11]Henry Bouillier, ed., *Stèles* (Paris: Plon, 1963), p. 276.

[12]Chow, p. 22.

allowing them to catch one off guard; "secrecy," whether political, poetic or corporal, is never tolerated in Confucian thought, for with "secrecy" comes disorder. This is why throughout his poetry, Segalen never misses an opportunity to sneer at Confucianism; this is also why Confucian virtue, with all the pettiness and prosaism it implies to Segalen, will bring its author the title of "boss of the school-teachers" awarded to him by Segalen.[13] As a result, it is this society crumbling under self-satisfaction, self-complacency, and the Golden Mean that he plans to leave, in "Departure":

> Here, the Empire at the center of the world . . .
> Where men stand, bow, greet according to their ranks. Where brothers know their categories; and where all is ordered by the clarifying influx of the Sky.
> There, the miraculous West. . . .

One must not conclude that Segalen rejects China for the West, Buddhism for Christianity for instance. It may be that, contrary to Confucianism, Buddhism never preaches a moral improvement of the world, since everything is considered transitory and fugitive. However, Buddhism, according to Segalen, goes too far when it claims, as do the Mahayanists, that only Mind is real and the outside world emanates from Mind; the supremacy of the mind is apparent in the Buddhist's effort to reach *nirvana*, a state of rest, untroubled by passion, evil, or desire. However, by promoting *nirvana*, Segalen contends, the Buddhist abolishes the complexity of human acts, does away with any going back beyond what is immediately visible, and establishes clarity by organizing a world without depth. For these reasons, he rejects Buddhism for the "mediocrity of its vital value."[14]

He will not accept Christianity any more readily. In any case, behind Buddhism, the *stèle* "on a Dubious Host" was aimed at Christianity, for the term "Savior of Men" fits Christ better than Buddha. There is no doubt in the *stèle* "In Praise of a Western Virgin": both Christianity and Confucianism (or Neo-Confucianism under the dynamic materialism of the philosopher Chu Hsi) come under attack by Segalen. First, Christianity is not alone in enjoying the privilege of miracles since the *Shih Ching* reports Hou Chi's miraculous birth, two thousand years before Christ; second, whereas "Reason is not offended" by such miraculous deeds, the tone of the *stèle* puts

---

[13]Bouillier, *Stèles*, p. 198. Incidentally, Confucius himself saw the failure of his moral and social system, when a group of female musicians and dancing girls ruined his efforts See Leon Wieger, *Textes historiques* (Paris: Imprimerie de Hien-hien, 1930), p. 147.

[14]Bouiller, p. 54.

forward the irrationality emerging from taking literally what pertains to a fictive domain. "Luminous Religion" gives the Chinese epigraph and sums up the content of the Nestorian stela of Hsianfu, but only to reject Nestorianism and Christianity which, according to Segalen, sacrifice sensual man to a hypothetical Hereafter: "Then come promises: an incarnation, an agony, a death, a resurrection. Now it is not good to have men know this too well." Once again, Segalen denounces Christianity's pretensions "to build forever," in "To the Ten Thousand Years" for instance. Indeed, under the pretext of liberating the mind and reaching for eternity, Western thought ends up in considering Time as an absolute and falls into technology, materialism and immobility. Confronting oriental architecture, Segalen addresses the same approach to the West: "Do you believe these palaces are motionless? Heavy like Western buildings?" In short, Christianity suffers from the same contradiction as Confucianism: both made to serve man, they reduce him to slavery. At least, this allows one to understand why Europe's interest in China, at first religious, became economic.

By the same token, Segalen never criticizes Chinese traditions in order to proclaim the superiority of their Western counterparts, for his attacks on China reflect a sharp criticism of Western ideology and, more specifically, a criticism of Cartesian rationalist thought. Indeed, Cartesianism is a mathematico-technical conception which reduces nature to an inert geometrical area; this mathematical idealism finds its basis in the idealism of the subjective and transcendental certitude of consciousness as a norm for all truth and for the evidence of clear and distinct ideas, the *Cogito*. As to the Cartesian God, it is again through the experience of the *Cogito* that the certitude of a Perfect Being can be attained; God becomes a guarantee of the fecund development of rationalist idealism. In other words, Cartesianism substitutes a subjective transcendency for a divine transcendency, but the result is the same: where Confucius repeats "It is the will of Heaven,"[15] where a Christian says "Thy will be done," the Cartesianist, bringing a logical conclusion to the concept of clarity in which things appear to mean something by themselves, declares: "My will be done!"

Now Segalen rejects any transcendency, whether divine or human, as well as all notions of rationalism. "Homage to Reason" is an antiphrastic title, for this *stèle* satirizes the fallacious edifices built by man in the name of Reason, such as religious beliefs, human equality, and the most fallacious concept in the West: democracy. With the disappearance of Reason comes that of the subjective consciousness, as in "Funeral Stela": "I the Emperor command my sepulture. . . . This pleasant tomb shall be mine." As for Time,

[15]Wieger, p. 122.

the absolute on which Cartesian philosophy is based, the *stèle* "Decree" confirms what the *stèle* "With No Dynasty Mark" hinted at, that is, "This is not Time that can be measured." In short, just as the Emperor faced South to give power to his decrees, Segalen also faces South but only to abolish all "decrees" and, with them, the Emperor of the Chinese tradition. By doing so, he brings hope to escape from the rigidity and immobility inherent in ritual.

Devoted to Friendship, the "Stelae facing North" gives a first glimpse of the remaking process at work. The first traditional concept to be remodeled is that of Time. In these *stèles*, Segalen uses the trivial theme of a broken friendship to conclude that the notion of continuity between the past and the present is an illusion: something has occurred between the past and the present, something responsible for the change in friendship but which cannot be accounted for when Time is considered as a linear process. As a consequence, this discovery calls into question not only Confucius' pretenses to establish a moral good for all men and all times but also the concept of dualism which sustains Cartesian philosophy (past-present, ephemeral-eternal, body-mind, mind-spirit, life-death), for it is unable to account for reality.

In order to account for reality, Segalen is led to create what the *stèle* "Vampire" calls an "equivocal being." Once again, the mythical theme of vampirism is almost trivial to the extent that it can be found in the oldest folk-tales, both in the West and China. But instead of characterizing the forces of Evil fighting against Goodness as in myths, Segalen's "vampire" appears as a fusion of opposites; whereas the Chinese epigraph of the *stèle* quotes verbatim the *Li Chi* and acknowledge the irreconcilability of antithetic concepts like life and death ("To treat the dead as completely dead is inhuman! To treat the dead as completely as alive is ignorant"), Segalen chooses "in spite of principles" to form "an equivocal being: neither genius nor dead nor alive." This "equivocal being" is important because just as it allows us to break away from the "principles," the fusion it is made of allows us to move from the realm of factual rationalism into a symbolic domain, in which Time and subjective certitude do not exist as such.

This symbolic world is never cut off from reality; as we mentioned, Segalen was compelled to create this being only to portray reality. Indeed, placed half-way between past and present, death and life, man and spirit, only an "equivocal being" is able to express what dualism could never have said, namely the movement taking place between the two parts of an opposition and accounting for the changes noticed in friendship. Moreover, by creating an "equivocal being" and venturing onto a symbolic ground, Segalen's interest in fiction explains itself. Fiction, however, paradoxical this may sound, is best suited to rescue reality from rationalism.

Consecrated to Woman, or "She" as Segalen calls her, the "Stelae facing

East" emphasizes and develops the same point, starting with "The Five Relationships." Whereas the *Li Chi* maintains a clear-cut distinction between the "five kinds of obligations common to men of all times and all places,"[16] Segalen concieves Woman as a fusion of the Five Relationships. "She" appears simultaneously as a friend, a sister, and a Princess, for only the blending of the different social categories will best express man's physical and spiritual needs:

> She who echoes within me more than any friend; whom I call delicious elder sister; whom I serve as a Princess, — O mother of all the impulses of my soul.

Again, the *stèle* "In Praise of a Young Lady" rebukes the faithful widow of Chinese tradition and celebrates the advent of "She" who, fusion of the opposites, is pregnant with every possibility, "rich with all that there is to come." With Woman, we penetrate deeper into Segalen's world because the fusion allows one to circumscribe the position of this world in human topology and epistemology. This symbolic world is the world before choices, before the divisions upon which hierarchy and rationalism rest were made. This is why such a world seems to be at the same time so close and so far from ours to the extent that its components are derived from a rationalist world but are reorganized according to a fusion which never results in chaos but in a movement, an unending richness and multiplicity of feelings and nuances absent from a dualist context; a symbolic approach to reality not only shows life but also is life at work.

If we do away with classification, simultaneity and multiplicity raise the question of Confucian and Cartesian clarity and certitude as well as the question of Confucius' correct "designations"; how can an "equivocal" world be expressed? This question is repeated with more pertinence in a *stèle* which is a discreet echo of "The Five Relationships" and whose title, not by chance, is "Equivocal Sister":

> By what name shall I call you, with what tenderness? Younger sister
> I never chose, wise accomplice of unawareness,
> Shall I proclaim you lover? No, you would not allow it. My relative?
> That tie might well have linked us. My beloved one? Nor you nor
> I knew how to love as yet.

In fact, there will be no direct answers to these questions, for it is not possible to "designate," to define the "equivocal." A definition, if this word is taken in its traditional acceptation, could only assign delimitations to a concept in order to fix it into what is already known; now this precisely what

Segalen, in this same *stèle*, reproaches the married woman with: "Here you are, settled from now on, given a name by rite, custom and lot." As a matter of fact, fixity and denominations would run counter to Segalen's project, since the "equivocal" constitutes the first stage of a world whose purpose is to do away with tradition and meaning. Therefore, a sure clue to its newness, the "equivocal" may only be exprssed by the "unutterable," as Segalen said in "With No Dynasty Mark."

This belief is reasserted in "Out of Respect," the last of the "*Stèles* facing East":

> No! Let her reign within me be secret. Let it never befall. Let me even forget: henceforward let her name never blossom in my depths,
> Out of respect.

The religious tone should not be mistaken for the belief that in some religions certain names are taboo under the pretense that a pure substance, God for instance, would only be degraded by receiving the material support of words. Nor should it be mistaken for Confucius' belief, in the *Analects*, that Heaven does not speak because it does not need sensitive language to manifest itself to man, for such a conviction implies that Heaven can speak if it wishes to, as Fung Yu-lan was prompt to notice.[17] Segalen knows that fiction cannot do without words, and is a matter of words, but whether these words are meant to be constraining definitions or express the "unutterable" is another matter which is better understood by drawing a parallel between Segalen's thoughts and the Taoist doctrine that they resemble.

When Segalen declares that his domain is that of the "unutterable," he could be said to resemble Lao Tzu, for whom the Principle of the Universe is the Something Else, variously described as the Self-So, the Nameless, or Non-Being:

> There is a thing confusedly formed
> Born before heaven and earth.
> Silent and void
> It stands alone and does not change,
> Goes round and does not weary.
> It is capable of being the mother of the world.
> I know not its name
> So I style it "the way."[18]

[17]Chow, pp. 24-25.
[18]Lao Tzu, *Tao Te Ching*, trans. D. C. Lau (London: Penguin Books, 1963), p. 82.

Moreover, if Confucian teaching is based on moralism and ritual, Lao Tzu rejects conventions; according to him, rites, moral and social laws are artificialities of a nature which needs to be freed. As to Segalen's Sage, he could be Taoist to the extent that he practices voluntary obscurity and self-effacement; *stèles* like "In Praise of a Solitary Sage" or "Table of Wisdom," whose Chinese epigraph is "Nobody knows him," have a Taoist flavor. The rejection of conventions finds its correlative in the doctrine of the Taoist "inaction," *wu wei*, which Segalen seems to adopt in the epigraph of "Stela to Desire": "Not to act is to accomplish." It is always according to a principle analogous to that of the *wu wei* that, in "Bad Craftsmen," Segalen refuses to enlist the zodiac constellations in man's service. Finally, the existence of a supreme ontological reality which can be apprehended in its absence and its namelessness, the *Tao* is suggested in many "Middle Stelae" with eloquent titles such as "Praise and Power of Absence," "Moment," whose epigraph "The name that can be named is not the constant name" is a direct quotation from the *Tao Te Ching*, "Forbidden Violet City" and "Hidden Name": "When the void gapes underground in the heart's cavern, / . . . . / under the vault, now accessible, the Name can be received." This last statement is directly inspired from Taoism. Only when all conventions are suppressed and man renounces his passions will the Union with the Absolute be possible; as he has Chuang Tzu say: "The soul will be void and will grasp reality; the Union with the Tao can be obtained through the void; the void is the fasting of the heart."[19]

However, it would be wrong to transform Segalen into a disciple of Lao Tzu, for there is one point on which they diverge. Whereas Taoist "inaction" is understood as a renunciation of passions, Segalen's poetry is the writing of desire, and what is said of "Provisional Stela" could be said of *Stèles* in general. It is "this poem, this gift, this desire." Only desire can render the symbolic aspect of plurality or "diversity," as Segalen calls it in "The Five Relationships." That "diversity" can be approached through desire is easily understood. Just as the multiple facets of "diversity" permit one to escape from the one-sided and geometrical world of rites and classifications, desire does not know the limits of Time and Space, and can embrace man and things in one movement; or rather, by embracing things at a distance, the distance inherent in desire, desire solves the paradox of enjoying without possessing; with desire, one enters a phantasmatic world. This is why, in a remodeling of Taoism, desire is considered not as a disrupting human activity but as the very expression of a symbolic and immensely human activity not to be disregarded. It is thus not surprising to see that the Taoist *wu wei* is used as an epigraph for the *stèle* named "Stela to Desire."

[19]Chow, p. 40.

> Therefore, erect this to Imagining-Desire; which, despite them, has delivered you the mountain, higher than you, the road farther than you.
> And laid, whether she wants or not, the pure girl under your mouth.

That phantasm is not cut off from reality, we know from the strong flavor of sensuality and eroticism that emanate from Segalen's poetry. Already detected in "Stelae facing North," sensuality becomes stronger in "Stelae facing East," and bursts out violently in "Stelae facing West": "Mongol Libation" depicts the Mongolians' ferocity when dismembering their victim, as well as the victim's unending desire to fight:

> / .... / We wish to become demons, and of the bloodiest kind:
> Out of a longing forever to bite and devour that lot!

And again, "At the Tip of the Sabre" relates the "Mongolians' joy in destruction," as well as the power and immensity of the world Segalen is creating, in what is a reminder and fulfillment of "With No Dynasty Mark":

> Without frontiers, sometimes without a name, we do not reign, we go.
> But all that there is to be cut and split, all there is to be nailed and divided. . . .
> All that which can be done, in the end, at the tip of the sabre, we did.

A sure sign that we are evolving on a phantasmatic level, it is noteworthy to consider the resolution of what seems to be a paradox: violence is never cruelty, and the torturing of a victim or the Mongolians' conquests are never conceived as acts of barbarism but as signs of chivalry and energy, the very same energy that is requested from the dragon in "Hymn to the Sleeping Dragon":

> Get up, show yourself, it is time. With one leap jump out of us;
> / .... /
> Lash us with the snake of your tail,
> / .... /
> but shine outside of us, – oh! shine!

Just as the dragon has lost its Chinese meaning of regulator for the seasons, the concepts of victor and vanquished disappear; such a duality does not exist as both parties are praised: "When you are reborn, Cheng-ho-chang, do us the honor of being reborn among us," "Mongol Libation" concludes; in any case, there is no victor and no vanquished, as in "Savage Oath." It is also characteristic that the emergence of energy and the disappearance of concepts such as victor-vanquished or cruelty, inherent to war in both the West and the East, are linked to the fact that the subjective consciousness has lost the solidity, the sacredness and immunity it enjoyed in a ritualistic and rationalist world. "Orders to the Sun" is a brilliant proof that we are in a symbolic domain where the power of the subjective certitude is lost, in that deeds those of Yang, the Chinese Joshua who gives direct orders to nature, are no longer possible. In Segalen's poetry, the deeds we witness may be less spectacular but are more durable and rewarding. "Roadside Stelae" constitutes this reward.

The "Roadside" direction, never mentioned in traditional China's cosmic world, demonstrates the originality of these *stèles*, shown by the title "Roadside Stories [*wai-chi*]," namely the stories "not incorporated in history."[20] Written by travellers, Chinese or foreign, these stories were about countries foreign to China. Now what was not incorporated in Chinese history, what could not have been incorporated, with all the novelty it implies, is precisely the faculty of embracing the multiplicity and infinity of life, in all its aspects, the most fugitive as well as the most subtly shaded, the most remote as well as the most intimate. By following such a direction, the traveller will not arrive

> / . . . . / at the swamps of immortal joys,
> But at the whirlpools full of ecstasies of the great river Diversity,

as indicated in "Counsels to the Good Traveller," the first of the "Roadside Stelae."

The departure from the "swamps" of traditional China takes place almost literally, geographically and historically speaking. Indeed, "Solid Tempest," the first stopping-place in Segalen's symbolic journey, is the name given to the country of Chin by the *Analects*. This is an indication first, that we are leaving the swamps of the Yellow River (in whose bend, incidentally, the Sage of "Table of Wisdom" works repairing the terraces which were always collapsing[21]) for the higher plateaux of the "Chan-hsi" whose description given by Segalen in "Yellow Earth" is not unlike that of Marcel Granet: "Separated by impassable lands, isolated by canyons with precipitous sides, the loess plateaux were divided up into sections insufficiently connected by narrow isthmuses and difficult passes."[22] Then, from a political standpoint,

---

[20] Bouillier, p. 191; and Wieger, p. 9.
[21] Wieger, p. 61.
[22] Marcel Granet, *Chinese Civilization* (New York: Alfred Knopf, 1930), pp. 73-74.

the country of Chin was considered during the feudal period as a "border country" in relation with the Ti and the Jong of the Barbarian countries.[23] Finally, geographical and historical considerations join together in "The Pass," in an allusion to the Great Wall which, in Northern Chan-hsi, is the gateway to Mongolia. Therefore, the foreign world onto which the "Roadside Stelae" open never breaks away from reality, nor does it coincide, however paradoxical it may sound, with a detachment from China. The detachment is only from tradition, for *stèles* like "Solid Tempest," "Yellow Earth," and "The Pass" plunge deep into the land of China.

The phenomenon of penetration of China and detachment from tradition is repeated on the philosophical level, where the impact of the phantasmatic world is best felt. Indeed, if the Sage's harangues of "Table of Wisdom" have been recorded in the *Analects*,[24] one fact the *Analects* has certainly failed to record: the fact that, as in Segalen, the harangues do not count as much as the Sage's blending with the stone which pays him a tribute. At the same time, the fusion of man and stone supersedes the notion of voluntary self-effacement as the Taoist tradition understands it. The same process is also responsible for the osmosis taking place in the *stèle* "In Praise of Jade": even when Segalen makes a "paraphrase of the *Book of Rites*,"[25] we realize that jade is not an "image" of virtue, with all the inertia inherent in an "image," as in Confucius; jade becomes a living entity and communicates its life to virtue. As a result, virtue ceases to be a tool for bureaucracy and human perfectibility, becomes a concrete and living reality, and is assimilated in the Sage himself. At this point, it goes without saying that the coming to life of the jade corresponds to Segalen's desire to resurrect China.

The resurrection is also felt in "The Pass." Once again, the epigraph of the *stèle* refers to an important concept of Chinese life, the *Yin Yang chieh*, namely the passage to another world, the underground world of the dead as indicated by the story which inspired the *stèle*.[26] However, if Segalen's "pass" opens onto a new world, this world is not that of death as in the Chinese tradition, but of life:

> It is all the promise: the journey, the riding through the plains, the ambling pace to the infinite leg, the boundless widening, the flight, dispersion.

By the same token, the detachment from Chinese tradition corresponds to

[23] Granet, *Chinese Civilization*, pp. 77-82.
[24] Wieger, p. 61.
[25] Bouillier, pp. 197-298.
[26] Bouillier, p. 206.

a detachment from Christian tradition; whereas the "Luminous Religion" offers "promises" only good after a resurrection in the Hereafter, Segalen's promises and resurrection are fulfilled in this world. Such a resurrection, obtained by freeing China from its constraints, signifies that Segalen does not create *another* world but succeeds in making *otherness* of the world, the other side of man and things emerge. Hence the "inverted" aspect of the "Roadside Stelae": "Yellow Earth" is an "inverted land" which can be read only through "inverted characters" made to "be read from the inner lining of space,–the pathless country travelled by fixed dead eyes," as we are told in "Stela of the Soul's Way," for these characters address the dead, that is, ourselves.

To sum up the "Roadside Stelae," the discovering of the Chinese land coincides with a discovering of the human soul, but it is surprising to note that for Segalen the soul is not located in some remote mystical place, deep in the earth or man, but spreads itself out, in the open, under the sky. However, this openness has nothing in common with the clarity and transparency of the Cartesian subjective certitude, for, this time, the secrecy and complexity of life are exposed, and become as tangible as the Chinese plain with which they are blended; through this osmosis, the Chinese earth becomes alive and man breathes the Chinese earth, whose immensity and richness he acquires. In short, the "Roadside Stelae" put the reader in the presence of the "unutterable," expressing simultaneously man and the universe. A river, man will "flow into the crowd" ("Counsels to the Good Traveller"); a human, the mountain "piles effort on effort as pilgrims pile stones: in homage" ("Solid Tempest"); "the spreading plain/Levels its yellow face under the quotidian Sky of the days it receives in its basin" ("Yellow Earth"); and "all Mongolia-in-grass unfolds its fan at the edge of the horizon" ("The Pass").

If the "Roadside Stelae" constitutes the "nameless," what are we to think of the "Middle Stelae"?

As we mentioned, the Middle, in ancient China, coincides with the capital as well as with the mystic center of the world. For Segalen, this is not the case; the Middle does not reveal anything that was not already known, to such a point that it not only sums up but also sends the reader back to the preceding directions. "Fall" denies transcendency, and our desires, "Underground Judges" held in captivity, call out for their "Liberation," since the "Secret Demon" constituted by our desires contains "diversity"; hence the anticipation of "that reversed hour," when the "desires will act themselves out against my nature."

The "backwards" reading of the "Middle Stelae" is important. It implies that Segalen's Middle will never be a center which organizes the other directions and gives them their significance; in a word, the center has lost its power, just as the traditional Emperor and subjective consciousness have done; in doing so Segalen is following the counsel he gave in the first of the "Middle Stelae," when he advised one to "Lose the Quotidian Meridian," and to

> . . . go backwards sometimes,
> And through a reversible network, lead astray, in the end,
>   the quadruple senses of the Points of the Sky.

Correlatively, this implies that, contrary to Buddhism, whose ultimate goal is *nirvana*, contrary to Taoism which consists of a movement of ascetism at the end of which the initiate is united with the Tao, contrary to Confucianism whose goal is human moral perfectibility, and contrary to Christianity which proclaims a "revelation" when everything is explained to man, there is no such final word for Segalen, not because such a word is not possible but because we must be aware that such a word can be said only in a ritual or rationalist world; but then it corresponds to the end and death:

> Only when there is great drought, when frostbound winter crackles,
>   when springs at their lowest ebb, spiral in shells of ice,
> When the void gapes underground in the heart's cavern,
>   —where blood itself has ceased to flow,
>   —under the vault, now accessible, the Name can be received.
>
> ("Hidden Name")

Now, in the final line of this *stèle*, Knowledge is precisely what Segalen refuses:

> But let the hard waters melt, let life overflow, let the devastating torrent surge rather than Knowledge!

Once again, the last *stèle* confirms the "backwards" movement of the "Middle Stelae," in that it returns to the other directions, and especially to "the whirlpools full of ecstasies of the great river Diversity" of the "Roadside Stelae."

In conclusion, from an epistemological standpoint, Segalen's poetry puts an end to the traditional and rationalist concept of linearity: beginning-end, past-present. As we have seen, there is no final word in his poetry. However, it is neither a return to the past, because such a movement would still be linear. His interest in the past is not a return to an ideal beginning which would have been lost, whether that past is the Garden of Eden of the Christian tradition or the prestige the Hsia Dynasty had for Confucius: their rejection by Segalen speaks for itself. Instead, his fascination for Ancient China takes the shape of a reflexive movement which comes back not to a past and a historical tradition as such, but to what has been said in order to call it into question and to extract what has not been said yet.

Thus conceived, the "nameless" appears as the expression of all the possibilities which were discarded when ritual and classification occurred. This implies also that the "nameless," if it breaks away from the tradition, is never cut off from reality. Reality is here to prove that fact, when considering China's past not as history but as a story, as a "fiction" and a "work of art," Segalen is faithful to both the spirit and the letter of ancient texts. According to Marcel Granet, all which concerns the periods prior to the year 841 B.C., namely Ancient China, was expressed in Sung poems, at an age when dates, and therefore history, were unknown, dates and history coming later with the commentators and new editions of these texts.[27]

Freed from temporal constraints, Segalen's fictive and reflexive approach to Ancient China coincides with a very modern perception of reality which takes its full originality when placed in the European literary context of the early twentieth century. Prolonging Rimbaud's *Lettre du Voyant*, in which "the Poet makes himself a *visionary* by a long immense and reasoned *derangement* of *all the senses*" and expresses "things unheard-of and nameless," *Stèles* nevertheless succeeds in breaking away from the spiritual aspect which still permeates Rimbaud's *Saison en Enfer* and *Illuminations*, and thus manages to harmonize two sides of the poet, literature and adventure, which left Rimbaud profoundly divided: on the one hand the poetic genius and, on the other hand, the arms trafficker in Harrar. Moreover, by presenting Chinese past as a fiction, Segalen's enterprise parallels and even precedes those of *Remembrance of Things Past, Ulysses* and *Finnegan's Wake*, and Freud's work in which psychoanalysis can be understood to be a reworking of the past which helps man to perceive the reality he has veiled by building a mythical and ritual prison for himself.

Far from aspiring to a union of East and West as Leibnitz wished, Segalen's "demythifying" and reworking of China is an experiment from which the West has much to benefit, for it might help the West to become conscious of the myths on which its values are based. True in 1912, Segalen's claim remains true today if we are to believe Edmund White, in his analysis of Barthes' *Mythologies*:

> During the first half of this century, for instance, Americans were fond of saying that the Chinese worshiped their ancestors and that the extended family was the one enduring—even sacred—institution

[27]Granet, *Chinese Civilization*, pp. 56-58.

of Chinese life. This exaggerated respect for the past and for the family had a special appeal for Americans. It was both exotic (excessive, foolish, foreign) and familiar (a heightened version of our own conservatism). There was only one catch—the Chinese changed in 1949. They gave up Confucianism and filial piety with surprising ease. Only now do we admit that this "eternal" aspect of the Chinese "essence" was in fact true of only the elite, a class trait, and even among the Mandarins a trait in process. Our myth of the Chinese character blinded us to Chinese realities.[28]

University of Southern California

[28]Edmund White, "A Rebel's Discourse: The Politics of Roland Barthes," *The Village Voice*, XXIV:52 (December 24, 1979), p. 40.

ASIA AND THE POETIC DISCOVERY OF AMERICA
FROM EMERSON TO SNYDER

Dan McLeod

> I see that my disquietudes come from having understood too late
> that we are in the Occident. Occidental Swamps! . . . to the devil, I
> said, with martyr's crowns, the beams of art, the pride of inventors,
> the ardor of plunderers; I returned to the Orient and the first and
> eternal wisdom.   (Arthur Rimbaud, *A Season in Hell*)

> The traditional cultures are in any case doomed, and rather than
> cling to their good aspects hopelessly it should be remembered that
> whatever is or ever was in any other culture can be reconstructed
> from the unconscious, through meditation.
>   (Gary Snyder, "Buddhism and
>   the Coming Revolution.")

> The study of the West's Journey to the East is a study of the
> West; it is of the soul of the West that one learns, rather than that
> of the East.   (Robert Ellwood, "Percival Lowell's
>   Journey to the East")

I

The attraction of Asian traditions for American poets has usually been
accompanied by dissatisfaction with a critical part of our transplanted European culture. Since our roots were shallow on this continent and the adoption
of American Indian cultures unlikely even if they were made available, a
nineteenth-century poet who rejected his European heritage was left with
little cultural identity at all. In such an alienated condition even remote traditions offered attracitive possibilities. Thus, when an American poet recognized one of his own intuitions or poetic insights expressed effectively in an
Asian work he was inclined not only to read on, but to pursue those directions in his own work. This situation accounts for much of what is particular

to American poetry from its beginnings with Emerson and Whitman through
Eliot and Pound to Gary Snyder and any number of other contemporary
American poets.

That American poets may have misconstrued their Asian sources or that
such sources lack the cultural continuity and immediacy of more familiar
European sources is beside the point in this argument. Given the history and
geography of American society relative to those of Europe and Asia, some
sort of creative misunderstanding may have been as inevitable as it is ultimately unimportant to all but cultural purists. And "cultural purity" is
hardly an American ideal. As Snyder has pointed out in his characteristically
syncratic American way, "every living culture and language is the result of
countless cross-fertilizations."[1] But of a couple of points regarding the use
of Asian sources in American poetry we can be fairly confident: 1) their use
is closely related to (may, even, have been provoked by) a rejection of European values, and 2) the way in which Asian sources figure in American poetry
accounts for much of its distinctness in theme and technique when compared
to that of other Western cultures. In short, the Asian sources in our poetry
contribute to its American identity.

These ideas are suggested by the sequence of quotations that head this
essay. Rimbaud's list of discontents manages to touch most of those aspects
of Western civilization that have repelled American poets: a religious tradition
that celebrates suffering, repressive artistic forms that stifle rather than
support original expression, technological interests that tend to estrange men
first from the natural world and then from their own natures, and a lust for
material wealth that drives nations to economic and political imperialism. As
a "myth of Asia" developed in nineteenth century Europe, Asian values
came to be associated with the cultivation of intuition, spirituality and non-
self as contrasted to the cultivation in the West of rationality, materialism,
and the individual self.[2] It was this perception of Asian values that provoked
such quintessentially American poets as Emerson, Thoreau, Whitman, Pound,
Eliot, Rexroth, Bly, Wright, and Snyder to turn East as well as West for
influence and inspiration. Gary Snyder, albeit with more optimism and considerably less stridancy than Rimbaud, recognized early in his career that
"perhaps the whole Western tradition ... [was] off the track," and that
this realization might lead "many people to study other major civilizations—
India and China—to see what they could learn."[3] And what American poets
have drawn from their Asian sources is whatever they needed to confirm the

---

[1] "Poetry and the Primitive," *Earth House Hold* (New York: New Directions, 1969),
p. 126.
[2] See John M. Steadman, *The Myth of Asia* (New York: McMillan, 1969), pp. 21-46.
[3] *Earth House Hold*, p. 114.

direction of their own poetic and personal development. Far from diluting and obscuring American values by whoring after strange gods, these Asian borrowings have enriched and helped to define our culture. Thus, as Robert Ellwood observed in his essay on the impact of Japan on Percival Lowell, "the study of the West's Journey to the East is a study of the West."[4]

II

It is probably not coincidental that at about the same time that reliable studies of Asian cultures first became available in the West, American poetry was beginning to establish its own distinctive voice. The first readable translations of early South Asian literature into European languages appeared in time to exert a considerable influence on America's first important literary movement, Transcendentalism. The first good translations of East Asian literature, which began to appear shortly after World War I, exerted a similar influence on the modern movement in American poetry, and that influence has increased with our contemporary generation of poets.

American poets, like the early settlers on the American continent, may be sorted into those who wished to establish an outpost of European values here and those who found European traditions inadequate to their social, spiritual or aesthetic aspirations. Settlers not content with the ways of European civilizations were responsible for the central event of American history, the Western migration to the Pacific; poets who held this view continued even further, in their imaginations at least, to Asia. And like Columbus in his quest for Oriental riches, those American poets who turned to Asia for themes or techniques have generally ended up discovering America. At every turn from Transcendentalism to Imagism, the Beat Movement and Post-Modernism, Asia has played this role in the development of American poetics.

Foreign literature in translation has figured prominently in every poetic revolution in English verse from Chaucer's time to Snyder's, and the emergence of a truly American poetic voice in the mid-nineteenth century presents no exception to this rule. In their pioneer studies of Asian influence on American literature, Frederic Carpenter and Arthur Christy demonstrated that most of the Asian philosophy and literature available in Western languages during the nineteenth century was read, transformed and re-expressed by Emerson, Thoreau, and their Concord circle.[5] At that time only Hindu

---

[4] "Percival Lowell's Journey to the East," *The Sewanee Review* LXXVII:2 (1970), pp. 285-309.

[5] Frederic Carpenter, *Emerson and Asia* (Cambridge: Harvard University Press, 1930); and Arthur Christy, *The Orient in American Transcendentalism* (New York:

and Islamic cultures had been thoroughly penetrated by Western nations, so
Vedantic thought (most particularly as expressed in the *Bhagavad Gita*) and
Sufi mysticism exerted the strongest influence on the Concord sages, with
Confucianism trailing a slow third. Familiarity with Buddhist traditions was
rare in America until the opening of Japan, and any notion of the actual
nature of Chinese or Japanese poetry had to wait on the translations of Waley
and Pound. Vedanta, because of its affinities with such transcendental ideas
as "the Oversoul," held an obvious appeal for Emerson and his circle. Possessed of strong religious inclinations but generally anticlerical views, they
appreciated the direct and ecstatic celebration of religious experience that
characterizes the Sufi tradition, particularly in the poetry it had inspired.
Confucianism was less attractive because of its worldliness and reflexive
appeal to traditional authority, but the transcendentalists approved of Confucianism's assumption of the goodness of men as a basis for a practical
morality.

The Oriental attitudes adopted by Emerson and Thoreau are apparent in
their poetry, but these ideas found a fuller and more appropriate expression
in their prose which is more original and distinctively American than their
poetry. Their Asian preoccupations had to wait for the revolutionary free
verse of Whitman's "Passage to India" and "Facing West from California
Shores" for a proper poetic context. His "Chanting the Square Deific"
manages, unlike a poem such as Emerson's "Brahma," to be a modern
religious poem without the slightest accommodation to Christian views.
The Hindu vision Whitman had absorbed through Emerson and the *Bhagavad-
gita* is also more appropriate to the organic form and radical personal vision
of *The Leaves of Grass* than the dominant Protestant culture of 19th century
America that he and the Concord Transcendentalists chafed against. It is
interesting that Emerson's *Essays*, Thoreau's *Walden*, and Whitman's
Leaves of Grass, works expressive of the most profound questions and aspirations of nineteenth-century American culture, have been recognized by
Asians as participating in their own traditions. Rabindranath Tagore declared
that "no American has caught the Oriental spirit so well as Whitman," and
Gandhi claimed Thoreau provided him with the intellectual link between
traditional Hindu thought and modern ideals of social justice.[6]

Columbia University Press, 1932). More recently Wong Kim-yuen of the University of
San Diego has done an exhaustive scholarly search of Emerson's Chinese sources, which
demonstrates even closer affinities between Emerson's idealism and Confucianism. ("A
Passage to Humanism: Chinese Influence on Emerson," an unpublished paper read at the
MLA Convention, San Francisco, December 29, 1979.)

[6]Carpenter, p. 250.

It is a commonplace of American literary study that the most characteristic attitudes of our culture (the Protestant ethic, for instance) have seldom
appealed to our best writers. Hawthorne's urbane skepticism, Melville's profound doubt, and Poe's morbidity account in part for their neglect in the
19th century, while the cheery tone of domesticated European Romanticism
adapted by America's fireside poets (Bryant, Whittier, Longfellow, Lowell
and Holmes) contributed to the inflation of their contemporary reputations
and their eventual relegation to the poetic dustbin of the elementary classroom curriculum. It is pessimism, both cultural and cosmic, that pervades
the finest literary productions of our abidingly optimistic culture. This
suggests, among other things, that the transplantation of European literary
culture to American soil was not an entirely happy move. The noteworthy
exceptions to this grim characterization of our most impressive writers are
Emerson, Thoreau and Whitman: all writers of a distinctly American stamp
and those most inspired by Asian thought. This comfortable combination
of Asian influence and affirmative American themes holds true through the
twentieth century in the works of our modern poetic masters, Pound and
Eliot, and is even more characteristic of contemporary poets. The pervasive
distress and Spenglerian pessimism of much of modern (that is early twentieth century) American poetry has roots in Europe, not Asia. Indeed, that
faint promise of hope that Eliot holds out for Western civilization toward the
end of *The Waste Land* is drawn less from the classic and Christian cultures
that he draws on in the earlier, gloomier sections of the poem, than from
the Buddha's "Fire Sermon" and the *Vedas*. The thunder that augers life-
giving rain rumbles in Sanskrit, "Datta, Dayadhvam, Damyatta," and the
benediction that ends the poem is "shantih," the formal closing of an *Upani-
shad*. Similarly, Pound's *Cantos* use Chinese history and Confucian ethics as
a means of clarifying and giving a hopeful perspective to his view of Western
values, particularly those of American founding fathers.

Eliot and Pound developed their interest in Asian culture at about the
same time, albeit quite independently. In 1911, while working on his doc-
torate at Harvard, Eliot undertook the study of Indic philology, learned
Sanskrit and studied Indian literature and philosophy for two years. At that
time in New England, Asian studies were still largely limited to India, but the
philosophy of the Asian subcontinent held at least as much fascination for
Eliot as it had earlier for Emerson, Thoreau and Whitman. The curious aspect
of Eliot's Asian interest is that after *The Waste Land* (and barring some
allusions to the Krishna of the *Bhagavad-gita* in *Four Quarters*) his later
work is relentlessly Christian and Western in its orientation, and this despite
his judgment in an essay on Dante that the *Bhagavad-gita* was "the next

greatest philosophical poem to the *Divine Comedy.*"[7] Perhaps the best explanation for this retreat can be found in a remark he made in a lecture delivered at the University of Virginia in 1933: "My only hope of really penetrating to the heart of that mystery," he confessed in an allusion to the 'inscrutable' East, "would lie in forgetting how to think and feel as an American or a European; which for practical as well as sentimental reasons I did not wish to do."[8] Shortly after delivering this lecture Eliot, who had been living in Europe for years, gave up his American citizenship. Other American poets have not been so timorous about "going Asiatic," and none that I know of have ceased being American. Indeed their various passages to India and other point East have inevitably led them ever deeper into the meaning of their homeland.

Imagism, the most significant movement in the development of modern American poetry after Transcendentalism, was accompanied and supported by the translations of Chinese and Japanese poetry by Pound and Amy Lowell. The publication of Pound's *Cathay* in 1915, prompted Eliot's claim that Pound was "the inventor of Chinese poetry for our time," a title that fairness decrees he must share with Arthur Waley.[9]

Like Emerson, Pound found in certain East Asian moral and aesthetic traditions just what he needed to support his own personal program for American poetry. From about 1910 to the time of his death Pound struggled to link Asian and European traditions in American poetry. His key critical statements on this effort are to be found in his "Vorticism" essay of 1914 and his probably wrong-headed but nevertheless influential reworking of Fenollosa's notes on the ideogramatic character of the Chinese written language as a medium for poetry, written a few years later. Wai-lin Yip has demonstrated how this controversial essay perfectly complements his 1913 manifesto, "A Few Don'ts by an Imagiste."[10] Even Pound's famous slogan "Make it New" derives from his understanding of the Confucian use of tradition as guide for the renewal of culture. In a similar fashion his fondness for the Confucian concept of the "rectification of names" provided a moral extension from his earlier admiration for the Flaubertian obsession with "*le mot juste*" as a corrective to the flabby, the sentimental, and the inexact in American poetry.

[7]"Dante," *Selected Essays of T. S. Eliot* (New York: Harcourt, Brace and World, 1964), p. 219.
[8]T. S. Eliot, *After Strange Gods: A Primer of Modern Heresy* (London: Faber and Faber, 1934), p. 41.
[9]The remark appears in his introduction to *Ezra Pound: Selected Poems*, ed. T. S. Eliot (London: Faber and Faber, 1928), p. 14.
[10]Wai-lim Yip, *Ezra Pound's Cathay* (Princeton: Princeton University Press, 1969), pp. 158-165.

Pound, like many American lyric poets, longed to write a long poem, an epic for the new world. His work with the Japanese No drama convinced him that a long, epic-like poem composed along imagistic lines was a real possibility if its themes were historic rather than merely personal and if images could be made to take on the significance of archetypes. Most of Pound's energy for original poetry after 1920 went into his *Cantos* where his constant concern was the achievement of the correct terms and images which would serve as a "vortex" around which each canto was to develop. In the late 1950's, a young student of Pound's work, Gary Snyder, began work on his book-length poem, *Mountains and Rivers without End*, drawing (probably quite independently) from No drama and the aesthetics of Zeami's *Kadensho* for both themes and an organizing principle. In these long and complex works, both Pound and Snyder are attempting to redefine the meaning of Western experience by reference to cultural and aesthetic ideas which they have drawn from Asia. I suspect that Chinese and Japanese scholars of American literature find the *Cantos* and *Mountains and Rivers without End* no easier to understand than American readers, despite their pervasive reference to East Asian traditions. This is, of course, because neither Pound nor Snyder are slavish borrowers of traditions but renewers and adapters of them to their own purposes. But China and Japan provided the catalyst to those purposes and so contributed to a distinctively American poetry.

Philip Rahv characterized those writers who continued to draw largely on European values and literary traditions for their themes and techniques as the "pale faces" of American literature.[11] Poets the likes of Taylor, Bryant, Longfellow, Whittier, Robinson, Eliot (for the most part), Ransom, Stevens, Robert Lowell, and Wilbur probably belong with this group. Writers who drew on, or attempted to create, a native tradition he called "red skins." Major poets in this tradition are Emerson, Thoreau, Whitman, Pound (to a considerable extent), Eliot (in part), Williams, Olson, Rexroth, Ginsberg and Snyder. These poets, the ground breakers and bearers of a distinctively American poetic tradition, like their American Indian namesake, have ties to Asia. Each succeeding literary generation from the Transcendentalists produced a movement of "red skins," with its own distinct sort of Asian encounter that almost invariably served as a means to develop peculiarly American themes in a consciously non-European, if not entirely convincing or authentic Asian, manner.

Although European influence has, of course, been more intense and continuous in the development of American poetry, the Asian influence has, in each poetic generation, offered vital options to the overwhelming presence

---

[11] Philip Rahv, "Paleface and Redskin," in *Image and Idea* (New York: New Directions, 1957), pp. 1-7.

of Western literary tradition.[12] The Asian impact on American poetry is
evident in the characteristic use of the image in lyric poetry since Pound, in
the treatment of history as process rather than end in epic material since
Whitman, and in diction and the poetics of the line in many kinds of contemporary poetry. Perhaps most importantly, Asian thought has provided an
alternative to themes rooted in the Judeo-Christian tradition for three
generations of American poets whose religious and philosophical impulses
could not be adequately expressed within the Western tradition.

The point which I am aiming at with this sketchy rehearsal of literary
history is that the figure that Asian influence has impressed on American
literature for over a century has not been stimulated by the discovery of an
entirely new realm of experience analogous to Keats' reading of Chapman's
Homer, much less any desire for the "exotic" as an escape from the burden
of one's own culture, but by motives quite the opposite of these. Escapism
(which we can see expressed in the Rimbaud quotation) and the rage for
Chinoiserie and the like were largely European phenomena. American poets
have been able to recognize their own deepest insights expressed in the Asian
literature and philosophy that attracted them. What links the Asian figure in
works as diverse as those of Whitman, Pound, and Snyder is that in each
instance their use of Asian sources advanced their development of authentic
personal or native American themes in directions clearly discernible before
they turned to Asia. Their use of Asian sources confirmed the direction of
their poetic experiments and lent substance and reference to their most
profound intuitions.

III[13]

No significant American poet has been more influenced by Asian culture
than Gary Snyder, and it is rare that any commentary on his poetry does
not consider his use of Asian sources. For the most part, however, such

---

[12] It should be noted, however, that even "paleface" poets have drawn on Asia, but
their use is characteristically limited to casual allusion or superficial exoticism. Such
poets usually come by their Asian sources at second- or third-hand, usually by way of
Europe. For instance, Wallace Stevens' Asian interest grew out of his enthusiasm for
the French symbolist poets whose interest in Asian culture has its own special history.
From as early as the eighteenth century, American poets have decorated their verses
with *Chinoiserie* and *Japanisme* drawn from the fashionable affectations of the European art world. This particular pattern of influence characterizes American poetry before
1850 and is little more than a shadow of similar allusive practices in British poetry from
the eighteenth century.

[13] In a slightly different form, section III of this essay appeared in the *Tamkang
Review*, X, 3 (Spring, 1980), pp. 369-383.

discussions are focused on Japan, particularly on the impact of Zen Buddhism. Since Snyder lived in Japan for nearly ten years, learned the language, studied as a Zen monk, and married a Japanese, the topic is irresistible. This firsthand use of Japanese culture separates Snyder from all but a few American poets.[14] Because Snyder's use of Japanese sources is not only familiar to his readers but rather particular to his own experience, his use of Chinese sources provides a more informative illustration of the characteristic ways in which American poets have used Asian material. Although Snyder is able to read classical Chinese better than Ezra Pound could, he has never visited Taiwan or China. Moreover, China has exerted a longer and probably more pervasive influence on American poetry than Japan has done. American poets have drawn on Chinese culture from Emerson's time to the present, but none (not even Pound) have done so more sensitively or knowledgeably than Snyder.

Chinese influence spans Snyder's entire literary career. In a draft of a long prose work dealing with Asian attitudes toward nature he describes his first encounter with Chinese poetry:

> I first came onto Chinese poems in translation at nineteen, when my ideal of nature was a 45° ice slope on a volcano, or an absolutely virgin rain-forest. They helped me to "see" fields, farms, tangles of brush, the azaleas in the back of an old brick apartment. They freed me from excessive attachment to wild mountains, with their almost subliminal way of presenting even the wildest hills as a place where people, also, live.[15]

as an example of what he means he provides his own translation of Wan Wei's "At Deer Hedge:"

> Empty mountains:
>   no one to be seen,
> Yet—hear—
>   human sounds and echoes.
> Returning sunlight
>   enters the dark woods:

---

[14] Other American poets who have drawn on firsthand experience with Japanese culture are Snyder's friends Kenneth Rexroth, Philip Whalen, and Allen Ginsberg, as well as four younger poets: Clayton Eshelmann, Richard Brautigan, John Tagliube, and Stephen Sandy.

[15] The quotation is from p. 54 of the typescript. Snyder calls this work-in-progress his "Hokkaido Book," and I shall use that title when referring to this TS hereafter.

Again shining
on green moss, above. [16]

Chinese poems of this man-integrated-in-a-natural-scene type, have provided
a tradition for Snyder's own poetic practice. Such poetry was, as I have
noted, unavailable in the West until Pound's *Cathay* poems and Waley's
translations appeared, except for those able to read classical Chinese, and no
Western poet could. Snyder first translated "At Deer Hedge" in 1953, while a
student in his early twenties at Berkeley, and the version I have just cited has
undergone considerable revision. [17] Some of the translations Snyder produced
at this time have been included in the major English language anthologies of
Chinese literature.

Snyder has, of course, expanded the range of his themes and developed a
wider variety of poetic modes since his Berkeley days in the early fifties, but
he has never abandoned the style and themes of his poetic apprenticeship. It
was during this period of his poetic career that the impact of classical Chinese
poetry on Snyder's work was most intense. The influence is particularly
evident in his use of monosyllabic diction and the peculiarly terse eliptical
phrasing of the poems in his first collection, *Riprap*. He is still given to omit-
ting articles and personal pronouns from his poems, a stylistic habit that
contributes to their detached, impersonal tone. Such omissions also blur

---

[16] "Hokkaido Book" p. 55.

[17] I have seen two other versions, both done over twenty years ago. The first of these
versions appeared in the *Phi Theta Annual*, Papers of the Oriental Language Honor
Society, vol. 5 (1954-5), p. 12. The second was collected by the late David Happell
Hsin-fu Wand and has never been published. (See his "Cathay Revisited: The Chinese
Tradition in the Poetry of Ezra Pound and Gary Snyder," Diss. University of Southern
California 1972, pp. 125-126.

      Empty, the mountain—
        not a man,
      Yet sounds, echoes,
        as of men talking.
      Shadows awing into the forest.
      Swift light
        flashes
      On dark moss, above.   1953
        * * *

      Empty the mountains
        not a man;
      Yet sounds, echoes
        as of men speaking.
      Returning shadows enter the
        dark woods;
      Again flashing
        on green moss, above.   1958

grammatical distinctions between his subjects and his objects. Just as in Chinese poetry (and the Wang Wei poem cited above may serve as an example), the effect this creates in Snyder's nature poetry is to merge man and his natural setting. [18] Many commentators have noted (and Snyder has acknowledged) the considerable influence of the five and seven syllable *shih* on the *Riprap* poems, most of which were written during his Berkeley period. *Myths and Texts*, his first long-sequence poem, was also being composed then, and it contains more allusions to Chinese history, mythology, philosophy, and painting as well as poetry than any of his books since then. The prose he was writing around this time, and since collected in *Earth House Hold*, also reveals his Chinese interests. The book contains a lively translation of the ninth-century Ch'an master, Po-chang Huai-hai, occasional references to his Chinese studies in journal entries, and frequent Chinese allusions in the essays. In short, then, Snyder's poetic apprenticeship may have been as much to Chinese poetry as it was to his American mentors: Pound, Williams, Jeffers, and Rexroth.

It might be argued that the Chinese influence on Snyder's later collections of short lyrics and those sections of *Mountains and Rivers without End* (the long poetic sequence he began after *Myths and Texts* was completed) that have been published, as well as his recent prose is nearly as pervasive as it was in *Riprap*, *Myths and Texts*, and *Earth House Hold*. But this influence is not nearly so evident because it has been absorbed so completely into his own poetic style.

Snyder moved to Japan in the mid-fifties to undertake formal Zen training. The decade or so he lived in Kyoto was spent in consciously deepening his awareness of the spiritual qualities he had earlier sensed living in the wilderness areas of the Pacific Northwest. Living in a modern Asian society while immersed in the study of its traditional culture afforded Snyder a splendid perspective from which to view the shortcomings as well as the possibilities of American life. His social concern and awareness matured, and this development is reflected in all his books after *Riprap*. Snyder pictures the modern societies of India, Japan, and China as every bit as burdensome to the social, personal and spiritual development of human beings as he does American society. For models of good social organization he reaches back to the prehistoric. "As a poet," he claims in a frequently quoted remark, "I hold the most archaic values on earth. They go back to the late Paleolithic; the fertility

---

[18] Consider the grammar of his slight, haiku-like poem called "Hiking in the Totsugawa Gorge" in *Regarding Wave* (New York: New Directions, 1970), p. 74:

    pissing
    watching
    a waterfall

of the soil, the magic of animals, the power vision in solitude, the terrifying
initiation and rebirth; the love and ecstasy of the dance, the common work of
the tribe."[19] He advocates that modern societies reconsider their earliest
common values, a heritage shared by Oriental as well as Occidental cultures
before neolithic tribalism gave way to monolithic civilizations. For this reason
Snyder's readers are likely to find few references to Chinese culture after the
T'ang dynasty.

Before turning to some specific examples of Chinese influence on Snyder's
writing I would like to comment on the rather Chinese nature of his character
which may account in some way for the influence that Chinese culture has
had on his work. In an interesting note, Wai-lim Yip reported that Snyder
thinks of himself as "Chinese in temperament,"[20] and a number of commentators have remarked on those aspects of his character that have a Taoist
cast: his nature mysticism, his spontaneous sense of fun, the informality of
his manners and dress, and the apprehension with which he views large
governing bureaucracies on both the left and right of the political spectrum.
But there is a Confucian side to his character most of these commentators
have missed. I suspect it has always been a part of his nature, but it has
become more clearly evident in recent years.

Although Snyder is a Buddhist, his conception of the Buddha Dharma is
remarkably similar to the Confucian doctrine of *hsiu chi chih p'ing* (the
development of society leading from the development of the self).[21] The
three traditional aspects of the Dharma path are *dhyana* (meditation),
prajna (wisdom) and *sila* (morality). Snyder, drawing on Hui-Neng's *Plat-
form Sutra*, views meditation and wisdom (that is, in Snyder's words, the
wisdom "that lies beneath one's ego driven anxieties and aggressions") as
occurring simultaneously and leading naturally to morality, which he describes as expressing the private insights achieved by meditation "through
personal example and responsible action, ultimately toward the true community (*sangha*) of all beings."[22] This movement from the examination of
the self to the exercise of social wisdom is clearly reflected in the development of Snyder's writing which has moved from the still, almost purely
meditative lyrics of *Riprap* to the celebration of the human family as a vital
part of a broad network of relationships linking all forms of life in *Regarding
Wave*, and to the eco-political poems and essays in *Turtle Island* which

[19]This remark is quoted on the back cover of *Earth House Hold.*

[20]Wai-lim Yip, "Classical Chinese and Modern Anglo-American Poetry: Convergence
of Language and Poetry," *Comparative Literature Studies*, XI, I (March, 1974), p. 47.

[21]This point was first made by Yao-fu Lin, "The Mountains Are Your Mind": Orientalism in the Poetry of Gary Snyder," *Tamkang Review*, VI, 2 (Oct., 1975), p. 360.

[22]*Earth House Hold*, p. 92.

contain his most didactic poetry. It is significant in this regard that over the last few years Snyder's didactic impulses have provoked a larger proportion of prose (which he calls "plain talk") to poetry than at any other stage of his writing career. And the title of his most recent collection of essays, *The Old Ways*, has a particularly Confucian ring. Most of the essays in this book deal with the renewal and imaginative application of man's "most archaic values" to modern American life which is, of course, the Confucian approach to maintaining social values. In an as yet uncollected essay, "Poetry, Community and Climax"[23] Snyder links the functions of poetry in society (to redeem the past, support a healthy present, and provide for a fertile future) to that of duff and detritus in climax forest ecology. While it is unlikely Confucius would have drawn such a comparison, this is indeed the way he thought music and poetry should figure in society.

In an interview conducted in 1967, Snyder observed that "Confucius said, as well as Plato, that as soon as you change the mode of music you change the government, that politics and music are related." When the interviewer pointed out that "Plato was for kicking all musicians out," Snyder remarked that "Confucius was all for bringing poets into government and letting them run it. He said that the study of poetry teaches you the names of flowers and trees and animals, then it gives you a proper sense of decorum, and thirdly it trains your character, so that people who know poetry can be good governors." Snyder went on to say (and, it appears to me, approvingly) that "the ideal in the Confucian government is that when everything is running smoothly, government consists of rites and music—the only important bureau is the bureau of rites."[24]

In the last few years Snyder has begun to exercise his Confucian responsibilities as a poet in society. He has become a leader in the community where he has settled, particularly in matters touching education and land use. Some of his most recent poetry draws on his experience working with government bureaucracy and his friendship with the former governor of California. In these poems are conscious echoes of such Confucian themes as thoughts of home while away on official business and the poet as the "reminder" to government. Both themes are treated in the Chinese manner in a recent uncollected poem "Talking Late with the Governor About the Budget:"[25]

[23] It has been published in *Field*, 20 (Spring, 1979), pp. 21-26.

[24] "Conversation between Gary Snyder and Dom Aelred Graham at the Snyders' home in Kyoto, September 4, 1967," in Graham's *Conversations: Christian and Buddhist* (New York: Harcourt, Brace and World, 1968), pp. 55-56.

[25] The poem has been published in *The Ohio Review*, XVIII, 3 (Fall, 1977), p. 106.

Entering the midnight
Halls of the capitol,
Iron carts full of printed bills
Filling life with rules.

At the end of many chambers
Alone in a large tan room
The Governor sits, without dinner,
Scanning the hills of laws—budgets—codes—
In this land of twenty million
From desert to ocean.

Til the oil runs out
There's no end in sight.

Outside, his car waits with driver
Alone, idling.
The great pines on then Capitol grounds
are less than a century old.

We walk to the street
Tired of the effort
Of thinking about "the people."
The half-moon travels west
In the elegant company
Of Jupiter and Aldebaran.

And east, over the Sierra,
Far flashes of lightning—
Is it raining tonight at home?

I do not wish to suggest that Snyder has abandoned the Taoist values of his early life and work in favor of a Confucian stance; it is simply a new and utterly appropriate development. He is, after all, past fifty. Confucianism figures in Snyder's life much as it does in the life of a traditional Chinese: Taoism for the private life, Confucianism for social living. Did Wang Wei or any of the other T'ang poets whose work Snyder admires find any difficulty in mixing Confucianism with Taoism or, for that matter, mixing both sets of values with Buddhism. A touch of coherent syncretism is not only a sign of sophistication but an indication of true maturity.

Chinese influence can be seen in almost every aspect of Snyder's work: most obviously in his translations, discursive essays, and literary allusions, less obviously in the themes and techniques of his poetry. I will conclude this essay by considering his use of Chinese sources in just this order: from the most obvious to the least.

Snyder's Chinese translations are all from the Buddhist tradition of the T'ang Dynasty. His only prose translation, "Record of the Life of the Ch'an Master Po-chang" was done while he was living in Japan, and the poems all date back to his Berkeley days. Indeed, his translations of poems by Wang Wei, Wei Ying-wu, Meng Hao-jen, and Liu Tsung-yuan were among the first tasks he undertook as a poet. That some were published in multiple versions may even indicate that back then Snyder was still uncertain of his own style. By the time he turned to Han Shan, however, his hand was sure. He once told Wai-lim Yip that the 'images in the Han Shan poems (in the original) were practically his own.'[26] And it is not only the clear images but the extreme terseness and colloquial language that characterize Han Shan's style and that we see reflected in Snyder's original *Riprap* poems.

Of the three hundred or so Han Shan poems extant, Snyder chose only those that express the T'ang recluse's joyous rejection of the civilized world of "boiling red dust" in favor of the purity of "Cold Mountain." In doing this Snyder has created a thematic rapport to complement the stylistic rapport that already existed between himself and Han Shan. Unlike Arthur Waley or Burton Watson, he translates none of the poems wherein Han Shan recalls his early life as a poor scholar or the wife, family, and farm he had to leave behind when he chose to live on the mountain. Instead of attempting a comprehensive sampling of Han Shan's poetry, Snyder arranged a thematically coherent sequence of twenty-four poems that begins with an introduction to the mountain and its physical difficulties and leads to a celebration of the beauty, freedom, and spiritual insight that living on the mountain bring. It ends with an invitation for the reader to try this way of life. One critic has called Snyder's *Cold Mountain Poems* "A kind of Zen Walden Pond," which suggests my general point about the use of Asian sources in American poetry; when serious American poets draw on Asian material it is usually to bring them closer to expressing an American experience.[27] Snyder has published little in the way of translation in recent years, but in light of his developing Confucianism it should come as no surprise that he hopes some day to translate Tu Fu.

Snyder's most allusive poem is *Myths and Texts*, and a good many of its allusions are to Chinese sources. So recondite are some of the references in this poem it has provoked a pamphlet of helpful notes similar to those T. S. Eliot's publisher insisted he appended to *The Waste Land*, a poem

---

[26] Yip, "Classical and Modern Anglo-American Poetry," p. 47.

[27] Herbert J. Fackler, "Three Versions of Han-Shan's Cold Mountain Poems," *Literature East and West*, XV, 2 (Fall, 1973), p. 274.

which may have provided Snyder with a structural model for his own long work.[28] *Myths and Texts* has, naturally enough, invited the attention of Ph.D. dissertation writers as no other work of Snyder's has, and this is no place to add to their learned elucidations. For those unfamiliar with the work, suffice it to say that it is made up of forty-eight poems arranged in three sections. "Logging" is concerned with the destruction of forests and the attitudes responsible for the loss of wilderness; "Hunting" celebrates the shaman-like rapport that primitive hunters established with their prey and explores man's relationships with the animal world; and "Burning" transforms the insights of wildlife ecology into a myth of human rebirth. The "texts" of the poem deal directly with the sensual perception of the phenomenal world; the "myths" develop out of these "texts" and provide symbolic descriptions of the mind's nature. Wai-lim Yip maintains that the "non-metaphoric, non-symbolic" textual portions of *Myths and Texts* are very close to Wan Wei's poetic method.[29] And the mythic sections are rich in Chinese allusions. The last stanza of the final poem of the "Logging" section may serve to illustrate Snyder's allusive method at its most direct and accessible:

> Pine sleeps, cedar splits straight
> Flowers crack the pavement.
>   Pa-ta Shan-jen
> (A painter who watched Ming fall)
>   lived in a tree:
> "The brush
> May paint the mountains and streams
> Though the territory is lost."

The stanza suggests that the damage man has done to nature and himself may be repaired after the manner of the great Ch'an painter, Pa-ta Shan-jen, much as Snyder himself is attempting with *Myths and Texts*.[30] In this allusion the speaker is clearly identified and his connection with logging established.

But other Chinese allusions in *Myths and Texts* are more complex and subtle. The opening stanza of the seventh poem in the "Burning" section

---

[28] Howard McCord, *Some Notes to Gary Snyder's Myths and Texts*, (Berkeley: The Tribal Press, 1971).

[29] In his *Hiding the Universe, Poems by Wang Wei* (New York: Grossman, 1972), p. 3.

[30] Yao-fu Lin takes this to be the ultimate value of Snyder's poetry: "Snyder's poetry, with its program for recreating the wilderness in the mind, is finally a poetry for human survival." Lin, p. 389.

links two seemingly disparate allusions within a poetic context which is itself none too clear:

> Face in the crook of her neck
>   felt throb of vein
> Smooth skin, her cool breasts
> All naked in the dawn
>   "byrdes
> sing forth from every bough"
>   where are they now
> And dreamt I saw the Duke of Chou

The quotation is from Marlowe's "Elegy," and it was Confucius who worried if he did not dream regularly of the exemplary Duke of Chou. The East-West cultural nexus is further complicated by the fact that the Marlowe passage is itself a translation of Ovid's *Amores*, and the allusion to Confucius' mythic model of the ideal statesman is transferred to the persona of *Myths and Texts*. While I cannot claim with any confidence that I understand this stretch of allusive writing (Snyder has not yet collected as many useful explicators as Eliot or Pound), it seems to be expressing an aspect of the old courtly love theme from medieval romance, truly to love a woman heightens man's sensitivities and ennobles his aspirations. At the very least, this interpretation is consonant with the themes of transcience (an Asian theme) and transformation (a Western theme) that run through the "Burning" section.[31]

Many of Snyder's Chinese allusions are tied to Western allusions as in the passage just cited, but all of them are, at least, implicitly connected to an American theme or setting. In the sixth poem of the "Burning" section, for instance, Snyder describes himself meditating on a famous Ch'an *koan*. The setting is probably a mountain fire lookout in one of the national parks of the the Pacific Northwest:

> March wind
>   blows the bright dawn
>   apricot blossoms down.
>   salty bacon smoking on the stove
>   (sitting on Chao-chou's *wu*
>   my feet sleep)

---

[31]See Bert Almon's "The Imagination of Gary Snyder" Diss. University of New Mexico 1971) pp. 208-268 for the most careful working out of Snyder's Asian references in *Myths and Texts*.

The apricot image here probably refers to the blossoms in Pound's "Canto XIII":

> The blossoms of the apricot
> "Blow from the East to the West,
> And I have tried to keep them from falling.

which is itself an allusion to Confucius' definition of his role as a preserver of culture. The flower of Chinese culture, Snyder subtly suggests, is settling in North America. The thirteenth poem of this section, which deals with the transforming vision that comes with Buddhist enlightenment, is among *Myths and Texts* most complex with its abrupt shifts of reference and setting. Its conclusion

> it was nothing special
> misty rain on Mt. Baker,
> Neah Bay at low tide.

is a trans-pacific poetic echo of an old Chinese poem. Snyder's friend, Alan Watts, writes that this poem is often used to suggest the *wu-shih* ("nothing special") nature of *satori*:[32]

> Mount Lu in misty rain; the River Che at high tide.
> When I had not been there, no rest from the pain of longing!
> I went there and returned. . . . It was nothing special:
> Mount Lu in misty rain; the River Che at high tide.

In all these allusions the general purpose is to thicken the poem's texture and enrich its mythical context by linking culturally disjunct parts of human experience. More particularly, Snyder has transported a number of images from Chinese culture to a North American setting where they function to comment on and clarify the American experience with its landscape and relate that experience to the nature of our minds and sensibilities.

Such allusiveness in the Pound-Eliot (and, one might add, Chinese) tradition tends to occur less frequently in Snyder's poetry after *Myths and Texts*. In his later work Asian attitudes and images tend to be incorporated into the overall fabric of his poems rather than expressed in discrete references. *Myths and Texts* was written while Snyder was a young student of Chinese culture.

[32] *The Way of Zen*, (New York: New American Library, 1957) pp. 126. I am indebted to Bert Almon's dissertation for this reference.

Poems written after 1958 deal with an Asian experience that has been absorbed and integrated into his character and is expressed with much less learned self-consciousness. To illustrate this less self-conscious use of Chinese sources, I will conclude this paper with a short discussion of that aspect of the Chinese imagination which has had the longest influence on Snyder's poetry but which has received very little consideration anywhere: Chinese landscape paintings.

In Snyder's unfinished book dealing with East Asian attitudes toward nature that I drew on earlier, he describes his introduction to Chinese culture in this way:

> The Cascades of Washington, and the Olympics, are wet, rugged, densely forested mountains that are hidden in cloud and mist much of the year. When I was a boy of nine or ten I was taken to the Seattle Art Museum, and was struck more by Chinese landscape paintings than anything I'd seen before, or maybe since. I saw first that they looked like real mountains, and mountains of an order close to my heart; second that they were different mountains of another place and true to those mountains as well; and third that they were mountains of the spirit and that these paintings pierced into another reality which both was and was not the same reality as "the mountains."
>
> That seed lodged in my store-house-consciousness to be watered later when I first read Arthur Waley's translations of Chinese poetry and then Ezra Pound's. I thought, here is a high civilization that has managed to keep in tune with nature. The philosophical and religious writings I later read from Chinese seemed to back this up. I even thought for a time that simply because China had not been Christian, and had been spared an ideology which separated humankind from all other living beings (with the two categories of redeemable and unredeemable) that it naturally had an organic, process-oriented view of the world. [33]

Further on in this typescript Snyder devotes six pages to elaborating upon what he has seen in Chinese landscape painting and what this has meant to him. He admires the ways in which the T'ang landscapes "are still half-tied to journeys, topographies or poems" and then how "with the Sung they opened out to great space: with the rock formations, plants and trees, seasons, ways of appearance and disappearance . . . [and how] vast scenes . . . become visionary timeless lands of mountain rocks and air-mist-breath and far calm vistas; in which people are small, but lovingly rendered, doing

[33] "Hokkaido Book," pp. 20-21.

righteous tasks, or reclining and enjoying their world." Of particular interest
to him are those Sung "Streams and Mountains without End" painters who

> didn't always walk the hills they portrayed. With a known vocabu-
> lary of forms and the freedom of the brush they could invent moun-
> tains that ... seemed to float in mist. But the life is what counts:
> this vision of earth surface as organism, in which water, cloud, rock,
> and plant growth all stream through each other.

He describes the mountains and rivers of the Sung dynasty painters as "magical and difficult, the routes are not clear. Yet they are passable." His description of post-Yuan painting might just as well serve as a description of his own
mission as a poet:

> For post-Yuan China, people living more in cities and farther from
> the hills, painting kept love of nature alive, but it came to be paint-
> ings done by people who had never walked the wild, for people who
> would never see it. Still, Wang Hui's "Landscape in the Style of
> Chu-jan and Yen Wen-Kuei" (1715) does one more turn, it draws
> out to sea at the end, where the sea-fog is twisting into scrolls that
> take us back to the very beginning. Fine. Mountains were meant to
> be deeply entered, on foot, where the naked energy can be touched
> anew.[34]

Snyder's most ambitious work to date is the book-length poem *Mountains and Rivers without End*, of which only seven sections have been published entire and only portions of other sections, in all, about sixty pages so
far. This work draws technical and thematic inspiration as well as its title
from Chinese horizontal landscape scrolls. In an interview he gave in 1964,
Snyder discussed the poem as an exploration of the landscape of consciousness; "more and more," he said, "I am aware of the very close correspondence between the external and internal landscape in my long poem ... I'm
dealing with these correspondences, moving back and forth."[35] Each section
of this poem, like each section of a Chinese landscape scroll, is a point in a
journey that unfolds inward and outward as well as onward. Occasionally
small descriptive details in *Mountains and Rivers without End* are rendered
as if the poet were aspiring to be a painter.

---

[34] "Hokkaido Book," pp. 59-64.
[35] Gene Fowler, "Interview with Gary Snyder," *Literary Times* (Chicago), IV, 2
(December, 1964), p. 7.

> Snow on the pines & firs around Lake Shasta
> —Chinese scene of winter hills & trees
> us "little travellers" in the bitter cold

Many of Snyder's short lyrics also show deft touches of Sung-like land-scape technique. "After Work" (from the "Far West" section of *The Back Country*) opens with an image of a small human dwelling adrift and obscured in an amorphous expanse of space after the principle of *hsu shis*, or vacant space punctuated by objects:

> The Shack and a few trees
> float in the blowing fog

Particularly in Snyder's nature poems it is clear that he is following what Wai-lim Yip has called "the age-old aesthetic in which the self easily dissolves into undifferentiated existence."[36] Fine early examples of this ego-dissolving aesthetic are "Mid-August at Sourdough Mountain Lookout" and "Piute Creek" from *Riprap*. Seeing clearly is central to Snyder's life and work, and his way of seeing has been splendidly conditioned by Chinese painting and Ch'an meditation. The vision of these poems is unobscured by any sort of elaborate poetic figure. There are no metaphors, the diction is notably simple and monosyllabic, and the images are concrete and clear. Even the natural world these poems evoke is spare and elemental when contrasted to sublime or picturesque landscapes favored by poets in the Western Romantic tradi-tion. The speaker in the landscapes of these poems is so utterly at home and so clearly absorbed in and by nature that his ego falls away and he is literally one with what he views, like the small people who figure as a part of the land-scape in Chinese painting. So involved in his setting is the speaker of "Sour-dough Mountain Lookout" that he can recall neither books nor friends as he looks "down for miles/Through high still air." Without the impediment of ego and the meanings it insists on, the figure who moves through the land-scape of "Piute Creek" becomes sharply aware of the fact that seeing is reciprocal in a world where stone, juniper, cougar, coyote, and poet are referred to as "we":

> A clear, attentive mind
> Has no meaning but that
> Which sees is truly seen.
> No one loves rock, yet we are here.

[36]Yip, "Classical and Anglo-American Poetry," p. 21.

> Night chills. A flick
> In the moonlight
> Slips into juniper shadow:
> Back there unseen
> Cold proud eyes
> of cougar or coyote
> Watch me rise and go.

A good example of painterly vision exercised in a recent poem is "Straight"-Creek–Great Burn" from *Turtle Island*. After five stanzas of stunning description of the transformations of spring on the landscape without once mentioning any observers, we suddenly come upon them much as viewers come upon figures as they unroll a landscape scroll:

> us resting on dry fern and
>   watching

Their "resting" and "watching," the principal occupations of the people who figure in Chinese landscape, focuses our attention on the scene:

> A whoosh of birds
> swoops up and round
> tilts back
> almost always flying all apart
> and yet hangs on!
> together;
>
> never a leader,
> all of one swift
>
> empty
> dancing mind.
>
> They arc and loop & then
> their flight is done.
> they settle down
> end of poem.

The last line of this poem functions in much the same way as the wooden rod that marks the end of a Chinese horizontal scroll painting. Both announce the completion of a work of art. Here, as in much of his work, Snyder has borrowed and transformed an aesthetic idea from China to deal with the American landscape. And, as with other American poets who have turned East for inspiration, the Asian influence has enabled him to see that landscape better and to express it more effectively.

San Diego State University

V

ART EAST AND WEST

PORTRAITURE IN THE WEST AND THE EAST

Robert E. Fisher

Portraiture has long been a popular art form in the Western world. Such famous artists as Rembrandt created images that not only captured the likeness but also penetrated appearances to reveal something of the inner state of that individual. With the coming of photography the art of the painted and sculptured portrait declined in favor of the more rapid and less expensive new medium, but the popularity of portraiture continued to grow. Today, most Westerners consider portraiture one of their major art forms and have come to expect a high degree of objective accuracy in such a work. In East Asia portraiture has also enjoyed a long and successful history, though different from the West in several fundamental respects. In China and Japan the portrait never achieved the same lofty stature among the various art forms as it did in the West. Generally, East Asian portraits were less realistic and more idealized than their Western counterparts, and the making of a portrait was a branch of figure painting, not to be regarded as highly as landscape painting or the making of religious images. This popularly-held belief that Western portraits are more "realistic" while those of the Orient are more "idealistic" is generally valid, but not without some important qualifications. A study of the traditions of each reveals that a considerable amount of Western portraiture is made up of established formulae while some East Asian examples (especially Japanese) can lay claim to as much "realism" as is generally found in the West. By dividing Western portraiture into a few main categories and then comparing those with evidence from the East one may come to realize that East and West may not be as far apart as they seem.

I

Portraiture has been a part of the Western artistic tradition at least as far back as the Egyptians. By the third millennium B.C. Egyptians were creating images of individuals for use in tombs, and though not accurate portrayals of a specific person they did carry a degree of verism that enables museum visitors today to recognize something of a personality-type and frequently tell the differences among the groups of images.[1] Not until the Age of Akhenaten (1370-1352 B.C.) could a true likeness be claimed, and this was but a brief break in an otherwise continuous flow of idealized images. Sometime after the fourth or third century B.C., perhaps because of the Greeks' curiosity and search for perfection, portraits began to appear that did show a concern with individuality. The Greeks even went so far as to utilize actual casts from living people,[2] but the Romans remain the primary source for most of our knowledge of ancient portraiture. Their portraits often achieve a remarkable degree of realism, even by today's standards (see Figure 1). This marble head from around 100 A.D. is typical of many that remain from a culture greatly interested in realistic portraiture, primarily as ancestor portraits, to a degree not found again for nearly a thousand years. From the fall of Rome through the Gothic period, portraiture ceased its Roman realism, preferring instead an idealized type that has more in common with its contemporary Byzantine neighbors to the east and to Egyptian art before. Indeed, realistic portraiture seems to be the preferred mode of representation the more secular the culture. Medieval and Gothic Europe, dominated by the Church, produced no realistic portraits. That remained for the humanists of the Renaissance, and by the sixteenth century portraiture had truly come into its own, led by the Venetian masters who used color, shading, and dramatic light to set the foundation or modern portraiture in the West. By the late eighteenth century, building on the descriptive brilliance of such portrait masters as Rembrandt, some artists began to probe deeper into the character of the subject. Psychologically powerful studies, at times disturbing and frightening in their revelations of one's hidden nature, added a new dimension to portraiture. Goya and later van Gogh are among the best known of many artists interested in taking the portrait well below surface realism and into the depths of one's soul. Other portrait masters, such as Daumier, used the art form for satirical effect. The invention of the camera in the early nineteenth century, though seriously reducing the demand for traditional portraiture, did increase its overall popularity by greatly simplifying the process. Today, portraiture is alive and well. The photo-realist school has generated a renewed interest, even to the extent of emulating the Hellenistic Greeks by utilizing moulds taken from real people to create statues of startling veracity.

---

[1] The subject of verism in ancient art has been reviewed by *The Journal of Roman Studies*, XLV (1955).

[2] T. B. L. Webster, *The Art of Greece: The Age of Hellenism* (New York: Crown Publishers, 1966), p. 184.

Figure 1. Portrait Head of a Man.
Italy, Roman, ca 100 A.D. The Cleveland Museum of Art. Gift from J. H. Wade.

In this long development, several categories of portraiture can be found. These four divisions, comprising the main themes of Western portraiture, will be the basis for a comparison with portraiture in the Far East.

The first category includes portraiture that is idealized or, more correctly, mostly idealized. This would include the Egyptian portraits, most Greek examples, medieval works, and any portrait that emphasizes a type rather than a specific individual. By far the greatest number of Western portraits fall into this category. It would appear that many portraits, even after the sixteenth century, that appear at first glance to be realistic are actually idealized, emphasizing character of a general sort but not one specific individual. Some artists mix the two in one work, such as Lorenzo Lotto, who portrays an idealized Virgin and Child in one part of a painting with devoted donors, rendered somewhat realistically, looking on from the other side of the scene.[3] Even though there is a tendency toward greater realism after the sixteenth century, much of the old idealization is maintained in the conventions of pose, gesture, gaze, and dress that play a major part in Western portraiture.

A second category, and the one most often considered typical of the Western tradition, is realistic or nearly realistic portraiture. Beginning at least as early as Imperial Rome (see Figure 1) and coinciding with the secularization of society, this tradition portrays the individual as he actually looks. Some of the finest examples come from the work of Dutch painters. Indeed, the northern European tradition favored realistic portrayals, in greater detail, than their Italian counterparts as early as the fifteenth century, and few portrait artists can exceed the often penetrating studies of Rembrandt. This realism became an inner realism in the nineteenth and twentieth centuries as artists such as van Gogh and Munch sought to reveal the inner reality beyond the surface. The development of Freudian psychology suggested new directions for portrait artists, and today many viewers have come to expect a portrait to reveal the "real" person as much as how he looks.

The third category of portraiture in the West includes satire, humor, and caricature. Though less common than either of the other categories, humorous portraiture has a long history in the West. Classical Greece indulged in this artistic form, but not until the Renaissance did it become more widespread. Leonardo da Vinci and Hieronymous Bosch have left studies of heads much too distorted to be mere realistic portraits. From the seventeenth century, politicians and Popes, rich and poor are frequently presented in humorous guise, and political cartoonists today actively carry on one of the most interesting traditions of portraiture in the Western world. So powerful

---

[3] T. Pignatti, *The Golden Century of Venetian Painting* (Los Angeles: Los Angeles County Museum of Art, 1979), p. 67.

has this tradition become that certain public figures, such as Richard Nixon or Ayatollah Khomeini, are remembered as much in caricatured form as they are in reality.

The last category is the self-portrait. This tradition is less well documented and would be a topic worthy of further research. There are examples from the Gothic era, including instances of the artist's putting his image (idealized, of course) into the corner of a stained glass window he created for a church.[4] The pivotal sixteenth century witnessed considerable popularity in self-portraits and dramatic examples from such Venetian masters as Titian remain unexcelled in artistic quality: "In the entire history of art few self-portraits can equal this one in the expression of the dignity of the artistic profession and the transcience of the artist himself."[5] During the nineteenth and into the twentieth century the popularity of self-portraits would almost seem to be a barometer of the growing independence and confidence of the artist, so many were done. Certain artists, such as van Gogh and Rembrandt, are remembered today for their penetrating self-portraits, and artists continue to pursue this type as both a form of expression and self-awareness.

III

Portraiture in the Far East includes works from three separate areas: China, Korea, and Japan, and their differences are sometimes greater than the variations in portraiture between major European countries such as France and Germany. However, the vast number of works lost over time has reduced the available material, and the influences that crossed borders, especially from China, makes it difficult to discuss one part only. The increased realism among some Japanese works does tend to set them apart, but the overall picture indicates associations between China and Japan despite the lack of artistic remains from the Chinese side. It is often difficult to treat East Asia as one unit, but in this study, where the comparison between East and West is the prime objective, the Asian areas will generally be considered as one cultural sphere.

In China, references to portrait painting are frequent by around 100 B.C. and the literature tells of generals and court beauties regularly painted upon imperial order.[6] The recently excavated silk banner from the Ma-Wang-tui

---

[4] *Encyclopedia of World Art* (London: McGraw-Hill Book Co., 1966), Vol. XIII, plate 160.

[5] Pignatti, p. 78.

[6] Soame Jenyns, *A Background to Chinese Painting* (New York: Schocken Books, 1966), p. 144.

tomb, Hunan Province,[7] of the Han Dynasty, may well include a portrait
of the deceased. With the coming of Buddhism the demand for figural art
increased and many of the beliefs that became basic to subsequent portraiture
in China were established, especially by the fourth and fifth centuries. From
late Han well into the Six Dynasties era there is ample evidence of a strong
interest in individual personality, often revealed by one's physiognomy, and
portraits from this time stressed such traits:

> Hsi K'ang (223-262 A.D.) . . . , was described by his Bamboo Grove
> colleague, Shan Tao (205-283 A.D.) as "lofty, like rocks piled on
> high, like the independence of a solitary pine. In his drunkenness he
> is rumbling, crumbling, like a mountain of jade about to fall." [8]

The culture of fourth- and fifth-century China, politically chaotic, was
nevertheless full of independent, eccentric individuals, and shows a remarkable shift from the Confucian conformity of the previous Han period. By the
fourth century Chinese artists were creating portraiture with a degree of
observation but failed to capture the subject's actual appearance, and these
means of expression formed the foundation for most of the rest of the history of Chinese portraiture. No actual paintings of portraits remain from
this era, only copies in other media, such as engraved stones or clay bricks.
It would appear, however, that what the Chinese considered "individual"
would be classified in Western terms as character studies or somewhat idealized. Certainly the evidence indicates less realism than the Roman portraits
of roughly the same date. The Chinese were more interested in portraying
something of the individual's nature in traits like thoughtfulness or alert-
ness, and this remains as the prime goal in subsequent portraiture. It is
interesting that this effort to capture the essential nature of the subject
becomes a dominant element in Western portraiture rather late, with artists
such as Goya in the late eighteenth century. The fifteenth century portrait
by Tu Chin, "The Poet Lin Pu Wandering in the Moonlight" (see Figure 2)
shows these ideals, telling us more about the poet's nature (serious, lost in
the process of creation, feeling for nature), than how he may have actually
appeared. These ideals, well formulated by the fifth century, were to remain
the guiding force throughout the next thousand years, until the influence
of Western portraiture began to alter them in the sixteenth century. Famous

---

[7] Fong Chow, "Ma-wang-tui: A Treasure-trove from the Western Han Dynasty,"
Artibus Asiae, Vol. XXV, 1/2 (1973), pp. 5-24.

[8] E. J. Liang, "Neo-Taoism and the Seven Sages of the Bamboo Grove in Chinese
Painting," *Artibus Asiae*, Vol. XXXVI, 1/2 (1974), p. 7.

Figure 2. The Poet Lin Pu Wandering in the Moonlight.
Tu Chin, active ca. 1465-ca. 1509, Chinese, Ming Dynasty, hanging scroll.
The Cleveland Museum of Art. Purchase, John L. Severance Fund.

artists, such as Wu Tao-Tzu in the T'ang or Li Lung-mien in the Sung Dynasty, built reputations for their brilliance as portrait painters, but this was
more for brush virtuosity than for any basic change in the manner of characterization established in the Six Dynasties period. A fourteenth century
author, critical of some people's preference for mere copying of a person's
likeness, summarizes the general Chinese view toward portraiture:

> In painting, figures are the most difficult to render skillfully, for if
> they are restricted by form-likeness and placing arrangement, they
> will miss in spirit consonance and take form-likeness as the standard.
> They do not know that ancient people regarded form-likeness as
> least in ranking. In the case of Li Kung-lin [Li Lung-mien], who
> was the only master after Wu Tao-Tzu, he was not troubled by
> lapses in form-likeness, for his marvelous quality lies in brushwork,
> spirit consonance, and expression. Form-likeness came last.[9]

The one major deviation from this pattern prior to the influence of Western realism was the use of portraits by the Ch'an sect of Chinese Buddhism.
These were much closer to visual reality because of their unique role in portraiture. These paintings of the master were given to each monk who had
attained enlightenment and testified to the close personal relationship between the teacher and student. There seems little doubt that the best of these
portraits surpassed any known Chinese secular portraits in terms of physical
likeness.[10]

In the case of Japan, most of the same values held by the Chinese were
adopted. The Japanese, who have preserved more of their artistic works than
the Chinese (and by collecting Chinese examples over the centuries saved
many more from destruction), do seem to differ from the Chinese in their
approach to portraiture. This apparent difference may be due in large part to
the relatively small number of portraits that exist from China, leaving only
fragmentary remains upon which to draw a comparison. From the remains
it does appear that the Japanese were often interested in capturing a greater
degree of realism, through their history, than were the Chinese. Alongside
their idealistic portraits, in the Chinese manner, appear rather remarkable
and life-like portraits such as the famous eighth century dry lacquer statue
of the Priest Ganjin.[11] This likeness may well have been made by an artist

[9] Chu-Tsing Li, *A Thousand Peaks and Myriad Ravines* (Ascona: Artibus Asiae
Publishers, 1974), Vol. I, p. 10.
[10] J. Fontein and M. L. Hickman, *Zen: Painting and Calligraphy* (Boston: Museum of
Fine Arts, 1970), p. xxxi.
[11] S. Noma, *The Arts of Japan: Ancient and Medieval* (Tokyo: Kodansha International, 1966), plate 58.

who knew the priest. This realism is also found later in secular portraiture and again to a degree not known in Chinese works. The Japanese seem generally to show more interest in how people look, in genre subjects, and in capturing details than do the Chinese. As in China, Western concepts of realistic portraiture also appear in Japan at least as early as the seventeenth century.

A direct comparison with the West, in the four categories noted above, is severely hampered by the loss of much East Asian portraiture. From what remains it is possible, however, to see some general parallels and perhaps a sense of some common values held between the two parts of the world.

Idealized portraiture, the largest category in the West, is also the most common type in East Asia. In this area the two cultures have much in common. Whether the subject is a ruler, an ancestor, or a deity, the favored mode of representation finds him presented as majestic, and larger than anyone else, with generalized features and symbolic paraphernalia to reinforce his lofty station. Examples remain from at least as far back as the eighth century in both China and Japan. The T'ang scroll of the "Thirteen Emperors" (now in Boston)[12] and the portrait of Shotoku Taishi (Imperial Household Collection) of the Nara Period,[13] are early examples of a tradition that goes back as far as the first imaginary portrait of the Buddha. These representations are often dramatic in their strong characterization, notably in portraits of arhats or holy men of superior powers, who are shown with exaggerated features, often in an imaginative landscape setting of equal emotional impact.[14] In Japan the exaggeration achieving such characterization is more pronounced than in China, with the individual's legendary features (eyebrows, neck, nose) emphasized and, in one case, real hair actually affixed to the chin of an idealized statue of a Zen monk.[15] In East Asia, idealized portraits enjoyed continuous popularity and, in Japan especially, there seemed to be a fascination with imaginative ways of enhancing certain qualities of the individual at times bordering on the grotesque to amplify the dramatic aspects of character. In the West, idealism was usually more tame, keeping to prescribed formulae, and perhaps closer to the Chinese restraint.

In the use of realism, there is generally a considerable difference between East and West. Ch'an Buddhism dictated the portrayal of realistic portraits, and in the examples that remain, all from the fourteenth century and later,

[12] K. Tomita, "Portraits of the Emperors," *Museum of Fine Arts, Boston, Bulletin*, 30, No. 117 (1932), pp. 2-8.

[13] H. Mori, *Japanese Portrait Sculpture*, trans. W. Chie Ishibashi (Tokyo: Kodansha International, 1977), p. 69.

[14] Helmut Brinker, "Ch'an Portraits in a Landscape," *Archives of Asian Art*, XXVII (1973-1974), pp. 8-25.

[15] Mori, plates 32 and 33.

Figure 3. Portrait of Hoto Kokushi (Priest Kakushin).
Japan, Kamakura Period, inscription datable to 1286.
The Cleveland Museum of Art. Purchase, Leonard C. Hanna Jr. Bequest.

Figure 4. Portrait of the Chinese Priest Dokuryu.
Kita Genki, Japanese, Edo Period, fl. 1664-1698, hanging scroll.
The Cleveland Museum of Art. Purchase, Mr. and Mrs. William H. Marlatt Fund.

there is some reluctance on the part of the Chinese to pull away from the more standard idealistic representation. Many of those portraits emphasize character, but whether they actual capture a realistic likeness of the subject cannot always be determined. Certainly realism in Chinese portraiture means the inner reality of the individual. Expressing these qualities pictorially must result in generalized types of portrayals, and the final result takes on the look of an idealized portrait. Whatever the degree of realism in Ch'an portraits, they are certainly more realistic than secular works, which held to the more rigid idealistic canons.[16]

The Japanese seem to go further towards realism in some of their portraits, although they too prefer the idealized type. Again, the role of Zen Buddhism is central to the development of realistic portraiture, but, as Noma has pointed out,[17] the Japanese have exhibited a feeling for intuitive and direct simplicity from ancient times. This statement, if true, helps explain the frequent interest Japanese artists have shown in rather direct and realistic portraiture over a longer period of time than known in China. The seated wooden statue of Hoto Kokushi (see Figure 3), carved in 1286, while the subject was alive, is an example of the Japanese ability to keep the idealized qualities of intense concentration, studious habits, and strength of character, while capturing visual realism in the high cheeckbones, shape of the head, and eyebrows, blending the two aspects into a striking portrait of convincing realism. There is additional evidence that the physical likeness is accurate, as Sherman Lee points out, for at least four other portraits of this same individual exist.[18] Japanese secular portraiture, unlike Chinese, is often remarkably realistic. Certainly no Asian image exceeds the portrait of Minamoto no Yoritomo[19] in capturing both the power of his character along with the realistic details of his face and the blending of the two elements into a portrait of idealism and realism that both symbolizes what he accomplished and expressed his inner personality.

One measure of the degree of realism in China and Japan can be found when Western influences arrive. The Chinese portraits generally remain idealistic, with minimal realism, while often Japanese portraiture continues toward greater realism, at times becoming strongly westernized and sometimes resulting in a curious blend of the two traditions. The seventeenth century portrait (Figure 4) is realistic in the "Western" treatment of facial details, rendered with minute care, but as one looks at the total figure it

[16] Fontein and Hickman, p. xxxi.

[17] Noma, p. 36.

[18] Sherman Lee, "Varieties of Portraiture in Chinese and Japanese Art," *Bulletin of the Cleveland Museum of Art*, LXIV, No. 4 (April 1977), p. 128.

[19] Noma, plate 161.

becomes clear that the angle of view shifts into a "bird's eye" effect at the bottom, resulting in a curious mix of East and West, not satisfactorily rendered in either fashion.[20]

Korean portraiture from the Yi Dynasty (1392-1910) seems to follow in a similar path; remarkable realism in the faces of some individuals accompanies idealized and even cursory treatment of the rest of the figure.[21] It is especially tragic that so few examples from this period of Korean art remain, for portraiture achieved its greatest stature during the Yi Dynasty and the highest honor for a portrait painter was a royal commission.[22]

The third major category of portraiture is that of humor, satire, and caricature. There seems to be little reference to this type in China, and though Korea is known for a long tradition of genre art and humorous, often irreverent, treatment of many subjects, one must turn again to the Japanese for some parallels with the West. The modern Western tradition of satirical cartoons (Daumier, Rowlandson) is preceded as early as the twelfth century in Japan by satirical attacks on Buddhism and humorous portrayals of human weaknesses. Many picture scrolls portray the frailties of individuals through exaggeration and comedy. Even the Buddha is portrayed as a giant frog,[23] and some of the portraits of Daruma are, in part, humorously conceived, especially the later works from the Zenga school, such as those by Sengai and Hakuin.[24] All these humorous or satirical works are based on an idealized image, and the Western nineteenth- and twentieth-century caricatures that clearly derive from an actual person, utilizing known physical traits, are not found in East Asia.

The last category is that of the self-portrait. This type is not frequently found in East Asia and is based upon idealized images. The almost methodical and year by year record of one's features, such as Rembrandt's, simply has no Asian counterpart. There is no Zen requirement for the self-portrait, as there had been for the realistic portrait, and thus the general preference for idealization is maintained. There are records of Zen monks who commissioned their own portraits, apparently not for the usual purpose of passing them on to their students,[25] but no record of a monk who

[20] Lee, p. 125.

[21] The National Museum of Korea, *5000 Years of Korean Art* (San Francisco: Asian Art Museum of San Francisco, 1979), plates 193 and 223.

[22] *5000 Years of Korean Art*, p. 178.

[23] H. Okudaira, *Narrative Picture Scrolls*, trans. E. ten Grotenhuis (New York: Weatherhill Publishers, 1973), fig. 25.

[24] Y. Arakawa, *Zen Painting*, trans. J. Bester (Tokyo: Kodansha International, 1970), plates 70, 71, and 122.

[25] Mori, p. 112.

consciously made self-portraits. The few self-portraits available are idealized to an extent that a label is necessary to clarify just whom they represent. The eighteenth-century master Tao-chi portrays himself seated under a tree while a young boy and a monkey play in front of him. The artist shows himself with a small goatee and mustache and robed as a monk, having otherwise no distinguishing details.[26] There is at least one Korean self-portrait, of the Yi Dynasty, that exhibits considerable character but is still not individualized beyond general features and lacks evidence of being a close physical likeness.[27] Likewise, Japanese examples are few, although one witty Zenga version summarizes the Asian attitude toward this form of portraiture. The artist is shown full figure, but from the rear![28]

The relative absence of the self-portrait in East Asia may largely have to do with the means of expression itself. The manner in which the artist handles the brush tells a great deal about his character. Western art has no such equivalent for interpreting the artist's nature. Since so much was revealed by the manner in which the East Asian artist painted, it may have seemed redundant to do self-portraits.

V

This brief overview of portraiture in East and West does serve to point out certain convergences and differences. Both traditions have favored the idealized portrait and have much in common prior to the age of scientific study in the West. East Asia had always sought to express the true character of the individual, rather than the physical appearance. This has resulted in a great many portraits that initially look alike and take on individuality only when one knows who is represented and something about him, the information often included in the calligraphy that usually is part of the painting. The West's growing interest in the physical world and its description meant that all things were equally eligible for such pictorial description. The Asian search for the real character below the surface seems to have come later in the Western tradition. The Asian technique of brush painting, itself so autobiographical, may have a great deal to do with the failure of the self-portrait to develop as it had done in the West. Overall, certain conventions remain throughout, and this pattern changes only when social or religious interests

[26] O. Siren, *Chinese Painting: Leading Masters and Principles* (New York: Hacker Art Books, 1973), Vol. VI, plate 388a.
[27] Korean Government, *5000 Years of Korean Arts* (Tokyo, 1976), plate 126 (text in Japanese with English captions).
[28] Arakawa, plate 113.

create new demands. Zen portraits are a response to a religious need, and Rembrandt's self-portraits are possible in a culture that takes an interest in the individual and his character.

University of Redlands

INTERPLAY

Proceedings of Colloquia in
Comparative Literature and the Arts

VOLUME ONE: *THE DREAM AND THE PLAY:*
Ionesco's Theatrical Quest
Includes three unpublished dream scenes by E. Ionesco

Richard N. Coe, Martin Esslin, George E. Wellwarth, Robert W. Corrigan, Emmanuel Jacquart, David I. Grossvogel, Rosette C. Lamont, Jan Kott, Moshe Lazar, Eugène Ionesco

VOLUME TWO: *THE ANXIOUS SUBJECT:*
Nightmares and Daymares in Literature and Film

Nicholas Kiessling, Joseph M. Natterson, Claude T. H. Friedman, Richard J. Rosenthal, Peter Hodgson, Geoffrey Green, Franca Schettino, Noel Carroll, Lindley Hanlon, Katherine S. Kovács, Vlada Petric, Marsha Kinder, Arnold Heidsieck

VOLUME THREE: *PLAY DÜRRENMATT*

Gerwin Marahrens, Arnold Heidsieck, Joseph P. Strelka, Peter Spycher, Renate Usmiani, Hans Bänziger, Nicole Dufresne, Joseph A. Federico, Gerhard P. Knapp, Martin Esslin, Robert E. Helbling, Armin Arnold, Enoch Brater, Cornelius Schnauber, Friedrich Dürrenmatt

VOLUME FOUR: *DISCOVERING THE OTHER:*
Humanities East and West

Robert S. Ellwood, Peter H. Lee, Hajime Nakamura, David Wei-yang Dai, San-pao Li, Robert A. Rosenstone, Dominic C. N. Cheung, Saralyn R. Daly, Noriko Mizuta Lippit, Jean-Luc Filoche, Dan McLeod, Robert E. Fisher

Published by Undena Publications under the auspices of
The Comparative Literature Program and
The Center for the Humanities, University of Southern California

VOLUME FIVE: *THE DOVE AND THE MOLE:*
Kafka's Journey into Darkness and Creativity
(forthcoming)

Walter H. Sokel, Peter Beicken, Geoffrey Green, Richard Caldwell, Joseph P. Strelka, Stanley Corngold, John M. Grandin, Bluma Goldstein, Arnold Band, Evelyn T. Beck, Franca Schettino, Peter Heller, Arnold Heidsieck, Gershon Shaked

VOLUME SIX: *KHRONOS AND MNEMOSYNE:*
Time in Literature and the Arts (forthcoming)

Paul Alkon, Carolyn Dewald, Mari Riess Jones, Gilbert Rose, Bonnie J. Barthold, Meir Sternberg, Tami Sternberg, Stephen Lansing, Alexander Moore, Gary Seaman, Robert Ellwood, George Hayden, Lawrence G. Thompson, Samuel L. Macey, Bruce Kawin, Seymour Chatman, Naima Prevots, Moshe Lazar, Barney Childs, Jonathan Kramer

VOLUME SEVEN: *MEDIEVAL LAUGHTER* (forthcoming)

Jeffrey Henderson, Alan E. Knight, Jean-Claude Aubailly, Gari Muller, George Hayden, Norman Roth, Edward E. Haymes, Josef Purkart, Franca Schettino, Norris J. Lacy, F. R. P. Akehurst, Joseph Dane, Barry Sanders, Anthony N. Zahareas, Antonio Jauregui, Moshe Lazar, Hendik van der Werf